Becker Professional Education, a global leader in professional education materials for the ACCA for more than 20 years. Thousands of students have succeeded in their professional examinations studying with its Plat centers in Central and Eastern Europe and Central Asia.

Nearly half a million professionals have advanced their careers through Becker Professional Education's courses. Throughout its 60-year history, Becker has earned a strong track record of student success through world-class teaching, curriculum and learning tools.

Becker Professional Education has been awarded ACCA Approved Content Provider Status for its ACCA materials, as well as materials for the Diploma in International Financial Reporting (DipIFR).

We provide a single solution for individuals and companies in need of global accounting certifications and continuing professional education.

Becker Professional Education's ACCA Study Materials

All of Becker's materials are authored by experienced ACCA lecturers and are used in the delivery of classroom courses.

Study Text: Gives complete coverage of the syllabus with a focus on learning outcomes. It is designed to be used both as a reference text and as part of integrated study. It also includes the ACCA Syllabus and Study Guide, exam advice and commentaries and a Study Question Bank containing practice questions relating to each topic covered.

Revision Question Bank: Exam style and standard questions together with comprehensive answers to support and prepare students for their exams. The Revision Question Bank also includes past examination questions (updated where relevant), model answers and alternative solutions and tutorial notes.

Revision Essentials Handbook*: A condensed, easy-to-use aid to revision containing essential technical content and exam guidance.

*Revision Essentials Handbook are substantially derived from content reviewed by ACCA's examining team.

ACCA

TAXATION
(UNITED KINGDOM) (TX-UK) (F6)

REVISION QUESTION BANK

Finance Act 2017
Applicable to Examinations from June 2018 to March 2019

No responsibility for loss occasioned to any person acting or refraining from action as a result of any material in this publication can be accepted by the author, editor or publisher.

This training material has been prepared and published by Becker Professional Development International Limited: www.beckeracca.com

Level 25, 40 Bank Street
Canary Wharf
London
E14 5NR
United Kingdom

SBN: 978-1-78566-568-4

Copyright ©2018 Becker Educational Development Corp. All rights reserved.

The trademarks used herein are owned by Becker Educational Development Corp. or their respective owners and may not be used without permission from the owner.

No part of this training material may be translated, reprinted or reproduced or utilised in any form either in whole or in part or by any electronic, mechanical or other means, now known or hereafter invented, including photocopying and recording, or in any information storage and retrieval system without express written permission. Request for permission or further information should be addressed to the Permissions Department, Becker Educational Development Corp.

Becker Professional Education is an **ACCA Approved Content Provider** for the ACCA Qualification. This means that this Revision Question Bank has been reviewed by the ACCA examining team. The objective of the review is to ensure that the material properly covers the syllabus and study guide outcomes, used by the examining team in setting the exams, in the appropriate breadth and depth. The review does not ensure that every eventuality, combination or application of examinable topics is addressed by the ACCA Approved Content. Nor does the review comprise a detailed technical check of the content as the Approved Content Provider has its own quality assurance processes in place in this respect.

Acknowledgement

Past ACCA examination questions are the copyright of the Association of Chartered Certified Accountants and have been reproduced by kind permission.

REVISION QUESTION BANK – TAXATION (TX-UK) (F6)

CONTENTS

Tax Rates and Allowances (vii)

OBJECTIVE TEST QUESTIONS

Introduction to Objective Test Questions (x)

Question	Name	Page	Answer	Marks	Date worked

SECTION A: OBJECTIVE TEST QUESTIONS [1]

1	General Concepts and Principles	1	147	18	
2	Income Tax Computations	3	148	16	
3	Property and Investment Incomes	4	149	16	
4	Employment Income	6	150	14	
5	Unincorporated Traders – Assessment and Profits	8	151	10	
6	Capital Allowances	9	152	12	
7	Unincorporated Traders – Relief for Trading losses	10	153	12	
8	Unincorporated Traders – Other Matters	12	154	12	
9	Chargeable Gains – Basic Principles	13	155	28	
10	Chargeable Gains – Chattels, Land and Buildings	17	157	12	
11	Chargeable Gains – Shares	18	158	8	
12	Chargeable Gains – Business Assets	19	158	12	
13	Corporation Tax – The Tax Computation	20	159	10	
14	Corporation Tax – Loss Reliefs	22	159	10	
15	Corporation Tax – Groups of Companies	23	160	10	
16	Inheritance Tax	25	160	22	
17	NIC, PAYE and Self-assessment	27	162	18	
18	Tax Compliance	30	163	16	
19	Value Added Tax	32	164	28	

CONCEPTS AND PRINCIPLES

20	Aspects of a Tax System	36	167	10	
21	Shiv and Shanker	36	168	10	

INCOME TAX AND NIC LIABILITIES

22	Bayle Defender *(ACCA J11)*	37	169	10	
23	Josie Jones *(ACCA D12)*	37	170	15	
24	Sophia Wong *(ACCA D12)*	39	171	10	
25	John Beach *(ACCA J13)*	39	173	15	
26	Phil Jones *(ACCA J13)*	40	174	10	
27	Richard Feast *(ACCA D13)*	41	175	15	
28	Fang and Hong *(ACCA D13)*	43	177	10	
29	KLM and Richard Morris *(ACCA D13)*	43	178	10	
30	Chi Needle *(ACCA J14)*	44	179	10	

---

[1] All OT questions are 2 marks each unless otherwise indicated.

TAXATION (TX-UK) (F6) – REVISION QUESTION BANK

Question	Name	Page	Answer	Marks	Date worked

INCOME TAX AND NIC LIABILITIES (continued)

31	Qi Pin *(ACCA J14)*	45	180	15	
32	Alfred King *(ACCA D14)*	47	181	15	
33	CBE: Edward King *(ACCA D14 adapted)*	48	183	10	
34	Sophie Shape *(ACCA J15 Specimen)*	49	184	10	
35	Fergus *(ACCA J15)*	50	185	10	
36	Wai *(ACCA J15)*	50	186	15	
37	Daniel, Francine and Gregor *(ACCA S15)*	51	187	10	
38	Samson & Delilah *(ACCA D15)*	52	188	15	
39	George *(ACCA M16)*	53	190	10	
40	Patience *(ACCA M16)*	54	191	15	
41	Stevie Dee	56	193	10	
42	Basil and Yoko	56	194	15	

CHARGEABLE GAINS FOR INDIVIDUALS

43	CBE: Winston King *(ACCA J12 adapted)*	57	195	10	
44	CBE: Aom and Leroy *(ACCA D13 adapted)*	58	196	10	
45	CBE: Mick Stone *(ACCA J14 adapted)*	59	197	10	
46	CBE: Patrick and Emily *(ACCA D14 adapted)*	61	198	10	
47	Ruby *(ACCA D15)*	62	199	10	
48	Jerome *(ACCA M16)*	63	200	10	

INHERITANCE TAX

49	CBE: Sam Shire *(ACCA D12 adapted)*	64	201	10	
50	CBE: Pere Jones *(ACCA J13 adapted)*	65	202	10	
51	CBE: Afiya *(ACCA D13 adapted)*	66	203	10	
52	CBE: Kendra Older *(ACCA J14 adapted)*	67	204	10	
53	CBE: Tobias *(ACCA D14 adapted)*	69	205	10	
54	Zoe *(ACCA J15)*	70	206	10	
55	Marcus *(ACCA D15)*	71	207	10	
56	James *(ACCA J16)*	71	208	10	

CORPORATION TAX

57	Black Ltd *(ACCA D11)*	72	210	10	
58	Heavy Ltd *(ACCA J12)*	73	211	10	
59	Soft Ltd and Greenstew Ltd *(ACCA J12)*	74	212	10	
60	Greenzone Ltd *(ACCA J13)*	75	213	10	
61	Opal Ltd *(ACCA J13)*	76	214	10	
62	Softapp Ltd *(ACCA D13)*	77	215	15	
63	CBE: Long Ltd *(ACCA J14 adapted)*	79	217	10	
64	E-Commerce plc *(ACCA D14)*	80	219	15	
65	CBE: Cairo Ltd and Kigali Ltd *(ACCA D14)*	82	220	10	
66	Retro Ltd *(ACCA J15)*	84	221	15	
67	Lucky Ltd *(ACCA S15)*	86	223	13	
68	Jump Ltd *(ACCA J16)*	87	225	15	

REVISION QUESTION BANK – TAXATION (TX-UK) (F6)

Question	Name	Page	Answer	Marks	Date worked
CHARGEABLE GAINS FOR COMPANIES					
69	CBE: Wiki Ltd *(ACCA J12 adapted)*	89	226	10	
70	CBE: Acebook Ltd *(ACCA D12 adapted)*	91	227	10	
71	Luna Ltd *(ACCA J15)*	92	228	10	
VALUE ADDED TAX					
72	CBE: Flick Pick *(ACCA J12 adapted)*	93	229	10	
73	CBE: Clueless Ltd *(ACCA D12 adapted)*	94	230	10	
74	CBE: Richard Famine *(ACCA D13 adapted)*	96	231	10	
75	CBE: Wrong Ltd *(ACCA J14 adapted)*	98	232	10	
76	CBE: DEE-Commerce plc *(ACCA D14)*	100	233	10	
77	Zim *(ACCA J15)*	101	234	10	
78	Smart Ltd *(ACCA S15)*	102	235	10	
79	Garfield *(ACCA J16)*	103	236	10	

Specimen Exam (applicable from September 2016)

Section A	15 Objective Test (OT) questions	105	237	30	
Section B	"OT-case" questions				
16-20	Delroy and Marlon	109	238	10	
21-25	Opal	110	238	10	
26-30	Glacier Ltd	112	238	10	
Section C	"Constructed response" questions				
31	Sarah	113	239	10	
32	Simon	114	240	15	
33	Naive Ltd	115	242	15	

September 2016 Exam

Section A	15 Objective Test (OT) questions	117	244	30	
Section B	"OT-case" questions				
16-20	Adana	121	245	10	
21-25	Kitten and Kat Ltd	122	245	10	
26-30	Alisa	124	245	10	
Section C	"Constructed response" questions				
31	Joe	125	246	10	
32	Ashura	126	248	15	
33	Tenth Ltd and Eleventh Ltd	127	249	15	

TAXATION (TX-UK) (F6) – REVISION QUESTION BANK

Question	Name	Page	Answer	Marks	Date worked

December 2016 Exam

Section A	15 Objective Test (OT) questions	129	251	30	
Section B	"OT-case" questions				
16-20	Zoyla	133	253	10	
21-25	Roman and Paris	135	253	10	
26-30	Ardent Ltd	136	253	10	
Section C	"Constructed response" questions				
31	Jack	138	254	10	
32	Array Ltd	139	255	15	
33	Wretched Ltd	140	256	15	

March/June 2017[2]

Section C	"Constructed response" questions				
31	Zhi	142	258	10	
32	Petula	144	259	15	
33	Online Ltd	145	261	15	

COMPUTER BASED EXAMINATIONS

> If preparing to sit the Computer Based Examination (CBE) you are strongly advised to attempt the CBE versions of ACCA's specimen exam and recent exams (above) which are available at www.accaglobal.com/taxation.

Constructed response questions in the CBE will require written and numerical answer to be inserted into blank word processing pages, blank spreadsheets or pre-formatted templates. The answer layouts used in the past exam questions reproduced in this question bank are blank word processing pages and blank spreadsheets. A **blank spreadsheet** is indicated with this icon:

ACCA recommends that students use the constructed response workspace, which can also be found at www.accaglobal.com/taxation, for additional practice. The icon highlighting the constructed response workspace tool alongside some of the questions is for guidance only – it is important to recognise that each question is different and that the answer space provided by ACCA in the exam is determined by both the technical content of the question as well as the quality assurance processes ACCA undertakes to ensure the student is provided with the most appropriate type of workspace.

---

[2] Since December 2016, ACCA publishes only a sample of questions from Section C of the March and June examinations and the September and December examinations.

The following supplementary instructions will be included in the exams to 31 March 2019:

SUPPLEMENTARY INSTRUCTIONS

Calculations and workings need only be made to the nearest £.
All apportionments should be made to the nearest month.
All workings should be shown in Section C.

TAX RATES AND ALLOWANCES

The following tax rates and allowances are to be used in answering the questions.

Income tax

		Normal rates	*Dividend rates*
Basic rate	£1 – £33,500	20%	7.5%
Higher rate	£33,501 – £150,000	40%	32.5%
Additional rate	£150,001 and over	45%	38.1%

Savings income nil rate band	– Basic rate taxpayers	£1,000
	– Higher rate taxpayers	£500
Dividend nil rate band		£5,000

A starting rate of 0% applies to savings income where it falls within the first £5,000 of taxable income.

Personal allowance

Personal allowance	£11,500
Transferable amount	£1,150
Income limit	£100,000

Residence status

Days in UK	Previously resident	Not previously resident
Less than 16	Automatically not resident	Automatically not resident
16 to 45	Resident if 4 UK ties (or more)	Automatically not resident
46 to 90	Resident if 3 UK ties (or more)	Resident if 4 UK ties
91 to 120	Resident if 2 UK ties (or more)	Resident if 3 UK ties (or more)
121 to 182	Resident if 1 UK tie (or more)	Resident if 2 UK ties (or more)
183 or more	Automatically resident	Automatically resident

Child benefit income tax charge

Where income is between £50,000 and £60,000, the charge is 1% of the amount of child benefit received for every £100 of income over £50,000.

Car benefit percentage

The relevant base level of CO_2 emissions is 95 grams per kilometre.

The percentage rates applying to petrol cars with CO_2 emissions up to this level are:

50 grams per kilometre or less	9%
51 grams to 75 grams per kilometre	13%
76 grams to 94 grams per kilometre	17%
95 grams per kilometre	18%

TAXATION (TX-UK) (F6) – REVISION QUESTION BANK

Car fuel benefit

The base figure for calculating the car fuel benefit is £22,600.

Individual savings accounts (ISAs)

The overall limit is £20,000.

Property income

Basic rate restriction applies to 25% of finance costs.

Pension scheme limits

Annual allowance	£40,000
Minimum allowance	£10,000
Income limit	£150,000

The maximum contribution that can qualify for tax relief without any earnings is £3,600.

Authorised mileage allowances: cars

Up to 10,000 miles	45p
Over 10,000 miles	25p

Capital allowances: rates of allowance

Plant and machinery
Main pool	18%
Special rate pool	8%

Motor cars
New cars with CO_2 emissions up to 75 grams per kilometre	100%
CO_2 emissions between 76 and 130 grams per kilometre	18%
CO_2 emissions over 130 grams per kilometre	8%

Annual investment allowance
Rate of allowance	100%
Expenditure limit	£200,000

Cash basis

Revenue limit	£150,000

Cap on income tax reliefs

Unless otherwise restricted, reliefs are capped at the higher of £50,000 or 25% of income.

Corporation tax

Rate of tax - Financial Year 2017	19%
- Financial Year 2016	20%
- Financial Year 2015	20%
Profit threshold	£1,500,000

Value added tax (VAT)

Standard rate	20%
Registration limit	£85,000
Deregistration limit	£83,000

Inheritance tax: tax rates

Nil rate band	£325,000
Residence nil rate band	£100,000
Excess – Death rate	40%
– Lifetime rate	20%

Inheritance tax: taper relief

Years before death	Percentage reduction
Over 3 but less than 4 years	20%
Over 4 but less than 5 years	40%
Over 5 but less than 6 years	60%
Over 6 but less than 7 years	80%

Capital gains tax

	Normal rates	Residential property
Rates of tax – Lower rate	10%	18%
– Higher rate	20%	28%
Annual exempt amount		£11,300
Entrepreneurs' relief – Lifetime limit		£10,000,000
– Rate of tax		10%

National insurance contributions

Class 1	Employee	£1 to £8,164 per year	Nil
		£8,165 to £45,000 per year	12%
		£45,001 and above per year	2%
Class 1	Employer	£1 to £8,164 per year	Nil
		£8,165 and above per year	13.8%
		Employment allowance	£3,000
Class 1A			13.8%
Class 2		£2.85 per week	
		Small profits threshold	£6,025
Class 4		£1 to £8,164 per year	Nil
		£8,165 to £45,000 per year	9%
		£45,001 and above per year	2%

Rates of interest (assumed)

Official rate of interest	2.50%
Rate of interest on underpaid tax	2.75%
Rate of interest on overpaid tax	0.50%

TAXATION (TX-UK) (F6) – REVISION QUESTION BANK

Introduction to Objective Test (OT) Questions

"Multiple choice – single answer" – is the standard OT type in paper-based examinations. In CBE this type is presented with radio bullets instead of A B, C, D options.

Illustration

Cate and Dani have traded in partnership for several years. Their profit-sharing arrangements are:

	Cate	Dani
Annual salaries	£5,000	£4,000
6% interest on capital account balances	£35,000	£20,000
Profit-sharing ratio	3 :	2

Adjusted trading profits for the year ended 31 March 2018 were £33,000.

What amount of profit will be allocated to Dani for the year ended 31 March 2018?

- £13,200
- £13,080
- £13,480
- £13,600

How to answer?

✓ Click on a radio button to select an answer from the choices provided.
✓ You can select only one.
✓ If you want to change your answer, click on your new choice and the original choice will be removed automatically.

Answer

- £13,480

	Cate £	Dani £	Total £
Profit			33,000
Salary	5,000	4,000	(9,000)
6% interest (on £35,000/£20,000)	2,100	1,200	(3,300)
Balance to share 3:2	x	8,280	20,700
		13,480	

OTHER OT TYPES

The following OT types appear **only** in CBE:

(1) Multiple response
(2) Pull down list
(3) Number entry
(4) Hot area
(5) Enhanced matching

These are illustrated below.

REVISION QUESTION BANK – TAXATION (TX-UK) (F6)

(1) Multiple response

Description – candidates are required to select more than one response from the options provided by clicking the appropriate tick boxes.

Illustration 1

Jasper is in full-time employment as a waiter in a restaurant.

Which TWO of the following items of Jasper's income are exempt for income tax purposes?

- ☐ Interest received on a repayment of income tax
- ☐ Interest received on a loan Jasper made to a friend
- ☐ Gratuities ("tips") received from restaurant customers
- ☐ Dividends received from an Individual Savings Account

How to answer?

- ✓ Two is the maximum you are permitted to select.
- ✓ You can deselect a chosen answer to clear it.
- ✓ When you have chosen the required number, deselecting an answer will allow you to select another answer.

Answer

- ☑ Interest received on a repayment of income tax
- ☑ Dividends received from an Individual Savings Account

(2) Pull down list

Description – candidates are required to select one answer from a list of choices within a drop down list.

Illustration 2

Since 6 April 2017, Nicolas has let out an unfurnished freehold office building. On that date, the tenant paid Nicolas a premium of £82,000 for the grant of a 15-year lease.

How much of the premium of £82,000 will Nicolas include when calculating his property business profit for the tax year 2017–18?

Select... ▼
£59,040
£22,960
£82,000
£5,467

TAXATION (TX-UK) (F6) – REVISION QUESTION BANK

Answer

82,000 – (82,000 × 2% × (15 – 1)) = **£59,040**

(3) Number entry

Description – candidates are required to key in a numerical response.

Illustration 3

Naomi is self-employed. For the year ended 5 April 2018 she made a trading loss of £110,000, having made a trading profit of £24,000 for the year ended 5 April 2017. Naomi also had employment income of £92,000 for the tax year 2016–17.

What is the maximum loss relief claim which Naomi can make against her total income for the tax year 2016–17?

£ ☐

How to answer?

- ✓ Enter a numerical value in the answer box.

- ✓ The **only** permitted characters for numerical answer are:
  - ❑ One full stop as a decimal point if required;[3]
  - ❑ One minus symbol at the front of the figure if the answer is negative.

  For example: -10234.35

- ✗ No other characters, including commas, are accepted.

- ✓ You can change your answer by adding permitted characters or deleting one or more highlighted characters.

Answer

24,000 + 50,000 = £ **74000**

(4) Hot area

Description – candidates are required to select one or more areas in an image as their answer(s).

Illustration 4

Mammoth Ltd commenced trading on 1 January 2015. The company's profits have been as follows:

Period	£
Year ended 31 December 2015	524,000
Year ended 31 December 2016	867,000
Year ended 31 December 2017	912,000

Throughout all of these periods, Mammoth Ltd had one related 51% group company.

---

[3] One of the exam instructions is to calculate to nearest £, so decimal points are not needed for monetary amounts.

Identify the first year for which Mammoth Ltd will be required to pay its corporation tax liability by quarterly instalments.

Year ended 31 December 2016	CORRECT	INCORRECT
None of the years ended 31 December 2015, 2016 or 2017	CORRECT	INCORRECT
Year ended 31 December 2017	CORRECT	INCORRECT
Year ended 31 December 2015	CORRECT	INCORRECT

How to answer?

✓ Click on a hotspot area to select an answer from the hotspot choices provided.
✓ You can select only one per line.
✓ The selected area will be highlighted.
✓ If you want to choose a different answer click on an alternative area.

Answer

Year ended 31 December 2016		INCORRECT
None of the years ended 31 December 2015, 2016 or 2017		INCORRECT
Year ended 31 December 2017	CORRECT	
Year ended 31 December 2015		INCORRECT

(5) Enhanced matching

Description – candidates are required to select and drag chosen answers to other areas of the screen.

Illustration 5

For the tax year 2017–18, identify the latest dates by which a taxpayer, who does not wish to incur a penalty, should file a self-assessment tax return on paper or online.

Date
31 October 2018
31 January 2019
31 October 2019
31 January 2020

Paper tax return	Online tax return

How to answer?

✓ Select an option (this case a date) by clicking on it.
✓ Drag and drop to an empty box.
✓ Repeat for as many times as there are empty boxes to fill.
✓ If you want to choose a different answer, click on an alternative option and drag and drop again.

Answer

Paper tax return	Online tax return
31 October 2018	31 January 2019

REVISION QUESTION BANK – TAXATION (TX-UK) (F6)

Question 1 GENERAL CONCEPTS AND PRINCIPLES

1.1 Which of the following UK taxes is an indirect tax?

    A   Capital gains tax
    B   Inheritance tax
    C   National insurance contributions
    D   Value added tax

1.2 Which of the following is responsible for the assessment and collection of UK taxes?

    A   Commissioners for Revenue and Customs
    B   HM Revenue and Customs
    C   HM Treasury
    D   Inland Revenue

1.3 Topaz is a sole trader.

Identify, by clicking on the relevant box in the table below, which of the following actions by Topaz would be tax evasion.

Failing to record cash sales	YES	NO
Claiming personal expenses through the business	YES	NO
Understating the value of closing inventory	YES	NO
Postponing a sale of shares from 5 April until 6 April	YES	NO

1.4 Having graduated from a university in the UK, Patrick is now working full-time overseas. He now wishes to be non-resident in the UK but expects to make return trips to the UK to visit friends.

What is the maximum number of days Patrick can spend in the UK and be non-resident?

    A   15
    B   45
    C   90
    D   120

1.5 Which of the following people would be treated as automatically non-resident in the UK for the tax year 2017–18?

    A   Anna, who stayed in the UK for 15 days during the tax year 2017–18

    B   Barbara, who was not previously UK resident and stayed in the UK for 50 days during the tax year 2017–18

    C   Carol, who was UK resident for the tax year 2015–16 and stayed in the UK for 40 days during the tax year 2017–18

    D   Danita, who stayed in the UK for 70 days during the tax year 2017–18, and who has left the UK to carry out part-time work overseas

TAXATION (TX-UK) (F6) – REVISION QUESTION BANK

1.6 **Which of the following statements correctly explains the difference between tax evasion and tax avoidance?**

- A Both tax evasion and tax avoidance are illegal, but tax evasion involves providing HM Revenue and Customs with deliberately false information
- B Tax evasion is illegal, whereas tax avoidance involves the minimisation of tax liabilities by the use of any lawful means
- C Both tax evasion and tax avoidance are illegal, but tax avoidance involves providing HM Revenue and Customs with deliberately false information
- D Tax avoidance is illegal, whereas tax evasion involves the minimisation of tax liabilities by the use of any lawful means

1.7 Samuel is planning to leave the UK to live overseas, having always previously been resident in the UK. He will not automatically be treated as either resident in the UK or not resident in the UK. Samuel has several ties with the UK and will need to visit the UK for 60 days each tax year. However, he wants to be not resident after he leaves the UK.

For the first two tax years after leaving the UK, what is the maximum number of ties which Samuel could keep with the UK without being treated as resident in the UK?

- A One
- B Four
- C Two
- D Three

1.8 **Identify, by clicking on the relevant box in the table below, which of the following companies will be treated as resident in the UK for corporation tax purposes.**

A Ltd, a company incorporated in the UK, with its central management and control exercised in the UK	RESIDENT	NOT RESIDENT
B Ltd, a company incorporated overseas, with its central management and control exercised in the UK	RESIDENT	NOT RESIDENT
C Ltd, a company incorporated in the UK, with its central management and control exercised overseas	RESIDENT	NOT RESIDENT
D Ltd, a company incorporated overseas, with its central management and control exercised overseas	RESIDENT	NOT RESIDENT

1.9 Taxes can be either capital taxes or revenue taxes, although some taxes are neither type of tax.

Match each of the classifications to the correct tax.

Classification	
Capital	
Revenue	
Neither	

Tax
Value added
National insurance contributions
Inheritance

(18 marks)

Question 2 INCOME TAX COMPUTATIONS

2.1 Jasper is in full-time employment as a waiter in a restaurant.

Which TWO of the following items of Jasper's income are exempt for income tax purposes?

☐ Interest received on a repayment of income tax

☐ Interest received on a loan Jasper made to a friend

☐ Gratuities ("tips") received from restaurant customers

☐ Dividends received from an Individual Savings Account

2.2 Matt's net income for the tax year 2017–18 is £116,000.

What is the highest effective marginal rate of income tax that Matt will suffer in the tax year 2017–18?

A 40%
B 45%
C 50%
D 60%

2.3 Frank is full-time employed. His gross salary for the tax year 2017–18 was £29,360. During the tax year 2017–18 his employer paid £3,517 income tax for Frank via PAYE.

How much income tax is payable by Frank under self-assessment for the tax year 2017–18?

A £55
B £2,355
C £3,572
D £5,872

2.4 Alphonso, who is self-employed, opened a personal pension scheme for the first time in the tax year 2015–16 and made pension contributions of £56,000 in that year. He made further contributions of £17,000 for the tax year 2016–17.

What is the maximum amount of pension contributions that Alphonso can make for the tax year 2017–18 without incurring an annual allowance tax charge?

A £23,000
B £40,000
C £47,000
D £63,000

2.5 Aubrey has made pension contributions of £33,000 a year for the last five years. He plans to make pension contributions of £113,000 for the tax year 2017–18. His annual income is £140,000.

What is the amount of the excess contribution subject to the annual allowance tax charge in the tax year 2017–18?

A £73,000
B £52,000
C £45,000
D £0

TAXATION (TX-UK) (F6) – REVISION QUESTION BANK

2.6 When a taxpayer's net income exceeds £100,000, the personal allowance is progressively decreased and can be lost altogether.

Identify, by clicking on the relevant box in the table below, who can reduce the loss of personal allowance by making contributions into a personal pension scheme.

Directors	YES	NO
Employees	YES	NO
Self-employed persons	YES	NO

2.7 For the tax year 2017–18, Chi has a salary of £53,000. She received child benefit of £1,771 during this tax year.

What is Chi's child benefit income tax charge for the tax year 2017–18?

- A £1,771
- B £0
- C £1,240
- D £531

2.8 **Which TWO of the following items of expenditure are deductible in the calculation of an individual's taxable income?**

- ☐ A contribution into a personal pension scheme
- ☐ A charitable gift aid donation
- ☐ A contribution into an employer's HMRC registered occupational pension scheme
- ☐ A charitable donation made under the payroll deduction scheme

(16 marks)

Question 3 PROPERTY AND INVESTMENT INCOMES

3.1 Luke acquired a residential property that was first let, unfurnished, on 1 August 2017 for an annual rental of £12,000 payable quarterly in advance. Expenditure for the period from 1 August 2017 to 5 April 2018 was:

	£
Buildings insurance	650
Minor repairs to doors and windows	1,150
Improvements to the property	1,500
Advertising for tenants	220
Council tax	1,600
	5,120

What is Luke's property business profit for the tax year 2017–18?

Select... ▼
£2,680
£4,380
£5,530
£8,380

3.2 Gloria lets out two furnished properties to holidaymakers from the beginning of March to the end of October on a weekly basis.

- Property A was actually let for a total of 140 days. These lettings included a holiday taken by some friends from 3 July to 14 August.

- Property B was actually let for 110 days. It was unoccupied for the rest of the time.

Identify, by clicking on the relevant box in the table below, which property qualifies as furnished holiday accommodation.

Property A	YES	NO
Property B	YES	NO

3.3 Kathleen owns a cottage which qualifies as furnished holiday accommodation (FHA). During the year ended 5 April 2018 she makes a loss from letting the cottage of £8,800 for tax purposes.

Against which of the following can Kathleen relieve this loss?

- A   Future business profits from FHA lettings only
- B   All future property business profits
- C   All future investment income
- D   Future business profits and unearned income

3.4 Abby, Babs, Caleb and Daniel are all employed:

(1) Abby is a higher rate taxpayer with no investments in stocks or shares
(2) Babs is a basic rate taxpayer with substantial investments in shares
(3) Caleb is a higher rate taxpayer with substantial investments in shares
(4) Daniel is a basic rate taxpayer with no investments in stocks or shares

Which taxpayer could potentially benefit the most by investing in a stocks and shares ISA?

- A   Abby
- B   Babs
- C   Caleb
- D   Daniel

3.5 Paul invested £6,000 in a stocks and shares Individual Savings Account (ISA) in January 2018.

How much can Paul invest in a cash ISA for the year 2017–18?

- A   £0
- B   £6,000
- C   £20,000
- D   £14,000

3.6 Since 6 April 2017, Nicolas has let out an unfurnished freehold office building. On that date, the tenant paid Nicolas a premium of £82,000 for the grant of a 15-year lease.

How much of the premium of £82,000 will Nicolas include when calculating his property business profit for the tax year 2017–18?

Select... ▼
£59,040
£22,960
£82,000
£5,467

3.7 Rackman's only source of taxable income is his property business consisting of unfurnished residential lettings. His profit for the tax year 2017–18 was £86,500 after incurring interest expenses of £24,000.

How much income tax is payable by Rackman under self-assessment for the tax year 2017–18?

- A £23,300
- B £24,500
- C £25,700
- D £29,100

3.8 Which TWO of the following statements are correct in relation to the restriction of tax relief for finance costs of a residential property business?

- ☐ It applies to residential lettings including furnished holiday lettings
- ☐ It applies to finance costs including those incurred for property repairs
- ☐ For the tax year 2017-18, 25% of property income finance costs are ineligible for tax relief
- ☐ The restriction is being phased in over four years

(16 marks)

Question 4 EMPLOYMENT INCOME

4.1 Sharon uses her own motor car for business travel. During the tax year 2017–18, she drove 15,600 miles in the performance of her duties, without any reimbursement from her employer.

What statutory approved mileage allowance can Sharon claim?

- A £0
- B £3,900
- C £5,900
- D £7,020

4.2 Jamie's employer has provided him with living accommodation since 13 August 2014. The apartment had been purchased in June 2007 for £126,000, and was valued at £209,000 on 1 July 2014. Improvements costing £14,000 were made to the property during October 2011.

On what figure will Jamie's additional living accommodation benefit be calculated for the tax year 2017–18?

- A £134,000
- B £140,000
- C £148,000
- D £209,000

4.3 Ben's employer provided him with an interest free loan throughout the tax year 2017–18. The balance outstanding at 6 April 2017 was £15,400 and at 5 April 2018 it was £9,800.

Using the average method, what is the taxable benefit for the tax year 2017–18?

- A £135
- B £245
- C £315
- D £385

4.4 Rose is liable to income tax at 40% and has received the following benefits during the tax year 2017–18:

- Childcare vouchers of £45 per week for 52 weeks; and
- Luncheon vouchers of £5 per day for 240 days.

What is the amount of Rose's taxable benefits for the tax year 2017–18?

- A £884
- B £1,200
- C £2,084
- D £3,540

4.5 Charles commenced employment on 1 July 2017 on an annual salary of £35,000. He was immediately provided with a diesel company car with a list price of £20,000 and CO_2 emissions of 160 grams per kilometre. Charles pays for all his private fuel.

What is Charles's car benefit for the tax year 2017–18?

- A £4,650
- B £5,100
- C £6,200
- D £6,800

4.6 Natalia is self-employed. Her accounts for the year to 30 September 2017 showed legal and professional fees amounting to £7,000.

Which TWO of the following costs will be disallowed in the calculation of Natalia's tax-adjusted trading profit?

- ☐ Renewal of a 10-year lease on business premises
- ☐ Legal fees of a successful appeal against a tax assessment
- ☐ Cost of taking out a new five-year lease on business premises
- ☐ Fees incurred in the recovery of a trade bad debt

4.7 Malachi commenced trading on 1 September 2017 preparing his first set of accounts for the nine months to 31 May 2018.

On 1 November 2017 Malachi purchased a car with emissions of 130grams per kilometre for £21,000. 40% of the mileage is for private journeys.

What is the maximum amount of capital allowance available for the car for the nine months ended 31 May 2018?

£ ☐

(14 marks)

TAXATION (TX-UK) (F6) – REVISION QUESTION BANK

Question 5 UNINCORPORATED TRADERS – ASSESSMENT AND PROFITS

5.1 During his accounting year ended 31 May 2018 Cedric incurred leasing costs of £3,100 in respect of a motor car with CO_2 emissions of 125 grams per kilometre.

How much of the leasing costs will be deductible in calculating Cedric's adjusted trading profit for the year ended 31 May 2018?

- A £3,100
- B £2,635
- C £465
- D £0

5.2 Pearl commenced trading on 1 January 2017 making up her first set of accounts to 28 February 2018. Her tax-adjusted profits after capital allowances are as follows:

	£
Period ended 28 February 2018	49,700
Year ending 28 February 2019	33,000 (estimate)

What is Pearl's trading profit for the tax year 2017–18?

- A £49,700
- B £48,308
- C £42,600
- D £33,000

5.3 Alan began trading on 1 October 2016 preparing accounts to 30 September each year. He prepared accounts with tax-adjusted trading profits as follows:

	£
Year ended 30 September 2017	19,660
Year ended 30 September 2018	22,440

What amount of profits will Alan be assessed on for tax year 2016–17?

- A £9,830
- B £11,220
- C £19,660
- D £22,440

5.4 Alan began trading on 1 October 2016 preparing accounts to 30 September each year. He prepared accounts with tax-adjusted trading profits as follows:

	£
Year ended 30 September 2017	19,660
Year ended 30 September 2018	22,440

What amount of overlap profits arises on the commencement of trade?

- A £9,830
- B £11,220
- C £19,660
- D £22,440

5.5 Morgan ceased trading on 30 September 2017. He prepared accounts with tax-adjusted trading profits as follows:

	£
Year ended 31 December 2016	16,500
Nine months to 30 September 2017	10,500

Unused overlap profits brought forward from the commencement of trade were £1,600.

What is the amount of assessable profits for tax year 2017–18?

Select... ▼
£7,000
£8,900
£13,025
£14,900

(10 marks)

Question 6 CAPITAL ALLOWANCES

6.1 Joseph is self-employed. During the year ended 5 April 2018 he bought a motor car with CO_2 emissions of 135 grams per kilometre. The motor car is used by an employee, and 40% of the mileage is for private journeys.

How should Joseph treat the motor car in calculating capital allowances?

A As a separate item at the main rate with a private use adjustment
B Included in the special rate pool
C Included in the main pool
D As a separate item at the special rate with a private use adjustment

6.2 The written down values brought forward on Deborah's main pool of assets at 6 April 2017 was £32,000. The balance on the special rate pool at 6 April 2017 was £15,000.

During the year 2017–18, Deborah spent £7,000 on equipment and sold main pool plant for £6,000 (original cost £8,000).

What is the maximum amount of capital allowances which Deborah can claim for the year 2017–18?

A £7,140
B £11,680
C £12,520
D £12,880

6.3 The written down value brought forward on Pedro's main pool of assets at 6 April 2017 was £300,000. There was no balance on the special rate pool.

During the year 2017–18, Pedro purchased items of plant and equipment for £150,000 and spent £250,000 on the installation of a cooling system as an integral feature of a factory used in Pedro's business.

What is the maximum amount of capital allowances which Pedro can claim for the tax year 2017–18?

£ _____

6.4 Coral Ltd purchased the following new cars during the year ended 31 March 2018:

	£
Car with CO$_2$ emissions of 120 grams per kilometre	24,000
Car with CO$_2$ emissions of 75 grams per kilometre	13,500

The car with CO$_2$ emissions of 120 grams per kilometre is used 25% for business purposes by the managing director.

What is the maximum total capital allowances available to Coral Ltd on the cars for the year ended 31 March 2018?

- A £3,510
- B £6,750
- C £14,080
- D £17,820

6.5 Verdite Ltd is registered for value added tax (VAT). It purchased a new car for a VAT-inclusive price of £11,220 which included £225 breakdown insurance cover for one year. The car is used by the marketing manager for business and private use.

What amount should be included in the capital allowance computation as the acquisition cost of this vehicle?

- A £11,220
- B £10,995
- C £9,350
- D £9,163

6.6 Wan ceased trading on 31 December 2017, having been self-employed since 1 January 2004. On 1 January 2017, the tax written down value of her plant and machinery main pool was £6,200. On 10 November 2017, Wan purchased a computer for £1,600. All of the items included in the main pool were sold for £9,800 on 31 December 2017.

What is the balancing charge which will arise upon the cessation of Wan's trade?

Select... ▼
£4,716
£3,404
£2,000
£3,600

(12 marks)

Question 7 UNINCORPORATED TRADERS – RELIEF FOR TRADING LOSSES

7.1 Frank has been trading for many years. His recent adjusted trading results are as follows:

		£
Year to 31 March 2016	Loss	(17,500)
Year to 31 March 2017	Profit	8,250
Year to 31 March 2018	Profit	11,150

The loss is not being relieved against other income or chargeable gains.

What is Frank's assessable trading income for the tax year 2017–18?

A	£11,150 profit	
B	£1,900 profit	
C	£6,350 loss	
D	£0	

7.2 Darek's business has a trading loss. As no specific claims have been made to relieve the loss it is being carried forward automatically.

What can the loss be set against?

- A Total income
- B Taxable income
- C Trading profits arising from any trade
- D Trading profits arising from the same trade

7.3 A claim to set a trading loss incurred in the tax year 2017–18 against total income must be made by what date?

- A 5 April 2018
- B 5 April 2019
- C 31 January 2019
- D 31 January 2020

7.4 Aubrey has been in business for several years. His recent adjusted trading results are as follows:

		£
Year to 30 September 2016	Profit	14,900
Year to 30 September 2017	Loss	(19,660)

Aubrey has other income of £3,900 in the tax year 2016–17 and £5,100 in the tax year 2017–18.

He wishes to claim maximum loss relief as soon as possible.

What is Aubrey's total income for the tax year 2016–17 (after loss reliefs but before deducting the personal allowance)?

- A £0
- B £3,900
- C £14,900
- D £18,800

7.5 **Identify, by clicking on the relevant box in the table below, which of the following statements about terminal loss relief is/are correct?**

Any remaining overlap profits arising from the commencement of trade is deducted from the loss for the last 12 months	CORRECT	INCORRECT
This relief is given against trading profits of the tax year of permanent discontinuance and the three preceding tax years on a LIFO basis	CORRECT	INCORRECT

7.6 Naomi is self-employed. For the year ended 5 April 2018 she made a trading loss of £110,000, having made a trading profit of £24,000 for the year ended 5 April 2017. Naomi also had employment income of £92,000 for the tax year 2016–17.

What is the maximum loss relief claim which Naomi can make against her total income for the tax year 2016–17?

£ ☐

(12 marks)

Question 8 UNINCORPORATED TRADERS – OTHER MATTERS

8.1 Vanessa and Josh have traded in partnership for several years, preparing accounts to 30 June each year. Phil was admitted to the partnership on 1 November 2017.

What is the basis period for Vanessa's share of the partnership profits for the tax year 2017–18?

- A Year to 30 June 2017
- B 1 July 2016 to 31 October 2017
- C 1 November 2017 to 5 April 2018
- D Year to 30 June 2018

8.2 Xavier and Yolanda have traded in partnership for several years. Their profit-sharing arrangements are:

	Xavier	Yolanda
Annual salaries	£6,700	£4,400
4% interest on capital account balances of	£33,000	£27,000
Profit-sharing ratio	2 :	1

The tax adjusted trading profits for the year ended 31 March 2018 were £42,300.

What amount of profit will be allocated to Xavier for the year ended 31 March 2018?

- A £27,220
- B £27,500
- C £27,920
- D £28,200

8.3 Larimar and Amber have been in partnership for many years. The partnership agreement allocates partners' interest at 5% annually on capital invested. The balance of any profits is shared 35% to Larimar and 65% to Amber.

On 31 December 2017 Larimar's capital account had a balance of £36,000 and Amber's balance was £24,000. For the year ended 31 December 2017 the partnership had a tax-adjusted trading profit of £120,000.

What is the amount of Larimar's trading profit for the tax year 2017–18?

- A £42,750
- B £43,000
- C £41,350
- D £40,950

8.4 Cate and Dani have traded in partnership for several years. Their profit-sharing arrangements are:

	Cate	Dani
Annual salaries	£5,000	£4,000
6% interest on capital account balances	£35,000	£20,000
Profit-sharing ratio	3 :	2

The tax adjusted trading profits for the year ended 31 March 2018 were £33,000.

What amount of profit will be allocated to Dani for the year ended 31 March 2018?

- A £13,200
- B £13,080
- C £13,480
- D £13,600

8.5 **Identify, by clicking on the relevant box in the table below, whether the following statements about taxation of partnerships are true or false.**

A partner who has a trading loss for a tax year can choose whichever form of loss relief best suits his individual circumstances.	TRUE	FALSE
Each partner is liable for any income tax due on their other partners' shares of the partnership profits.	TRUE	FALSE

8.6 Laurel and Hardy have traded in partnership for many years, preparing accounts to 31 December each year and sharing profits equally. The adjusted trading profit for the year to 31 December 2017 was £48,000.

With effect from 1 October 2017 they changed their profit sharing agreement. Profits are now allocated one-third to Laurel and two-thirds to Hardy.

What amount of profit will be allocated to Laurel for the year ended 31 December 2017?

- A £16,000
- B £22,000
- C £24,000
- D £26,000

(12 marks)

Question 9 CAPITAL GAINS TAX – BASIC PRINCIPLES

9.1 Pieter purchased a holiday home in July 2008. The holiday home cost £95,000 and he paid legal fees of £2,600 relating to the purchase.

During 2013 he spent £6,700 on an extension to the kitchen and in 2016 he spent £3,300 on roof repairs following a storm. Pieter anticipates selling the house in the next few months.

What is the total amount of allowable expenditure on the disposal of the holiday home?

- A £97,600
- B £100,900
- C £104,300
- D £106,600

TAXATION (TX-UK) (F6) – REVISION QUESTION BANK

9.2 For the tax year 2017–18 Arthur's taxable income is £27,985. During the year he sold an antique chair which gave rise to a chargeable gain of £33,600.

What is Arthur's CGT liability for the tax year 2017–18?

A £2,230
B £3,908
C £4,460
D £6,168

9.3 **What will an individual taxpayer achieve by making sufficient disposals in the tax year 2017–18 so that chargeable gains are at least £11,300?**

The rate of CGT will be minimised	TRUE	FALSE
The due date will be delayed as long as possible	TRUE	FALSE
The benefit of the basic rate tax band will be maximised	TRUE	FALSE
The benefit of the annual exempt amount will be maximised	TRUE	FALSE

9.4 Jade has calculated her taxable gains for the tax year 2017–18 to be £35,000. She is not sure about the correct treatment of the following items:

(1) A gain of £3,900 on the sale of her five-year old racehorse which she has included in her calculation

(2) Auctioneer's fees of £600 which she has deducted from the £14,000 of sale proceeds for a painting which she sold at auction

What effect will the correct treatment of each of these items have on Jade's taxable gains?

	Item (1)	Item (2)
A	No effect	Decrease
B	Decrease	No effect
C	Increase	Decrease
D	No effect	Increase

9.5 In March 2004, Morgan purchased the freehold of an office building for £642,000. Morgan sold the building in March 2018 for £1,250,100 and incurred £120,000 estate agents' fees on the sale.

He made no other disposals of chargeable assets during the tax year 2017–18 and his taxable income in the tax year 2017–18 was £37,495.

What is Matthew's capital gains tax liability for the tax year 2017–18?

A £47,680
B £95,360
C £97,620
D £119,360

9.6 Jet Ltd realised the following gains and losses on the disposal of assets during the year ended 31 March 2018:

(1) Gain of £86,000 on the sale of an investment property.
(2) Loss of £5,900 on the sale of two cars used in the business. Each car cost and was sold for more than £6,000.

Drag and drop the correct treatment of each of these sales in the corporation tax computation of Jet Ltd for the year ended 31 March 2018.

Treatment
Allowable capital loss
Chargeable gain
Exempt

Investment property	Two cars

9.7 Alexandrite Ltd bought a factory on 12 February 2004 for £156,000. At acquisition, professional fees incurred in acquiring the factory were £4,500. In May 2009 an extension was added to the factory at a cost of £32,000.

In October 2017 Alexandrite Ltd sold the factory, which had always been used in its trade, for £321,000. Prior to the sale, Alexandrite Ltd repaired damage to fire doors following a break-in at a total cost of £3,000.

What is the amount of the unindexed gain on the sale of the factory?

- A £125,500
- B £128,500
- C £133,000
- D £160,500

9.8 Desperado Ltd sold a warehouse on 7 June 2018 for £315,000. The factory was purchased on 22 January 2001 for £154,000. Assume retail price indices are 171.1 for January 2001 and 281.8 for June 2018.

What is Dash Ltd's chargeable gain on the disposal of the factory?

- A £61,362
- B £104,167
- C £106,638
- D £161,000

9.9 For the tax year 2017–18 Samantha has chargeable gains of £23,100. She has unused capital losses of £25,700 brought forward from the tax year 2016–17.

What amount of unused capital losses can Samantha carry forward to the tax year 2018–19?

- A £2,600
- B £11,800
- C £13,900
- D £25,700

9.10 For the tax year 2017–18, Nog has a chargeable gain of £23,700 and a capital loss of £10,400. She has unused capital losses of £6,100 brought forward from the tax year 2016–17.

What amount of capital losses can Nog carry forward to the tax year 2018–19?

£ _____

9.11 On 31 March 2018, Jessica sold a copyright for £28,800. The copyright had been purchased on 1 April 2012 for £21,000 when it had an unexpired life of 15 years.

What is Jessica's chargeable gain in respect of the disposal of the copyright?

- A £0
- B £20,400
- C £16,200
- D £7,800

9.12 Identify, by clicking on the relevant box in the table below, whether the following statements are true or false.

An individual is subject to capital gains tax on the disposal of chargeable assets during any tax year in which they are resident in the UK	TRUE	FALSE
A company is subject to corporation tax on gains from the disposal of chargeable assets if it is resident in the UK	TRUE	FALSE
The disposal of a chargeable asset between civil partners is an exempt disposal	TRUE	FALSE
The transfer of chargeable assets between companies in a chargeable gains group is automatically treated as an exempt disposal	TRUE	FALSE

9.13 Vicki Ltd has chargeable gains in the current period of £26,000, capital losses in the current period of £20,000, brought forward capital losses of £10,000, and current period trading profits of £45,000.

What is the taxable total profits of Vicki Ltd upon which corporation tax will be charged?

- A £71,000
- B £51,000
- C £45,000
- D £41,000

9.14 Identify, by clicking on the relevant box in the table below, whether the following statements are true or false.

When a limited company has a capital loss, it is first set off against any chargeable gains arising in the same accounting period	TRUE	FALSE
Any remaining capital loss may be set against other income of the accounting period	TRUE	FALSE
Any capital loss unutilised in the accounting period is then carried forward and set off against the first available chargeable gains of future accounting periods	TRUE	FALSE
Any capital loss unutilised in the accounting period may be carried back and set off against the chargeable gains of the immediately preceding accounting period	TRUE	FALSE

(28 marks)

REVISION QUESTION BANK – TAXATION (TX-UK) (F6)

Question 10 CAPITAL GAINS TAX – CHATTELS, LAND AND BUILDINGS

10.1 On 21 March 2018 Jason sold six acres of land for £69,000. He had originally purchased nine acres on 17 July 2008 for £56,000. The market value of the unsold three acres as at 21 March 2018 is £27,600.

What is cost of the six acres of land that Jason has sold for CGT purposes?

A £37,333
B £40,000
C £49,286
D £55,200

10.2 In 2012, Finlay bought a painting for £75,000. In November 2017 it was damaged by smoke in a fire. In December 2017 it was valued at £60,000 and Finlay received compensation from the insurance company of £20,000 for the damage. Finlay spent none of the money on restoration.

What is the chargeable gain or allowable loss arising on the receipt of the compensation?

Select... ▼
£15,000 loss
No gain/no loss
£1,250 gain
£5,000 gain

10.3 On 28 October 2018 Leroy sold an antique vase for £12,100. The vase had been purchased on 28 February 2009 for £1,700.

What is Leo's chargeable gain on the disposal of the vase?

A £3,660
B £6,100
C £10,167
D £10,400

10.4 Anna bought a house on 2 April 1991 which she sold on 31 March 2018, realising a gain of £150,000. The house was Anna's principal private residence from the date of purchase until 30 September 2013, when she elected for another house to be her principal private residence.

What chargeable gain arose on the sale?

A £8,333
B £16,667
C £20,000
D £25,000

10.5 **Which of the following statements about a taxpayer's principal private residence is/are correct?**

(1) It is a chargeable asset for capital gains tax purposes.
(2) Even if part of it is used exclusively for business purposes, the whole of any gain arising on its disposal is exempt from capital gains tax.

A 1 only
B 2 only
C Both 1 and 2
D Neither 1 nor 2

10.6 On 10 January 2018, a freehold property owned by Winifred was damaged by a fire. The property had been purchased on 29 May 2004 for £73,000. Winifred received insurance proceeds of £37,200 on 23 February 2018, and she spent a total of £41,700 during March 2018 restoring the property. Winifred has elected to disregard the part disposal.

What is the base cost of the restored freehold property for capital gains tax purposes?

£ ☐

(12 marks)

Question 11 CAPITAL GAINS TAX – SHARES

11.1 Under the identification matching rules a disposal of shares in a quoted company can be matched to which of the following subsequent acquisitions?

(1) The same class of shares in the same company
(2) The same class of share in a similar company
(3) A different class of share in the same company

A 1 only
B 1 and 2 only
C 1 and 3 only
D 1, 2 and 3

11.2 Jenifer made the following transactions in the ordinary shares of Easter plc:

Date	Transaction	Number of shares
20 July 2016	Bought	2,000
22 August 2018	Bought	1,200
22 August 2018	Sold	350
31 August 2018	Bought	400
30 September 2018	Bought	500

Against which acquisition will the disposal of shares on 22 August 2018 be matched?

A 20 July 2016
B 22 August 2018
C 31 August 2018
D 30 September 2018

11.3 Jordan purchased ordinary shares in Birthday plc as follows:

Date	Number of shares	Cost £
31 July 1991	500	1,250
31 March 2018	1,500	4,400
10 April 2018	1,500	4,850

Jordan sold 500 shares on 15 May 2018 for £4,500. He made no further acquisitions of shares during 2018.

What amount of cost should be deducted in determining the chargeable gain on the disposal of shares?

A £1,250
B £1,467
C £1,500
D £1,617

11.4 On 31 August 2015, Fernando bought 2,400 ordinary shares in Party plc at a cost of £6,600. On 31 March 2016 the company made a 1 for 10 bonus issue. On 31 March 2018, Fernando sold 400 shares for £900.

What is the chargeable gain or allowable loss arising on the disposal?

A   £200 loss
B   £100 loss
C   £100 gain
D   £200 gain

(8 marks)

Question 12 CAPITAL GAINS TAX – BUSINESS ASSETS

12.1 Christos sold his business, which he had owned for 25 years, in January 2018. He realised a gain of £176,000 on the sale of business premises and a loss of £16,500 on the disposal of goodwill. Christos has no other chargeable gains or losses. His taxable income for the tax year 2017–18 is £35,500.

Assuming entrepreneur's relief is claimed, what is Christos' liability to capital gains tax arising for the tax year 2017–18?

A   £14,820
B   £15,950
C   £17,600
D   £29,640

12.2 Peter sold a warehouse on 27 June 2017 which resulted in a chargeable gain.

During what period must reinvestment take place if Peter wishes to claim rollover relief in respect of this gain?

A   27 June 2016 to 27 June 2019
B   27 June 2016 to 27 June 2020
C   27 June 2017 to 27 June 2020
D   27 June 2017 to 27 June 2021

12.3 In February 1996, Ronald bought land and buildings for use in his trade for £155,000. In June 2017 the land and buildings were sold for £620,000. In September 2017 Ronald bought replacement buildings for £420,000.

What is the amount of the gain that can be rolled over?

A   £0
B   £200,000
C   £265,000
D   £465,000

12.4 Janice owned shares in her personal trading company, Navros Ltd, which had cost £23,700. In August 2017 she gave the shares to her brother. At that date the market value of the shares was £82,500 and all of the chargeable assets of Navros Ltd were chargeable business assets.

What amount of the gain can be held-over?

A   £0
B   £23,700
C   £58,800
D   £82,500

TAXATION (TX-UK) (F6) – REVISION QUESTION BANK

12.5 Which THREE of the following are qualifying business assets for roll-over relief?

- ☐ Motor cars
- ☐ A warehouse
- ☐ Fixed plant and machinery
- ☐ Furnished holiday accommodation
- ☐ Moveable plant and equipment

12.6 Alice is in business as a sole trader. On 13 May 2017, she sold a freehold warehouse for £184,000, and this resulted in a chargeable gain of £38,600. Alice purchased a replacement freehold warehouse on 20 May 2017 for £143,000. Where possible, Alice always makes a claim to roll over gains against the cost of replacement assets. Both buildings have been, or will be, used for business purposes by Alice.

What is the base cost of the replacement warehouse for capital gains tax purposes?

£ _____

(12 marks)

Question 13 CORPORATION TAX – THE TAX COMPUTATION

13.1 Lapis Ltd commenced trading on 1 February 2016 and had the following periods of account:

1 February 2016 to 31 July 2017
1 August 2017 to 30 April 2018

The business was not successful and Lapis ceased to trade on 30 April 2018.

What is the last day of Lapis Ltd's first corporation tax accounting period?

- A 31 July 2016
- B 31 January 2017
- C 30 April 2017
- D 31 July 2017

13.2 Which TWO of the following expense items are deductible in arriving at the trading income of a company?

- ☐ Employer's national insurance contributions
- ☐ Gift of a £15 bottle of wine to a customer
- ☐ Interest on overdue corporation tax
- ☐ Replacement of roof tiles on the company's head office building

13.3 Which TWO of the following items are treated as income or expense on non-trading loan relationships for Brilliant Ltd?

☐ Bank overdraft interest

☐ Finance lease interest payable on the purchase of a company car for Brilliant Ltd's sales manager

☐ Interest payable on a loan to purchase an investment property

☐ Interest payable on a loan to purchase shares in Dim Ltd, another trading company

13.4 In the year ended 31 July 2018, Cat's Eye Ltd had bank interest receivable of £97,000 and loan interest payable as follows:

	£
On loan to acquire new factory premises	27,200
On loan to acquire an investment property	13,400
On loan to acquire shares in a subsidiary company	5,300

Identify the net amount assessable under the loan relationship rules for the year ended 31 July 2018 and the amount of interest which is deductible in arriving at Cat's Eye Ltd's trading profit.

Amount
£18,700
£27,200
£40,600
£51,100
£69,800
£78,300
£91,700

Net amount assessable	Deductible interest

13.5 Warovski Ltd has taxable total profits of £230,000 for the year ended 31 March 2018. However, this figure is before taking into account the following items, which were omitted from the financial statements:

(1) Qualifying charitable donations
(2) Recovery of trade debts previously written off as irrecoverable

What effect will each item have on Warovski Ltd's taxable total profits?

	Donations	Debt recovery
A	No effect	Increase
B	Decrease	No effect
C	Increase	Decrease
D	Decrease	Increase

(10 marks)

TAXATION (TX-UK) (F6) – REVISION QUESTION BANK

Question 14 CORPORATION TAX – LOSS RELIEFS

14.1 Kew Ltd has the following trading results to 31 December:

		£
2016	Loss	(37,600)
2017	Profit	19,500

The trading loss of £37,600 is carried forward.

The company also has bank interest receivable of £2,150 in 2016 and £3,200 in 2017.

What is the amount of Kew Ltd's taxable total profits for the year to 31 December 2017?

A £0
B £3,200
C £19,500
D £22,700

14.2 Highway Ltd has the following results for the years to 31 March 2017 and 31 March 2018:

	2017	2018
	£	£
Adjusted trading profit/(loss)	72,000	(90,000)
Property business profits	9,000	8,100
Chargeable gains	8,100	2,300
Qualifying charitable donations	1,800	1,800

The company makes all possible claims to relieve the trading loss against total profits.

What is the amount of total taxable profits for the year to 31 March 2017?

Select... ▼
£7,700
£9,500
£87,300
£89,100

14.3 Xiao Ltd has the following results for the two accounting periods to 31 March 2018:

	9 months to	Year to
	31 March 2017	31 March 2018
	£	£
Trading profit/(loss)	21,900	(24,800)
Chargeable gains	3,500	6,600

Assuming that Xiao Ltd makes all possible claims to relieve the trading loss against total profits, what is the total taxable profit for the nine months to 31 March 2017?

A £0
B £7,200
C £11,750
D £21,900

14.4 Zing Ltd made a trading profit in the year to 30 June 2016 and again for the nine months to 31 March 2017. It made a trading loss in the year to 31 March 2018.

The company made all possible claims to relieve the trading loss against total profits and a repayment of corporation tax became due for the year to 30 June 2016.

From what date will interest on the repayment of corporation tax for the year to 30 June 2016 accrue?

- A 31 January 2017
- B 1 April 2017
- C 1 January 2018
- D 1 January 2019

14.5 Sunny Ltd has had the following results:

Period	Trading profit/(loss) £
Year ended 31 December 2017	(120,000)
Five-month period ended 31 December 2016	47,000
Year ended 31 July 2016	90,000

The company does not have any other income.

How much of Sunny Ltd's trading loss for the year ended 31 December 2017 can be relieved against its total profits of £90,000 for the year ended 31 July 2016?

£ ⬜

(10 marks)

Question 15 CORPORATION TAX – GROUPS OF COMPANIES

15.1 Grebe Ltd owns 100% of the ordinary share capital of Bird Ltd. For the year ended 31 March 2018 Grebe Ltd had taxable total profits of £225,000. For the nine-month period ended 31 December 2017 Bird Ltd had a trading loss of £145,000.

How much of Blue Ltd's trading loss can Green Ltd claim against its taxable total profits for the year ended 31 March 2017?

£ ⬜

15.2 **Which of the following is NOT available for group relief?**

- A Unrelieved trading losses
- B Unrelieved capital losses
- C Unrelieved property business losses
- D Unrelieved qualifying charitable donations

15.3 Apple Ltd owns 85% of the ordinary share capital of Banana Ltd. Banana Ltd owns 75% of the ordinary share capital of Custard Ltd. Custard Ltd owns 100% of the ordinary share capital of Dairy Ltd and 75% of the ordinary share capital of Eden Ltd.

Identify, by clicking on the relevant box in the table below, which of the following companies form a chargeable gains group with Apple Ltd.

Banana Ltd	YES	NO
Custard Ltd	YES	NO
Dairy Ltd	YES	NO
Eden Ltd	YES	NO

15.4 Cranky Ltd owns 100% of the ordinary share capital of Mither Ltd. Both companies make up their accounts to 31 December. On 20 July 2017 Mither Ltd sold a factory building which resulted in a chargeable gain. On 27 December 2017 Cranky Ltd sold an office building that resulted in a capital loss.

By what date must Cranky Ltd and Mither Ltd make an election if they want their respective capital loss and chargeable gain to be matched?

- A 31 December 2018
- B 20 July 2019
- C 27 December 2019
- D 31 December 2019

15.5 Ten Ltd is the parent company for a group of companies. The group structure is as follows:

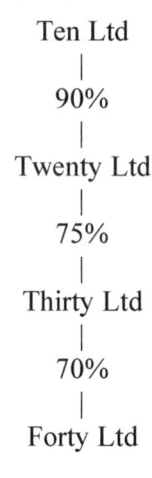

Ten Ltd
|
90%
|
Twenty Ltd
|
75%
|
Thirty Ltd
|
70%
|
Forty Ltd

Each percentage holding represents a holding of ordinary share capital.

What is the group relationship between Forty Ltd and Ten Ltd?

- A They form a group for both group relief and chargeable gains purposes
- B They form a group for group relief purposes but not for chargeable gains purposes
- C They form a group for chargeable gains purposes but not for group relief purposes
- D They do not form a group for either group relief or chargeable gains purposes

(10 marks)

Question 16 INHERITANCE TAX

16.1 Lily wishes to make gifts to her grandchildren, Andrew and Patrick rather than her daughter Kim.

Why might this be beneficial for inheritance tax (IHT) purposes?

A   To avoid a double charge to IHT
B   To maximise the use of the nil rate band
C   Because it postpones the payment of the IHT liability
D   Because there is a greater chance of the gift becoming exempt

16.2 Katrina made a gift of 3,000 £1 ordinary shares in CTS Ltd, an unquoted investment company. CTS Ltd has 20,000 £1 ordinary shares in issue. Before the transfer Katrina owned 11,000 of these shares. The shares are worth £18 each for a holding of 14%, £24 each for a holding of 40%, and £37 each for a holding of 55%.

What value has been transferred by Katrina in making the gift?

A   £54,000
B   £72,000
C   £111,000
D   £215,000

16.3 On 1 August 2017 Amanda made a gift to a trust of £550,000 (after deducting available exemptions). Amanda will pay the inheritance tax arising from the gift. She has not made any previous lifetime gifts.

What is Amanda's lifetime inheritance tax liability in respect of the gift?

A   £45,000
B   £56,250
C   £90,000
D   £137,500

16.4 Margaret died on 12 March 2018 leaving an estate valued at £450,000. On 12 July 2010 Margaret had made a gift of £15,000 to her daughter, and on 27 December 2012 she had made a gift of £75,000 to her son. These figures are after deducting available exemptions. Her estate is left equally between her two children and includes the property where she had lived, valued at £350,000.

What is the inheritance tax liability in respect of Margaret's estate?

A   £46,000
B   £40,000
C   £80,000
D   £180,000

16.5 Ben died on 14 February 2018. When his wife, Bella, died on 13 September 2008, only 35% of her nil rate band of £312,000 for the tax year 2008-09 was used. Ben and Bella did not have any children.

How much nil rate band may be claimed by Ben's personal representatives against his estate?

A   £325,000
B   £527,800
C   £536,250
D   £637,000

16.6 On 14 July 2016 Ray made a gift of £5,000 to his daughter, Wanda. On 17 October 2017 he made another gift of £6,700 to Wanda.

What is the value of the potentially exempt transfer to Wanda made on 17 October 2017?

A £700
B £2,700
C £3,700
D £6,700

16.7 On 6 November 2017 Andre made a gift to a trust which resulted in a lifetime inheritance tax liability of £39,450.

On what date is this liability due?

Select... ▼
31 December 2018
30 April 2018
6 May 2018
31 May 2018

16.8 Chan died on 8 December 2017, having made a lifetime cash gift of £500,000 to a trust on 16 October 2016. Chan paid the inheritance tax arising from this gift.

Who will be responsible for paying the additional inheritance tax arising from the gift made to the trust as a result of Chan's death, and when will this be due?

Select... ▼
The trustees on 30 June 2018
The personal representatives of Chan's estate on 8 June 2018
The personal representatives of Chan's estate on 30 June 2018
The trustees on 8 June 2018

16.9 Indicate which of the following obligations are deducted when calculating the value of a person's chargeable estate for inheritance tax purposes.

Obligations
An outstanding repayment mortgage
Funeral expenses
An outstanding interest-only mortgage
An outstanding endowment mortgage
A verbal promise to pay a friend's debt
Credit card debts

Deducted	Not deducted

REVISION QUESTION BANK – TAXATION (TX-UK) (F6)

16.10 Benjamin died on 30 November 2017 leaving an estate valued at £890,000. Inheritance tax of £276,000 was paid in respect of the estate. Under the terms of his will, Benjamin left £260,000 to his wife, a specific legacy of £120,000 (free of tax) to his brother, and the residue of the estate to his grandchildren.

What is the amount of inheritance received by Benjamin's grandchildren?

£ [   ]

16.11 Heng is a wealthy 45 year old who would like to reduce the potential inheritance tax liability on her estate when she dies.

Identify, by clicking on the relevant box in the table below, which of the following actions will be effective in achieving Heng's aim of reducing the potential inheritance tax liability on her estate when she dies.

Changing the terms of her will so that the residue of her estate goes to her grandchildren rather than her children	EFFECTIVE	NOT EFFECTIVE
Making lifetime gifts to trusts up to the value of the nil rate band every seven years	EFFECTIVE	NOT EFFECTIVE
Changing the terms of her will so that the residue of her estate goes to her husband rather than her children	EFFECTIVE	NOT EFFECTIVE
Making lifetime gifts to her grandchildren early in life	EFFECTIVE	NOT EFFECTIVE

(22 marks)

Question 17 NIC, PAYE AND SELF-ASSESSMENT

*17.1 – 17.4 are not exam standard and provided for revision only. An exam standard question would require two dates for two marks (e.g. Specimen Exam item 13) or include an extra level of complexity.

17.1* Andrea received a gross salary of £72,000 in the tax year 2017–18. She also received property income of £800 per month from an investment property that she has held for many years. On 20 September 2018 Andrea submitted her self-assessment tax return for the tax year 2017–18.

What is the due date of payment of the balance of tax due on Andrea's return for the tax year 2017–18?

A   31 January 2019
B   20 June 2019
C   30 September 2019
D   31 January 2020   (1 mark)

17.2* Angela submitted her self-assessment tax return for the tax year 2017–18 on 20 September 2018. On 31 December 2018 she found an error in her return.

What is the time limit for Andrea to correct her return for the tax year 2017–18?

A   31 January 2019
B   20 September 2019
C   30 September 2019
D   31 January 2020   (1 mark)

17.3* By which date must an employer submit forms P11D for the tax year 2017–18 to HM Revenue and Customs to avoid a late filing penalty?

- A 31 May 2018
- B 6 July 2018
- C 19 July 2018
- D 22 July 2018

(1 mark)

17.4* By which date must an employer provide employees with a form P60 for the tax year 2017–18?

- A 5 April 2018
- B 19 May 2018
- C 31 May 2018
- D 6 July 2018

(1 mark)

17.5 Bluish Ltd has prepared its corporation tax return for the year ended 31 March 2018.

Jasmine, a sole trader for many years, has just finished preparing her accounts to 31 December 2017.

Indicate to what dates Bluish Ltd and Jasmine must keep their business records in respect of the above periods.

Date
31 March 2023
31 January 2024
31 March 2024
31 January 2025

Bluish Ltd	Jasmine

17.6 Andrew has been trading for many years. His adjusted trading profits for the tax year 2017–18 are £25,000.

What is the total amount of national insurance contributions payable by Andrew for the tax year 2017–18?

- A £1,515
- B £1,663
- C £2,250
- D £2,398

17.7 Which classes of national insurance contribution is an employer responsible for paying?

- A Both Class 2 and Class 4
- B Class 1 only
- C Both Class 1 and Class 1A
- D Class 2 only

17.8 Abdul's tax liabilities for the tax years 2016–17 and 2017–18 are as follows:

	2016–17 £	2017–18 £
Income tax payable	300	2,400
Class 4 national insurance contributions	320	1,260
Capital gains tax liability	240	0
	860	3,660

What payment on account will Abdul have to make on 31 July 2018 in respect of his tax liability for the tax year 2017–18?

£ ☐

17.9 Mammoth Ltd commenced trading on 1 January 2015. The company's profits have been as follows:

Period	£
Year ended 31 December 2015	524,000
Year ended 31 December 2016	867,000
Year ended 31 December 2017	912,000

Throughout all of these periods, Mammoth Ltd had one related 51% group company.

Identify the first year for which Mammoth Ltd will be required to pay its corporation tax liability by quarterly instalments.

Year ended 31 December 2016	CORRECT	INCORRECT
None of the years ended 31 December 2015, 2016 or 2017	CORRECT	INCORRECT
Year ended 31 December 2017	CORRECT	INCORRECT
Year ended 31 December 2015	CORRECT	INCORRECT

17.10 Lorna has the choice of being either employed or self-employed. If employed, Lorna's gross annual salary for the tax year 2017–18 will be £36,000. If self-employed, Lorna's trading profit for the year ended 5 April 2018 will be £36,000.

How much more national insurance contributions will Lorna suffer for the tax year 2017–18 if she chooses to be employed rather than self-employed?

Select... ▼
£835
£932
£687
£1,080

17.11 For the tax year 2017–18, identify the latest dates by which a taxpayer, who does not wish to incur a penalty, should file a self-assessment tax return on paper or online.

Date
31 October 2018
31 January 2019
31 October 2019
31 January 2020

Paper tax return	Online tax return

(18 marks)

Question 18 TAX COMPLIANCE

18.1 Identify, by clicking on the relevant box in the table below, which of the following statements concerning the appeals procedure is correct.

(1)	A taxpayer can appeal against a determination and apply for postponement of payment	CORRECT	INCORRECT
(2)	The taxpayer must first apply for an internal review before making an appeal to the First-tier Tribunal	CORRECT	INCORRECT
(3)	A taxpayer can appeal against and apply to postpone the tax due under an assessment raised as a result of an enquiry into a tax return	CORRECT	INCORRECT

18.2 Esther, a higher-rate taxpayer, submitted her tax return for the tax year 2017–18 on 1 December 2018. She had omitted to include rental income of £18,000 because she did not want to disclose this source of income to HM Revenue and Customs (HMRC).

In response to HMRC's enquiries into her return Ethel made full disclosure of the rental income.

What is the minimum amount of penalty that HMRC could charge Esther for her misdeclaration?

A £1,260
B £2,520
C £5,040
D £4,500

18.3 Carmen commenced trading on 1 January 2017 and her profit for the year ended 31 December 2017 was £56,000. She has not contacted HM Revenue and Customs (HMRC) to advise that she has commenced to trade and has never been issued with nor completed a self-assessment return.

What is the latest date by which Carmen should have notified HMRC of her new business?

A 31 January 2017
B 5 October 2017
C 31 January 2018
D 5 October 2018

18.4 Landsend Ltd is a "small" company not required to pay corporation tax by instalments. It estimated its corporation tax liability for the year ended 31 December 2016 to be £90,000 and paid this on 1 November 2017. After filing the company's return, the corporation tax liability was amended to £102,000. The company paid the £12,000 further tax due on 31 January 2018.

How much is the interest on late paid tax?

A £82
B £110
C £206
D £316

18.5 Andre's income tax liability of £12,000 which was due for payment on 31 January 2018 was not paid until 31 March 2018.

How much interest will Andre be charged by HM Revenue and Customs in respect of the late payment of this income tax liability?

A £55
B £82
C £330
D £655

18.6 Quinn will not make the balancing payment in respect of her tax liability for the tax year 2016–17 until 17 October 2018.

What is the total percentage of penalty which Quinn will be charged by HM Revenue and Customs in respect of the late balancing payment for the tax year 2016–17?

Select...
15%
10%
5%
30%

18.7 For the tax year 2016–17, Willard filed a paper self-assessment tax return on 10 August 2017.

What is the deadline for Willard to make an amendment to his tax return for the tax year 2016–17, and by what date will HM Revenue and Customs (HMRC) have to notify Willard if they intend to carry out a compliance check into this return?

	Amendment	Compliance check
A	10 August 2018	31 January 2019
B	10 August 2018	10 August 2018
C	31 January 2019	10 August 2018
D	31 January 2019	31 January 2019

18.8 For the year ended 30 June 2017, Forgetful Ltd had a corporation tax liability of £166,250, which it did not pay until 31 July 2018. Forgetful Ltd is not a large company.

How much interest will Forgetful Ltd be charged by HM Revenue and Customs in respect of the late payment of its corporation tax liability for the year ended 30 June 2017?

Select... ▼
£1,385
£2,667
£4,953
£1,524

(16 marks)

Question 19 VALUE ADDED TAX

19.1 Which TWO of the following statements concerning VAT registration of Sug, a trader, are correct?

☐ He can register voluntarily if he makes only exempt supplies

☐ He can register voluntarily if he makes only zero-rated supplies

☐ If he makes both zero-rated and standard-rated supplies he must register only if taxable supplies exceed the VAT registration limit

☐ If he makes exempt supplies he must register if these supplies exceed the VAT registration limit

19.2 Emerald commenced business as a sole trader on 1 March 2017 making only taxable supplies. Her turnover in the first 15 months of trade was as follows:

1 March 2017 to 30 September 2017	£7,500 per month
October and November 2017	£10,500 per month
From December 2017 onwards	£12,000 per month

By what date should Emerald have notified HM Revenue and Customs that she was required to become VAT registered in order to avoid a penalty for late registration?

- A 1 March 2017
- B 30 November 2017
- C 31 December 2017
- D 31 January 2018

19.3 Dan is a VAT registered sole trader. Dan sold goods to Gus for £126 without charging any VAT as Gus had assured him that the goods were exempt from VAT. Dan subsequently found out that the goods were subject to the standard rate of VAT.

Indicate, by clicking on the relevant boxes in the table below, the amount of VAT payable on this sale and by whom.

Amount	£21.00	£25.20
Payable by	Dan	Gus

19.4 Gosia, is registered for VAT and operates the cash accounting scheme. She delivers some goods to a customer on 23 May in respect of an order received on 15 May. Gosia issued the invoice on 27 May and received payment from the customer on 14 June.

What is the tax point of the supply?

A	15 May
B	23 May
C	27 May
D	14 June

19.5 Charlie is a VAT registered trader making only standard-rated supplies. He received an order from a customer on 19 May 2018 enclosing a payment of £2,250 which represented a 15% deposit (including VAT).

Charlie dispatched the goods on 19 May and issued an invoice for the full amount of £15,000 on 1 June. The balancing payment of £12,750 was received on 13 July.

Charlie does not operate the cash accounting scheme.

Identify the amounts of output tax to be accounted for in the VAT returns for the quarters to 31 May and 31 August 2018.

Amount
£0
£250
£375
£2,125
£2,250
£2,500

31 May	31 August

19.6 Beryl is registered for VAT and is preparing her VAT return for the three-month period ended 31 March 2018. During this period she made zero-rated supplies of £14,450 and standard-rated supplies of £19,650. These figures exclude VAT.

What amount of output VAT should Beryl account for on her VAT return for the three months ended 31 March 2018?

A	£3,275
B	£3,330
C	£3,930
D	£6,820

19.7 Barbara is registered for VAT and is preparing her VAT return for the three-month period ended 31 March 2018.

Barbara incurred input tax of £1,338 related to zero-rated supplies and input tax of £600 related to standard-rated supplies.

What amount of input VAT should Barbar account for on her VAT return for the three months ended 31 March 2018?

A	£600
B	£738
C	£1,338
D	£1,938

19.8 Smoky Ltd is a VAT registered company that only makes standard-rated supplies. The company incurred the following VAT-inclusive costs:

(1) £13,600 for the purchase equipment. The VAT invoice was inadvertently destroyed and cannot be replaced.

(2) Purchase of a new car for the marketing manager for £18,500. The car is used 70% for business purposes.

Drag and drop the correct descriptor of recoverability to indicate to what extent Smoky Ltd can recover the input tax on each of these costs.

Recoverability
Irrecoverable
Partially recoverable
Fully recoverable

Equipment	New car

19.9 Johnnie, a sole trader, completed a VAT return for the quarter to 31 December 2017 showing output tax of £215,000 and input tax of £126,000.

In July 2018 Johnnie's accountant discovered that the input tax on the VAT return had been overstated by £7,500. This was the first time that Johnnie had made an error on a VAT return. HM Revenue and Customs (HMRC) was notified and the outstanding tax paid.

What is the minimum amount of penalty that HMRC could charge Johnnie for the error?

A   0% of tax lost
B   15% of tax lost
C   20% of tax lost
D   30% of tax lost

19.10 Which TWO of the following statements are correct in relation to the cash accounting scheme for VAT?

☐ A VAT return is completed once a year

☐ Relief for impairment losses on trade debts is given automatically

☐ Output VAT is accounted for when cash is received from the customer

☐ VAT is paid over to HM Revenue and Customs in quarterly instalments

19.11 Which THREE of the following statements are correct in relation to the flat rate scheme for small businesses?

☐ The flat rate scheme may be used in conjunction with the annual accounting scheme

☐ A trader can join if VAT exclusive turnover for the next 12 months is not expected to exceed £150,000

☐ There is no recovery of input VAT

☐ The flat rate is applied to the VAT exclusive turnover

☐ The scheme gives automatic relief for bad or impaired debts

19.12 Violet Ltd provides one of its directors with a company motor car which is used for both business and private mileage. For the quarter ended 31 March 2018, the total cost of petrol for the car was £600, of which 30% was for private use by the director. The relevant quarterly scale charge is £408. Both these figures are inclusive of value added tax (VAT).

Identify the amounts of the output VAT and input VAT entries that Violet Ltd should include on the VAT return for the quarter ended 31 March 2018 in respect of the company motor car.

Amount
£0
£68
£70
£100
£2,250
£2,500

Output VAT	Input VAT

19.13 Yui commenced trading on 1 April 2017, and registered for value added tax (VAT) from 1 January 2018. Her first VAT return is for the quarter ended 31 March 2018. During the period 1 April 2017 to 31 March 2018, Yui incurred input VAT of £110 per month in respect of the hire of office equipment.

How much input VAT in respect of the office equipment can Yui reclaim on her VAT return for the quarter ended 31 March 2018?

£ _____

19.14 Brian is registered for VAT and is registered for the flat rate scheme. He has previously been applying a rate of 14%, however from April 2017 the limited cost flat rate of 16.5% has been applicable.

For the quarter ended 30 September 2017 Brian made standard rated sales of £30,000 and purchases of £600 (both figures are exclusive of VAT).

How much more VAT will Brian have to pay for the quarter than if the previous 14% rate had still been available?

A £625
B £750
C £882
D £900

(28 marks)

TAXATION (TX-UK) (F6) – REVISION QUESTION BANK

Question 20 ASPECTS OF A TAX SYSTEM

Required:

(a) Give four main objectives of taxation in a developed economy. (2 marks)
(b) List the main sources of tax law effective in the UK. (3 marks)
(c) Explain the meaning of the terms "tax avoidance" and "tax evasion". (5 marks)

(10 marks)

Question 21 SHIV AND SHANKER

(a) Shiv and Shanker are brothers. Up until the tax year 2015–16 they have both been considered UK resident for income tax purposes.

Shiv is single and lives with his mother, Poppy, in her house in London. His employment as a mining engineer has been UK-based but in May 2017 and again in September he was sent on overseas assignments of seven weeks each. On 1 December 2017 he moved abroad to start a two-year posting. He made a return visit to the UK for three weeks over the Christmas and New Year holidays.

Shanker lives in East Anglia with his wife and daughter. He won a place as a crew member in a one year round-the-world yacht race and, after several weeks training in the UK, the yacht departed on 1 July 2017.

Required:

Explain whether or not Shiv and Shanker will be treated as UK resident for income tax in the tax year 2017–18. (4 marks)

Note: You should ignore any possible split year treatment.

(b) Poppy owns and manages a bookstore. She has one full-time employee, two other workers employed on a part-time job share basis, and also regularly uses unpaid volunteers looking for work experience.

The employees are paid on a monthly basis. Poppy uses a payroll software package to comply with real time information (RTI) reporting and payment requirements, but has recently had some problems with this. Her returns to HM Revenue and Customs for January, February and March 2018 were all submitted late.

Poppy has been speaking to her sister Holly, who works as an accounts assistant. Part of Holly's job is preparing accounts in iXBRL format and Poppy is worried that this is another area of compliance that her bookshop business should have already adopted.

Required:

(i) **State the reporting deadlines for a full payment submission and for end of year returns, and also the related payment deadlines. Advise when penalties may apply.**

(ii) **Describe what is meant by iXBRL and explain what action if any Poppy needs to take.** (6 marks)

(10 marks)

Question 22 BAYLE DEFENDER

You should assume that today's date is 20 November 2017.

Bayle Defender is self-employed as a lawyer.

On 1 December 2017 Bayle Defender is planning to bring a newly qualified lawyer, Fyle Guardian, into her business. Fyle will either be taken on as Bayle's only employee, being paid a gross monthly salary of £3,300, or join Bayle as a partner, receiving a 20% share of the new partnership's profits.

Bayle has forecast that her tax adjusted trading profit will be £216,000 for the year ended 30 September 2018, and £240,000 for the year ended 30 September 2019.

Fyle does not have any other income for the tax year 2017–18.

Required:

(a) **Assuming that Fyle Guardian is employed from 1 December 2017, calculate the total amount of national insurance contributions (NIC) that will be paid by Bayle Defender and Fyle Guardian, if any, in respect of his earnings for the tax year 2017–18.**

Note: You are not expected to calculate the national insurance contributions that will be paid in respect of Bayle Defender's earnings. (4 marks)

(b) **Assuming that Fyle Guardian becomes a partner from 1 December 2017:**

(i) **Calculate his trading income assessments for the tax years 2017–18 and 2018–19.**

Note: You are not expected to calculate any overlap profits. (3 marks)

(ii) **Calculate the total amount of national insurance contributions that will be paid by Bayle Defender and Fyle Guardian, if any, in respect of his trading income assessment for the tax year 2017–18.**

Note: You are not expected to calculate the national insurance contributions that will be paid in respect of Bayle Defender's trading income assessment. (3 marks)

(10 marks)

Question 23 JOSIE JONES

On 30 June 2017 Josie Jones ceased self-employment as a graphic designer. On 1 August 2017 she commenced employment with Typo plc as a creative director. The following information is available for the tax year 2017–18:

Self-employment

- Josie's trading profits for the final two periods of trading were as follows:

	£
Year ended 30 April 2017	56,500
Two-month period ended 30 June 2017	16,600

Both these figures are before taking account of capital allowances.

TAXATION (TX-UK) (F6) – REVISION QUESTION BANK

- The tax written down value of the capital allowances main pool at 1 May 2016 was £13,200. On 21 May 2017 Josie purchased computer equipment for £3,600. All of the items included in the main pool were sold for £7,700 on 30 June 2017, with no item being sold for more than its original cost.

- Josie has no unused overlap profits brought forward.

Employment

- Josie is paid a salary of £15,100 per month by Typo plc. The salary is paid on the last day of each calendar month.

- During August 2017 Typo plc paid £11,600 towards Josie's removal expenses when she permanently moved to take up her new employment with the company as she did not live within a reasonable commuting distance. The £11,600 covered both her removal expenses and the legal costs of acquiring a new main residence.

- On 1 September 2017 Typo plc provided Josie with an interest free loan of £33,000 that she used to renovate her new main residence. This loan was still outstanding at 5 April 2018.

- During the period from 1 August 2017 to 5 April 2018, Josie was provided with free meals in Typo plc's staff canteen. The total cost of these meals to the company was £1,340. The canteen is available to all of the company's employees.

Other information

- Josie owns two properties, which are let out. Property one qualifies as a trade under the furnished holiday letting rules, whilst property two is let out unfurnished. The income and allowable expenditure for the two properties for the tax year 2017–18 are as follows:

	Property one £	Property two £
Income	6,600	7,200
Allowable expenditure	9,700	2,100

- During the tax year 2017–18 Josie received building society interest of £11,200 and dividends of £7,200.

- On 2 October 2017 Josie received a premium bond prize of £100.

- During the tax year 2017–18 Josie made gift aid donations totalling £4,400 (net) to national charities.

Required:

Calculate the income tax liability of Josie Jones for the tax year 2017–18.

Note: You should indicate by the use of zero any items that are non-taxable/exempt from tax.

(15 marks)

Question 24 SOPHIA WONG

You should assume that today's date is 15 March 2017.

Sophia Wong is self-employed. For the year ended 5 April 2018 Sophia has forecast that her tax adjusted trading profit will be £80,000. This will be her only income for the tax year 2017–18. Sophia's total income tax liability and national insurance contributions (NIC) for this year if she continues to trade on a self-employed basis will be £25,231 as follows:

	£
Income tax	20,700
Class 2 NIC	148
Class 4 NIC	4,015
	24,863

Sophia understands that she could save tax and NIC if she instead traded as a limited company, and she is therefore considering incorporating her business on 6 April 2017. The forecast taxable total profits of the new limited company for the year ended 5 April 2018 are unchanged at £80,000 (before taking account of any director's remuneration).

Required:

Assuming that Sophia Wong incorporates her business on 6 April 2017, advise her whether or not there will be an overall saving of tax and national insurance contributions (NIC) for the tax year 2017–18 if she withdraws all of the profits from the new company as:

(a) **director's remuneration (after allowing for employer's class 1 NIC, gross director's remuneration will be £71,289); or** (5 marks)

(b) **dividends.** (5 marks)

Note: For both alternatives, you are expected to calculate the corporation tax liability (if any) of the new limited company for the year ended 5 April 2018, the income tax payable by Sophia Wong, and the class 1 NIC (if any) payable by Sophia and the new company.

(10 marks)

Question 25 JOHN BEACH

John is employed by Surf plc as a sales director The following information is available for the tax year 2017–18:

(1) During the tax year 2017–18, he was paid gross director's remuneration of £184,000.

(2) During the tax year 2017–18, John contributed £28,000 into Surf plc's HM Revenue and Customs' registered occupational pension scheme. The company contributed a further £12,000 on his behalf. Both John and Surf plc have made exactly the same contributions for the previous five tax years.

(3) During the period 6 April to 31 October 2017, John used his private motor car for both private and business journeys. He was reimbursed by Surf plc at the rate of 60p per mile for the following mileage:

	Miles
Normal daily travel between home and Surf plc's offices	1,180
Travel between Surf plc's offices and the premises of Surf plc's clients	4,270
Travel between home and the premises of Surf plc's clients (none of the clients' premises were located near the offices of Surf plc)	510
Total mileage reimbursed by Surf plc	5,960

(4) During the period from 1 November 2017 to 5 April 2018, Surf plc provided John with a petrol powered motor car which has a list price of £28,200 and an official CO_2 emission rate of 182 grams per kilometre. Surf plc also provided John with fuel for both his business and private journeys.

(5) During 2014 Surf plc provided John with a loan which was used to purchase a yacht. The amount of loan outstanding at 6 April 2017 was £84,000. John repaid £12,000 of the loan on 31 July 2017, and then repaid a further £12,000 on 31 December 2017. He paid loan interest of £1,090 to Surf plc during the tax year 2017–18. The taxable benefit in respect of this loan is calculated using the average method.

(6) John owns a holiday cottage which is let out as a furnished holiday letting, although the letting does not qualify as a trade under the furnished holiday letting rules. The property business profit for the year ended 5 April 2018 was £6,730.

Required:

(a) **Calculate John Beach's income tax liability for the tax year 2017–18.** (14 marks)

(b) **Calculate the class 1 national insurance contributions that will have been suffered by John Beach in respect of his earnings and benefits for the tax year 2017–18.** (1 mark)

(15 marks)

Question 26 PHIL JONES

(a) On 23 August 2012 Phil Jones received a house valued at £420,000 as a wedding gift from Pere, his father. Phil let it out unfurnished until it was sold on 5 April 2018. The following income and outgoings relate to the property for the tax year 2017–18:

	£
Rent received	22,000
Sale proceeds	504,000
Cost of new boundary wall around the property (there was previously no boundary wall)	(5,300)
Cost of replacing the property's chimney	(2,800)
Legal fees paid in connection with the disposal	(8,600)
Property insurance	(2,300)

Phil has no other income or outgoings for the tax year 2017–18.

Required:

Calculate Phil's income tax and capital gains tax liabilities for the tax year 2017–18.

(7 marks)

(b) **State the tax advantages of a rental property qualifying as a trade under the furnished holiday letting rules.** (3 marks)

(10 marks)

Question 27 RICHARD FEAST

(a) On 6 April 2017, Richard Feast commenced in self-employment, running a restaurant. Richard's statement of profit or loss for the year ended 5 April 2018 is as follows:

	Note	£	£
Gross profit			73,440
Expenses			
Motor expenses	1	7,660	
Property expenses	2	16,200	
Repairs and renewals	3	6,420	
Other expenses	4	10,960	
			(41,240)
Net profit			32,200

Note 1 – Motor expenses

Motor expenses are as follows:

	£
Cost of running Richard's motor car	4,710
Cost of running a motor car used by the restaurant's chef	2,670
Parking fines incurred by Richard	280
	7,660

Richard's motor car is used 70% for private journeys, and the chef's motor car is used 20% for private journeys.

Note 2 – Property expenses

Richard lives in an apartment which is situated above the restaurant, and one-fifth of the total property expenses of £16,200 relate to this apartment.

Note 3 – Repairs and renewals

Repairs and renewals are as follows:

	£
Decorating the restaurant	5,100
Decorating the apartment	1,320
	6,420

The property was in a usable state when it was purchased.

Note 4 – Other expenses

The figure of £10,960 for other expenses includes legal fees of £2,590 in connection with the purchase of the restaurant property. The remaining expenses are all allowable.

Additional information

Plant and machinery

The following motor cars were purchased during the year ended 5 April 2018:

	Date of purchase	Cost £	CO_2 emission rate
Motor car [1]	6 April 2017	14,000	94 grams per kilometre
Motor car [2]	6 April 2017	16,800	108 grams per kilometre

Motor car [1] is used by Richard, and motor car [2] is used by the restaurant's chef.

Required:

Calculate Richard Feast's tax adjusted trading profit for the year ended 5 April 2018.

(8 marks)

Notes:

(1) Your computation should commence with the net profit figure of £32,200, and should list all of the items referred to in notes (1) to (4), indicating by the use of zero (0) any items which do not require adjustment.

(2) In answering this part of the question you are not expected to take account of any of the information provided in part (b) below.

(b) Richard had three employees working for him in his restaurant during the tax year 2017–18 as follows:

(1) A chef who was employed throughout the tax year 2017–18 on a gross annual salary of £46,000. The chef was provided with a petrol powered motor car (see the plant and machinery information in part (a) above) throughout the tax year. The list price of the motor car is the same as its cost. Richard did not provide any fuel for private journeys.

(2) A part-time waitress who was employed for 20 hours per week throughout the tax year 2017–18 on a gross annual salary of £7,400.

(3) An assistant chef who was employed for eight months from 6 August 2017 to 5 April 2018 on a gross monthly salary of £2,200.

Required:

Calculate the employers' class 1 and class 1A national insurance contributions which Richard Feast would have incurred in respect of his employees' earnings and benefit for the tax year 2017–18. (7 marks)

Note: You are not expected to calculate the national insurance contributions suffered by the employees or by Richard in respect of his self-employment.

(15 marks)

Question 28 FANG AND HONG

(a) Fang commenced self-employment on 1 August 2015. She has a trading profit of £45,960 for the year ended 31 July 2016, and a trading profit of £39,360 for the year ended 31 July 2017.

Required:

(i) **Calculate the amount of trading profit which will have been assessed on Fang for each of the tax years 2015–16, 2016–17 and 2017–18, and state the amount of any overlap profit.** (3 marks)

(ii) **Explain how Fang would have obtained relief for trading expenditure incurred prior to 1 August 2015 and for computer equipment which Fang already owned which was brought into business use on 1 August 2015.** (2 marks)

(b) Hong has been in self-employment since 2006, preparing accounts to 5 April. For the year ended 5 April 2018 she made a trading loss of £45,800, and has claimed this against her total income and chargeable gain for the tax year 2016–17.

For the year ended 5 April 2017 Hong made a trading profit of £29,700. She also has a property business profit of £3,900 for the tax year 2016–17. Hong has an unused trading loss of £2,600 brought forward from the tax year 2015–16.

During the tax year 2016–17 Hong disposed of an investment property and this resulted in a chargeable gain (before the annual exempt amount) of £17,800. Hong has unused capital losses of £6,200 brought forward from the tax year 2014–15.

Required:

After taking account of the loss relief claims made, calculate Hong's taxable income and taxable gain for the tax year 2016–17, and state the amount of any trading loss carried forward. (5 marks)

Note: You should assume that the tax allowances for the tax year 2017–18 apply throughout.

(10 marks)

Question 29 KLM AND RICHARD MORRIS

(a) Kang, Ling and Ming have been in partnership since 2008, preparing accounts to 30 June. Ming left the partnership on 31 October 2016. Profits have always been shared equally.

The partnership had a trading profit of £148,800 for the year ended 30 June 2016, and a profit of £136,800 for the year ended 30 June 2017. Each partner has unused overlap profits brought forward of £29,400.

Required:

Calculate the trading income assessments of Kang, Ling and Ming for each of the tax years 2016–17 and 2017–18. (5 marks)

(b) During the tax year 2017–18 Richard Morris had employment income of £65,000, trading profit of £15,000 and investment income of £10,000. Richard did not make any personal pension contributions during the tax year 2017–18. He has never been a member of a pension scheme.

Required:

(i) Assuming that Richard Morris received child benefit of £1,752 during the tax year 2017–18, advise him of the amount of child benefit income tax charge which he will be subject to and how this will be collected. (2 marks)

(ii) Advise Richard Morris why the maximum amount of tax relievable personal pension scheme contribution which he could have made for the tax year 2017–18 is £40,000, and the method by which tax relief would have been given if he had made this amount of contribution. (3 marks)

(10 marks)

Question 30 CHI NEEDLE

Chi Needle commenced self-employment on 6 April 2017, and for the year ended 5 April 2018 her trading profit using the normal accruals basis was £52,400, calculated as follows:

	£	£
Revenue		71,900
Expenses		
Motor expenses	4,400	
Other expenses	8,200	
Capital allowances	6,900	
		(19,500)
Trading profit		52,400

Additional information

Chi has no other income for the tax year 2017–18.

She did not make any payments on account in respect of the tax year 2017–18.

Required:

(a) Based on the trading profit of £52,400 for the year ended 5 April 2018:

(i) Calculate Chi Needle's income tax liability for the tax year 2017–18. (2 marks)

(ii) Calculate the Class 2 and Class 4 national insurance contributions payable by Chi Needle for the tax year 2017–18. (3 marks)

(iii) Determine the amount of income tax and national insurance contributions which will be due for payment under self-assessment by Chi Needle on 31 January 2019. (3 marks)

(b) Advise Chi Needle of the latest date by which a paper self-assessment tax return can be filed for the tax year 2017–18, and the deadline should she wish to make an amendment to this return. (2 marks)

(10 marks)

Question 31 QI PIN

(a) Qi Pin commenced self-employment as an acupuncturist on 6 April 2017, and for the year ended 5 April 2018 her trading profit using the normal accruals basis was £52,400, calculated as follows:

	Note	£	£
Revenue	1		71,900
Expenses			
Motor expenses	2	4,400	
Other expenses	3	8,200	
Capital allowances	4	6,900	
			(19,500)
Trading profit			52,400

Note 1 – Revenue

The revenue figure of £71,900 includes receivables of £1,600 which were owed as at 5 April 2018.

Note 2 – Motor expenses

The total motor expenses for the year ended 5 April 2018 were £5,500, of which 20% was for private journeys. This proportion has been disallowed in calculating the trading profit. During the year ended 5 April 2018, Qi drove 13,200 business miles.

Note 3 – Other expenses

The other expenses figure of £8,200 includes payables of £900 which were owed as at 5 April 2018.

Note 4 – Capital allowances

Capital allowances consist of an annual investment allowance claim of £4,020 in respect of office equipment purchased on 6 April 2017, and a writing down allowance of £2,880 claimed in respect of Qi's motor car. The motor car had cost £20,000 on 6 April 2017.

Required:

Calculate Qi Pin's trading profit for the year ended 5 April 2018 if she had used the cash basis instead of the accruals basis. (5 marks)

Notes:

(1) Where relevant, expenses should be claimed on a flat rate basis.
(2) You are not expected to calculate the income tax liability or the national insurance contributions payable.

(b) **You should assume that today's date is 15 March 2018.**

Mobias has recently inherited the residue of his aunt's estate. Mobias will use some of his inheritance for the following purposes:

Personal pension contribution

Mobias will make an additional personal pension contribution for the tax year 2017–18, having already made contributions of £10,000 during this tax year. He has been self-employed since 6 April 2015, and has been a member of a personal pension scheme from the tax year 2016–17 onwards. Mobias' trading profits and gross personal pension contributions since he commenced self-employment have been as follows:

Tax year	Trading profit £	Pension contribution £
2015–16	32,000	0
2016–17	44,000	26,000
2017–18	78,000	10,000

Individual savings accounts (ISAs)

Mobias will invest the maximum possible amounts into individual savings accounts for the tax year 2017–18. He has already invested £2,400 in a cash individual savings account during this tax year, having previously invested £3,200 in a cash individual savings account during the tax year 2016–17.

Required:

(i) **Advise Mobias of the maximum amount of additional gross personal pension contribution which he is permitted to make for the tax year 2017–18, and how much of this maximum contribution will qualify for tax relief.** (3 marks)

(ii) **Advise Mobias as to what options he has as regards making full use of his individual savings account limits for the tax year 2017–18.** (2 marks)

(c) Road Ltd's recently appointed bookkeeper has asked your advice about the company's VAT and pay as you earn (PAYE) tax reporting obligations. Road Ltd pays its employees at the end of each calendar month, with some employees receiving taxable benefits. The bookkeeper understands that the company must report PAYE information to HM Revenue and Customs in real time. However, she does not know how PAYE real time reporting works in practice, having previously only produced payroll manually.

Required:

(i) **Explain how and when VAT registered businesses have to submit their quarterly VAT returns and pay any related VAT liability.** (2 marks)

Note: You are not expected to cover annual VAT returns, the election for monthly returns or substantial traders.

(ii) **Explain how and when Road Ltd will have to report real time PAYE information to HM Revenue and Customs, and state what forms, if any, will have to be provided to employees or submitted to HM Revenue and Customs following the end of the tax year.** (3 marks)

(15 marks)

Question 32 ALFRED KING

(a) Alfred King is trying to calculate his balancing payment for the tax year 2017–18, and the following information is available:

- He has been in partnership with Anne Royal and Mary Regal running a retail shop since 6 April 2008, but Mary resigned as a partner on 1 January 2018.

- The partnership's tax adjusted trading profit for the year ended 5 April 2018 is £228,000. This figure is before taking account of capital allowances.

- The tax written down value of the partnership's capital allowances main pool at 6 April 2017 was £10,000. The only capital expenditure during the year ended 5 April 2018 was the cost of £82,000 for refurbishing the second floor of the partnership's shop during January 2018. The cost was made up as follows:

	£
False ceiling	17,600
Display units	15,100
Tiled flooring	32,200
Moveable partition walls	17,100
	82,000

- The partners have always shared profits equally and continued to do so after Mary resigned.

- During the tax year 2017–18, Alfred received dividends totalling £6,060, of which £720 were from investments within an individual savings account (ISA).

- During the tax year 2017–18, Alfred made gift aid donations totalling £1,920 (net) to national charities.

- Alfred's payments on account of income tax and class 4 national insurance contributions in respect of the tax year 2017–18 totalled £20,200.

Required:

Calculate Alfred King's balancing payment for the tax year 2017–18. (13 marks)

Note: You should take account of class 4 national insurance contributions when calculating the balancing payment for Alfred King.

(b) For the tax year 2017–18, Alfred wants to file his self-assessment tax return online.

Required:

(i) **Advise Alfred King of the latest date by which his self-assessment tax return for the tax year 2017–18 should be filed.** (1 mark)

(ii) **Advise Alfred King as to how long he must retain the records used in preparing his tax return for the tax year 2017–18.** (1 mark)

Note: You should ignore the possibility of HM Revenue and Customs carrying out a compliance check.

(15 marks)

Question 33 EDWARD KING

The following scenario relates to questions 1–5.

Edward King is trying to calculate his balancing payment/repayment for the tax year 2017–18, Information for 2017–18 includes the following:

- Edward is employed by Stately Ltd as a marketing director. During the tax year 2017–18, he was paid gross director's remuneration of £179,000.

- On 1 December 2017, Stately Ltd provided Edward with an interest-free loan which he used to purchase a holiday cottage.

- Stately Ltd has provided Edward with a home entertainment system for his personal use since 6 April 2014. The home entertainment system had been purchased by Stately Ltd on 6 April 2014 for £5,200. The company gave the home entertainment system to Edward on 6 April 2017 for no charge, although its market value at that time was £2,200.

- During the tax year 2017–18, Edward contributed 4% of his gross director's remuneration of £179,000 into Stately Ltd's HM Revenue and Customs' registered occupational pension scheme. The company contributed a further 6% on his behalf.

- During the tax year 2017–18, Edward donated £200 (gross) per month to charity under the payroll deduction scheme.

- During the tax year 2017–18, Edward used his private motor car for business purposes. He drove 12,000 miles in the performance of his duties for Stately Ltd, for which the company paid an allowance of 35p per mile.

- On 1 January 2018, Edward paid a professional subscription to the Guild of Marketing, an HM Revenue and Customs' approved professional body.

- For the tax year 2017–18, Stately Ltd deducted a total amount of £62,600 in PAYE from Edward's earnings.

1 What mileage allowance will be deducted in calculating Edward's taxable income for the year 2017–18?

£ _____

2 What benefit for the home entertainment system will be included in calculating Edward's taxable income for the tax year 2017–18?

Select...
£2,200
£3,000
£2,080
£3,240

3 **What is the total amount of deductions for pension contributions and charitable donations which will be allowed in calculating Edward's taxable income for the tax year 2017–18?**

- ○ £20,350
- ○ £7,160
- ○ £9,560
- ○ £11,950

4 **Assuming that Edward's taxable income for 2017–18 is £171,670 what will be his balancing payment or repayment of income tax for this year?**

Select... ▼
£6,709 repayment
£1,939 repayment
£4,724 repayment
£451 payment

5 **Assuming that Edward has no other sources of income, identify which of the following statements is/are correct in respect of 2017–18.**

If Edward completes a paper tax return by 31 October 2018, then HM Revenue and Customs will prepare a self-assessment tax computation on his behalf	CORRECT	INCORRECT
Edward's tax records must be retained until 31 January 2022	CORRECT	INCORRECT

(10 marks)

Question 34 SOPHIE SHAPE

Sophie Shape has been a self-employed sculptor since 1998, preparing her accounts to 5 April. Sophie's tax liabilities for the tax years 2016–17 and 2017–18 are as follows:

	2016–17 £	2017–18 £
Income tax liability	5,240	6,100
Class 2 national insurance contributions	146	148
Class 4 national insurance contributions	1,240	1,480
Capital gains tax liability	0	4,880

No income tax has been deducted at source.

Required:

(a) **Prepare a schedule showing the payments on account and balancing payment which Sophie Shape will have made, or will have to make, during the period from 1 April 2018 to 31 March 2019.** (4 marks)

Note: Your answer should clearly identify the relevant due date of each payment.

(b) **State the implications if Sophie Shape had made a claim to reduce her payments on account for the tax year 2017–18 to nil without any justification for doing so.** (2 marks)

(c) Advise Sophie Shape of the latest date by which she can file a paper self-assessment tax return for the tax year 2017–18. (1 mark)

(d) State the period during which HM Revenue and Customs (HMRC) will have to notify Sophie Shape if they intend to carry out a compliance check in respect of her self-assessment tax return for the tax year 2017–18, and the possible reasons why such a check would be made. (3 marks)

Note: You should assume that Sophie will file her tax return by the filing date.

(10 marks)

Question 35 FERGUS

You should assume that today's date is 15 March 2017.

Fergus is currently self-employed, and if he continues to trade on a self-employed basis, his total income tax liability and national insurance contributions (NIC) for the tax year 2017–18 will be £33,263.

However, Fergus is considering incorporating his business on 6 April 2017. The forecast taxable total profits of the new limited company for the year ended 5 April 2018 are £100,000 (before taking account of any director's remuneration). Fergus will pay himself gross director's remuneration of £18,000 and dividends of £40,000. The balance of the profits will remain undrawn within the new company.

Required:

Determine whether or not there will be an overall saving of tax and national insurance contributions (NIC) for the year ended 5 April 2018 if Fergus incorporates his business on 6 April 2017.

Notes:

1. You are expected to calculate the income tax payable by Fergus, the class 1 NIC payable by Fergus and the new limited company, and the corporation tax liability of the new limited company for the year ended 5 April 2018.

2. You should assume that the rates of corporation tax remain unchanged.

(10 marks)

Question 36 WAI

Wai is employed as a sales manager by Qaz plc, and the following information is available in respect of the tax year 2017–18:

(1) During the tax year 2017–18, Wai was paid a gross monthly salary of £10,200.

(2) In addition to her salary, Wai has been paid the following bonuses:

Amount £	Date of payment	Date of entitlement	In respect of the six-month period ended
4,600	25 April 2017	31 March 2017	31 December 2016
8,100	20 August 2017	3 July 2017	30 June 2017
2,900	3 May 2018	15 April 2018	31 December 2017

(3) During the period 6 April to 31 August 2017, Wai used her private motor car for both private and business journeys. She was reimbursed by Qaz plc at the rate of 55p per mile for the following mileage:

	Miles
Normal daily travel between home and Qaz plc's offices	2,420
Travel between home and the premises of Qaz plc's clients (none of the clients' premises were located near the offices of Qaz plc)	8,580
Travel between home and a temporary workplace (the assignment was for 10 weeks)	2,860
Total mileage reimbursed by Qaz plc	13,860

(4) During the period 1 September 2017 to 5 April 2018, Qaz plc provided Wai with a petrol powered motor car which has a list price of £13,370, and an official CO_2 emission rate of 86 grams per kilometre. Qaz plc does not provide Wai with any fuel for private journeys.

(5) During January 2018, Wai spent 10 nights overseas on company business. Qaz plc paid Wai a daily allowance of £10 to cover the cost of personal incidental expenses, such as telephone calls to her family.

(6) Throughout the tax year 2017–18, Qaz plc allowed Wai the use of two mobile telephones. The telephones had each cost £400 when purchased by the company in March 2017.

(7) Throughout the tax year 2017–18, Qaz plc provided Wai with living accommodation. The company had purchased the property on 1 June 2014 for £149,600, and it has been provided to Wai since 1 February 2016. Improvements costing £14,400 were made to the property during October 2014, and further improvements costing £9,800 were made during August 2016. The annual value of the property is £4,600.

Required:

(a) **Calculate Wai's taxable income for the tax year 2017–18.** (12 marks)

(b) **Briefly outline the information to be included in PAYE forms P60 and P11D, and state the dates by which they should have been provided to Wai for the tax year 2017–18.**

(3 marks)

Note: Your answer should be confined to the details which are relevant to Wai, although no figures are required.

(15 marks)

Question 37 DANIEL, FRANCINE AND GREGOR

(a) Amanda, Beatrice and Claude have been in partnership since 1 November 2011, preparing accounts to 31 October annually. Daniel joined as a partner on 1 May 2017. Profits have always been shared equally. The partnership's recent tax-adjusted trading profits are as follows:

	£
Year ended 31 October 2016	147,000
Year ended 31 October 2017	96,000
Year ended 31 October 2018 (forecast)	180,000

Required:

Calculate Daniel's trading income assessment for the tax year 2017–18.

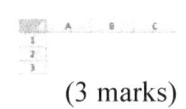

(3 marks)

TAXATION (TX-UK) (F6) – REVISION QUESTION BANK

(b) Francine is employed by Fringe plc. On 1 August 2017, Fringe plc provided Francine with a loan of £96,000 to help her purchase a holiday cottage. On 1 October 2017, the loan was increased by a further £14,000 so that Francine could renovate the cottage. Francine pays interest at an annual rate of 1·5% on this loan.

The taxable benefit in respect of this loan is calculated using the average method.

Required:

Calculate Francine's taxable benefit for the tax year 2017–18 in respect of the loan from Fringe plc. (3 marks)

(c) Gregor has been self-employed since 6 April 2004. He has the following income and chargeable gains for the tax years 2016–17 and 2017–18:

	2016–17 £	2017–18 £
Trading profit/(loss)	14,700	(68,800)
Business property profit/(loss)	4,600	(2,300)
Building society interest	1,300	900
Chargeable gain/(loss)	(2,900)	17,400

Required:

On the assumption that Gregor relieves his trading loss of £68,800 as early as possible, calculate the amount of trading loss carried forward to the tax year 2018–19.

(4 marks)

Note: You should assume that the tax allowances for the tax year 2017–18 apply throughout.

(10 marks)

Question 38 SAMSON & DELILAH

Samson and Delilah are a married couple. They are both employed by Rope plc, and Delilah is also a partner in a partnership. The following information is available in respect of the tax year 2017–18:

Samson

During the tax year 2017–18, Samson was paid a gross annual salary of £112,000 in respect of his employment with Rope plc.

Delilah

(1) During the tax year 2017–18, Delilah was paid a gross annual salary of £184,000 in respect of her employment with Rope plc.

(2) Throughout the tax year 2017–18, Rope plc provided Delilah with a petrol powered motor car which has a list price of £67,200, and an official CO_2 emission rate of 187 grams per kilometre. Rope plc does not provide Delilah with any fuel for private journeys. Delilah was unable to drive her motor car for a period during the tax year 2017–18 because of a skiing accident, and during this period Rope plc provided her with a chauffeur at a total cost of £9,400.

(3) Delilah pays an annual professional subscription of £450 which is relevant to her employment with Rope plc. Delilah also pays an annual membership fee of £1,420 to a golf club which she uses to entertain Rope plc's clients. Rope plc does not reimburse Delilah for either of these costs.

(4) During the tax year 2017–18, Delilah donated £250 (gross) per month to charity under the payroll deduction scheme operated by Rope plc.

(5) Delilah has been in partnership with Esther and Felix for a number of years. The partnership's tax adjusted trading profit for the year ended 31 December 2017 was £93,600. Esther is paid an annual salary of £8,000, with the balance of profits being shared 40% to Delilah, 30% to Esther and 30% to Felix.

(6) During the tax year 2017–18, Delilah paid interest of £6,200 (gross) on a personal loan taken out to purchase her share in the partnership.

(7) During the tax year 2017–18, Delilah made charitable gift aid donations totalling £6,000 (gross).

Joint income – Building society deposit account

Samson and Delilah have savings in a building society deposit account which is in their joint names. During the tax year 2017–18, they received building society interest totalling £9,600 from this joint account.

Required:

(a) **Calculate Samson and Delilah's respective income tax liabilities for the tax year 2017–18.**

Note: The following mark allocation is provided as guidance for this requirement:

Samson   (3.5 marks)
Delilah   (9.5 marks)   (13 marks)

(b) **Calculate Samson's income tax saving for the tax year 2017–18 if the building society deposit account had been in Delilah's sole name instead of in joint names for the entire year.**   (2 marks)

(15 marks)

Question 39 GEORGE

You should assume that today's date is 1 March 2017.

George, a software developer, has accepted a one-year contract to update software for Xpee plc.

(1) The contract will run from 6 April 2017 to 5 April 20178 with a fee of £40,000 payable for the entire year of the contract. A condition of the contract is that George will have to do the work personally and not be permitted to sub-contract the work to anyone else.

(2) George will work from home, but will have to attend weekly meetings at Xpee plc's offices to receive instructions regarding the work to be performed during the following week.

(3) George will not incur any significant expenses in respect of the contract apart from the purchase of a new laptop computer for £3,600 on 6 April 2017. This laptop will be used 100% for business purposes.

(4) During the term of the contract, George will not be permitted to work for any other clients. He will therefore not have any other income during the tax year 2017–18.

(5) George's tax liability for the tax year 2016–17 was collected through PAYE, so he will not be required to make any payments on account in respect of the tax year 2017–18.

TAXATION (TX-UK) (F6) – REVISION QUESTION BANK

George has several friends who are also software developers. He understands that his employment status is not clear cut but that his income tax liability for the tax year 2017–18 will be the same regardless of whether he is treated as employed or as self-employed. However, George appreciates that there are advantages to being classed as self-employed.

Required:

(a) List FOUR factors which are indicators of George being treated as an employee in relation to his contract with Xpee plc rather than as self-employed.

Note: You should confine your answer to the information given in the question.

(2 marks)

(b) Calculate George's income tax liability and national insurance contributions for the tax year 2017–18 if he is treated as self-employed in respect of his contract with Xpee plc.

(4 marks)

(c) If George is treated as being an employee of Xpee plc instead of self-employed:

(i) Explain why his income tax liability will be payable earlier. (2 marks)

(ii) Calculate the additional amount of national insurance contributions which he personally will suffer for the tax year 2017–18. (2 marks)

(10 marks)

Question 40 PATIENCE

Patience retired on 31 December 2017, and on that date ceased employment and self-employment. The following information is available in respect of the tax year 2017–18:

Employment

(1) Patience was employed by a private school as a teacher. From 6 April to 31 December 2017, she was paid a salary of £3,750 per month.

(2) During the period 6 April to 31 December 2017, Patience contributed 6% of her monthly gross salary of £3,750 into her employer's HM Revenue and Customs' (HMRC's) registered occupational pension scheme. Patience's employer contributed a further 10% on her behalf.

(3) During the period 6 April to 30 June 2017, Patience's granddaughter was provided with a free place at the private school run by Patience's employer. The normal fee payable would have been £4,600. The additional marginal expense of providing the place for the grandchild was £540.

(4) On 25 June 2017, Patience was given a clock valued at £600 as an award for her 25 years of teaching at her employer's school. She has not previously received any similar awards.

(5) Patience's employer provided her with an interest-free loan so that she could purchase a season ticket for the train to work. The balance of the loan outstanding at 6 April 2017 was £8,000, and Patience repaid the loan in full on 31 December 2017.

Self-employment

(1) Patience was self-employed as a private tutor. Her trading profit for the year ended 31 July 2017 was £14,800. This figure is after taking account of capital allowances.

(2) Patience's trading profit for the final five-month period of trading from 1 August to 31 December 2017 was £6,900. This figure is before taking account of capital allowances.

(3) The tax written down value of the capital allowances main pool at 1 August 2017 was £2,200. On 10 August 2017, Patience purchased a laptop computer for £1,700.

On the cessation of trading, Patience personally retained the laptop computer. Its value on 31 December 2017 was £1,200. The remainder of the items included in the main pool were sold for £800 on 31 December 2017.

(4) Patience has unused overlap profits brought forward of £3,700.

Personal pension contributions

During the period 6 April to 31 December 2017, Patience contributed a total of £3,600 (net) into a personal pension scheme.

Pension income

During the period 1 January to 5 April 2018, Patience received the state pension of £2,025, a pension of £6,000 from her employer's occupational pension scheme, and a private pension of £2,725. These were the total gross amounts received.

Property

Patience owned two properties which were let out unfurnished until both properties were sold on 31 December 2017. The following information is available in respect of the two properties:

	Property one £	Property two £
Rent received during the tax year 2017–18	3,600	7,200
Sale proceeds on 31 December 2017	122,000	98,000
Allowable revenue expenditure during the tax year 2017–18	(4,700)	(2,600)
Purchase cost	(81,400)	(103,700)

Patience has never occupied either of the two properties as her main residence.

Required:

Calculate Patience's income tax and capital gains tax liabilities for the tax year 2017–18.

Notes:
1. You should indicate by the use of zero (0) any items which are not taxable or deductible.
2. The following mark allocation is provided as guidance for this question:

   Income tax 13 marks
   Capital gains tax 2 marks

(15 marks)

Question 41 STEVIE DEE

Assume today's date is 1 March 2017.

Stevie Dee is employed as a service engineer by Acme Alarms and Security Ltd, and currently receives an annual salary of £40,000. Stevie is the sole user of a company van provided by Acme for his regular site visits, however his private use is minimal. All of the van's running costs and fuel are paid by the company, but Stevie reimburses the cost of fuel for any private use.

Stevie is considering leaving Acme and setting up his own business as a self-employed engineer with effect from 6 April 2017. He is confident that with his experience and contacts he will be able to achieve gross earnings of £45,000 in the tax year 2017–18. Stevie would use the cash basis for small businesses and understands that he will be able to claim a flat rate deduction of £18 per month for working from his home. He will use his own car for customer visits which will involve business mileage of 500 miles per month; the actual cost of these additional motor expenses will be £1,800 for the year. Other allowable business expenses will amount to £3,000 for the year.

All income and expenditure will be realised and paid within the year.

Stevie does not have any other sources of income in the year.

Required:

Calculate by how much Stevie's net income would increase or decrease for the tax year 2017–18 if he becomes self-employed rather than continuing in employment.

Note: You are expected to calculate income tax and national insurance liabilities for each scenario and take account where appropriate of costs incurred.

(10 marks)

Question 42 BASIL AND YOKO

Assume today's date is 1 March 2017.

Basil and Yoko are a married couple reviewing their tax position for 2017–18. Basil will receive a salary of £96,000 and dividend income of £5,000. He has unused capital losses brought forward from earlier years of £30,000.

Yoko will receive taxable property income of £18,000 and dividend income of £2,000. She is also planning to sell some quoted shares which will create a chargeable gain of £32,000. (This gain will not be eligible for entrepreneurs' relief).

Basil and Yoko have savings deposits in their joint names which will generate taxable interest of £8,000 for the year. They have always treated this income as being split 50:50 between them.

Required:

(a) **Calculate the overall tax saving that can be made by the couple if the quoted shares are transferred to Basil before disposal and the savings deposits are arranged so that Yoko receives all of the interest income.** (12 marks)

(b) **Assuming the planning ideas in (a) are effected, reply to the following further questions raised by Basil and Yoko:**

  (i) **How much capital loss, if any, will Basil have available to carry forward?** (1 mark)
  (ii) **Would it also be beneficial to transfer some of Basil's dividend income to Yoko, and if so, how much?** (2 marks)

(15 marks)

Question 43 WINSTON KING

The following scenario relates to questions 1–5.

On 19 May 2017 Winston King disposed of a painting, and this resulted in a chargeable gain of £45,960. For the tax year 2017–18 Winston has taxable income of £21,690 after the deduction of the personal allowance.

Winston is considering the sale of a business that he has run as a sole trader since 1 July 2009. The business will be sold for £260,000, and this figure, along with the respective cost of each asset, is made up as follows:

	Sale proceeds £
Freehold shop (cost £80,000)	140,000
Freehold warehouse (cost £102,000)	88,000
Net current assets	32,000
	260,000

The assets have all been owned for more than one year. The freehold warehouse has never been used by Winston for business purposes.

Where possible, Winston will claim entrepreneurs' relief in respect of this disposal.

1 What is Winston's capital gains tax (CGT) liability for the tax year 2017–18 assuming that he does not sell his sole tradership business?

Select... ▼
£3,466
£6,932
£5,751
£8,011

2 If Winston sells his business on 25 March 2018 what amount of capital gains will qualify for entrepreneurs' relief?

£ [   ]

3 If Winston sells his business on 25 March 2018, what amount of capital gains (after deducting the annual exempt amount) will be taxable at 28%?

- o £68,850
- o £31,960
- o £20,660
- o £8,850

4 If Winston sells his business on 25 March 2018 what effect would it have on his CGT liability if his income was £31,690 instead of £21,690?

Select... ▼
Increase by £2,000
Increase by £1,000
Decrease by £1,000
No effect

5 Identify, by clicking on the relevant box in the table below, which of the following statements is/are correct.

Chattels may be defined as tangible moveable property, so include items such as paintings and securities	CORRECT	INCORRECT
Chattels are exempt from CGT if they are wasting assets	CORRECT	INCORRECT
Chargeable disposals of chattels cannot give rise to a CGT loss	CORRECT	INCORRECT
Marginal relief can apply to the gain on disposal of a chattel if the sale proceeds are less than £6,000	CORRECT	INCORRECT

(10 marks)

Question 44 AOM AND LEROY

The following scenario relates to questions 1–5.

Aom

Aom is in business as a sole trader. On 3 February 2018, she purchased a freehold factory for £168,000. Aom also owns two freehold warehouses, and wants to sell one of these during March 2018. The first warehouse was purchased on 20 March 2013 for £184,000, and can be sold for £213,000. The second warehouse was purchased on 18 July 2006 for £113,000, and can be sold for £180,000.

All of the above buildings have been, or will be, used for business purposes by Aom. She will make a claim to roll over the gain on whichever warehouse is sold against the cost of the factory.

Leroy

On 2 April 2018, Leroy sold 12,000 £1 ordinary shares in Jerk-Chic plc for £83,400. He has had the following transactions in the shares of the company:

1 March 2009	Purchased 20,000 shares for £19,800
20 July 2013	Purchased 8,000 shares for £27,800
23 October 2017	Made a gift of 4,000 shares

The gift of 4,000 shares on 23 October 2017 was to Leroy's daughter. On that date the shares were quoted on the Stock Exchange at £7·80–£8·20. Holdover relief is not available in respect of this disposal.

Neither disposal of Jerk-Chic plc shares during the tax year 2017–18 qualifies for entrepreneurs' relief.

For the tax year 2017–18 Leroy is a higher rate taxpayer, and will remain so for the tax year 2018–19. Leroy regularly makes disposals of other investments, so no annual exempt amount is available for either of the tax years 2017–18 or 2018–19.

1 What will be the chargeable gain if Aom sells the first warehouse?

- A £67,000
- B £45,000
- C £29,000
- D £0

2 What will be the chargeable gain if Aom sells the second warehouse?

    A   £67,000
    B   £12,000
    C   £55,000
    D   £0

3 Which of the following statements is correct in relation to Leroy's gift of shares on 23 October 2017?

    A   As the consideration given is zero a capital loss will arise
    B   The shares should be at a price one quarter-up within the quoted spread
    C   The cost of the shares should be established on a FIFO basis rather than LIFO
    D   The shares should be valued at the market mid-price

4 What is the chargeable gain arising from Leroy's sale of shares on 2 April 2018?

    A   £71,520
    B   £61,580
    C   £(12,600)
    D   £63,000

5 Why would it have been beneficial if Leroy had delayed the sale of the 12,000 shares in Jerk-Chic plc until 6 April 2018?

    A   In a falling market the delay would result in a smaller chargeable gain
    B   The annual exempt amount would reduce the amount chargeable
    C   The tax liability would be due later resulting in a cash flow benefit
    D   Entrepreneurs' relief would become available in 2018–19

(10 marks)

Question 45 MICK STONE

The following scenario relates to questions 1–5.

Mick Stone disposed of the following assets during the tax year 2017–18:

Warehouse

On 19 May 2017, Mick sold a freehold warehouse for £522,000. The warehouse was purchased on 6 August 2005 for £258,000, and was extended at a cost of £99,000 during April 2007. In January 2011, the floor of the warehouse was damaged by flooding and had to be replaced at a cost of £63,000. The warehouse was sold because it was surplus to the business's requirements as a result of Mick purchasing a newly built warehouse during 2016. Both warehouses have always been used for business purposes in a wholesale business run by Mick as a sole trader.

Land

On 12 August 2017, Mick sold an acre of land for £81,700. He had originally purchased five acres of land on 19 May 2001 for £167,400. The market value of the unsold four acres of land as at 12 August 2017 was £268,000. The land has never been used for business purposes.

Shares in Rolling Ltd

On 24 September 2017, Mick sold 700,000 £1 ordinary shares in Rolling Ltd, an unquoted trading company, for £3,675,000. He had originally purchased 500,000 shares in Rolling Ltd on 2 June 2009 for £960,000. On 1 December 2014, Rolling Ltd made a 3 for 2 bonus issue. Mick has been a director of Rolling Ltd since 1 January 2009.

TAXATION (TX-UK) (F6) – REVISION QUESTION BANK

Shares in Sugar plc

On 19 January 2018, Mick made a gift of his entire holding of 24,000 £1 ordinary shares in Sugar plc, a quoted investment company, to his son, Keith. On that date the shares were quoted on the Stock Exchange at £6·98–£7·10, with recorded bargains of £6·85, £6·90, £7·00 and £7·05. The shares had been purchased on 8 May 2012 for £76,800. Mick's shareholding was less than 1% of Sugar plc's issued share capital, and he has never been an employee or a director of the company.

1. Assuming no rollover relief is available, what is the chargeable gain arising in respect of the disposal of the warehouse?

    £ ⬚

2. What TWO pieces of further information regarding the replacement warehouse would be required to establish whether rollover relief is available?

    ☐ Whether it was purchased in 2015–16 or 2016–17

    ☐ Whether it was purchased before or after 19 May 2016

    ☐ Whether it cost more or less than £522,000

    ☐ Whether it cost more or less than £258,000

3. What is the chargeable gain arising in respect of the disposal of the acre of land?

Select... ▼
£36,460
£42,591
£48,220
£100,600

4. What is the chargeable gain arising in respect of the disposal of the shares in Rolling Ltd?

    £ ⬚

5. What is the chargeable gain arising in respect of the disposal of the shares in Sugar plc?

    A £92,160
    B £0
    C £90,000
    D £91,440

(10 marks)

Question 46 PATRICK AND EMILY GRANT

The following scenario relates to questions 1–5.

You should assume that today's date is 15 December 2017.

Patrick and Emily Grant are a married couple. They have both always been resident in the United Kingdom (UK), being in the UK for more than 300 days each tax year up to and including the tax year 2016–17. However, following Patrick's retirement, the couple decided to move overseas, purchasing an overseas property on 6 April 2017.

Patrick and Emily still have a house in the UK, and will stay there on the 105 days which they spend in the UK during the tax year 2017–18. Neither Patrick nor Emily works full-time, and neither of them will do any substantive work in the UK during the tax year 2017–18.

For the tax year 2017–18, Patrick will have taxable income of £7,200, and Emily will have taxable income of £46,400. During May 2017, Emily disposed of an investment, and the resultant chargeable gain fully utilised her annual exempt amount for the tax year 2017–18.

Patrick and Emily urgently need to raise £80,000 in order to renovate their overseas property, and have two alternative assets which can be sold. They would like to sell the asset which will provide them with the highest net of tax proceeds. The alternatives are as follows:

Alternative 1 – Unquoted shares

Emily owns 8,000 £1 ordinary shares in Shore Ltd, an unquoted trading company with a share capital of 100,000 £1 ordinary shares. Shore Ltd's shares have recently been selling for £13·00 per share, but Emily will have to sell at £11·50 per share given that she needs a quick sale. The sale will be to an unconnected person. Emily subscribed for her shares in Shore Ltd at par on 1 June 2008, and she has been a director of the company since that date.

Alternative 2 – Quoted shares

Patrick and Emily jointly own 32,000 £1 ordinary shares in Beach plc, a quoted trading company. The shares are currently quoted on the Stock Exchange at £2·88. Patrick and Emily originally purchased 54,000 shares in Beach plc on 23 May 2006 for £75,600, but they had sold 22,000 shares on 17 November 2015 for £44,440.

The shareholding is less than 1% of Beach plc's issued share capital, and neither Patrick nor Emily has ever been an employee or a director of the company.

1 Based on the information given, how many UK ties do Patrick and Emily each have when considering their residency status for 2017–18?

    A   1
    B   2
    C   3
    D   4

2 Based on the information given, what would be Emily's taxable gain if she sells the shares in Shore Ltd?

    A   £72,700
    B   £84,000
    C   £84,700
    D   £96,000

TAXATION (TX-UK) (F6) – REVISION QUESTION BANK

3 Assume that Emily's chargeable gain from the sale of the shares in Shore Ltd is only £70,000 as a result of unexpected selling costs.

What will Emily's net proceeds from the sale be after taking account of capital gains tax?

A   £64,000
B   £56,000
C   £71,000
D   £63,000

4 **If Patrick and Emily sell the jointly held shares in Beach plc, what would be the capital gains tax liability arising for Patrick?**

A   £1,238
B   £2,368
C   £2,476
D   £1,958

5 **If Patrick and Emily sell the jointly-held shares in Beach plc, which of the following statements would be correct in respect of the sale?**

(1)   Patrick and Emily will have the same CGT liability as each other
(2)   Patrick and Emily will have the same taxable amount as each other
(3)   Patrick and Emily will suffer the same rate of CGT as each other

A   1 and 2
B   2 only
C   2 and 3
D   None of the statements

(10 marks)

Question 47 RUBY

You should assume that today's date is 1 March 2018.

(a) On 27 August 2017, Ruby disposed of an investment property, and this resulted in a chargeable gain of £45,800.

For the tax year 2017–18, Ruby has taxable income of £17,600.

Required:

Calculate Ruby's capital gains tax liability for the tax year 2017–18 if this is her only disposal in that tax year.

(2 marks)

(b) In addition to the disposal already made on 27 August 2017, Ruby is going to make one further disposal during the tax year 2017–18. This disposal will be of either Ruby's holding of £1 ordinary shares in Pola Ltd, or her holding of £0.50 ordinary shares in Aplo plc.

Shareholding in Pola Ltd

Pola Ltd is an unquoted trading company, in which Ruby has a 10% shareholding. The shareholding was purchased on 14 July 2010 for £23,700 and could be sold for £61,000. Ruby has been an employee of Pola Ltd since 2008.

Shareholding in Aplo plc

Aplo plc is a quoted trading company, in which Ruby has a shareholding of 40,000 £0.50 ordinary shares. Ruby received the shareholding as a gift from her father on 27 May 2013. On that date, the shares were quoted on the stock exchange at £2·12–£2·24. The shareholding could be sold for £59,000.

Neither entrepreneurs' relief nor holdover relief is available in respect of this disposal.

Required:

Calculate Ruby's revised capital gains tax liability for the tax year 2017–18 if, during March 2018, she also disposes of either (1) her shareholding in Pola Ltd; or alternatively (2) her shareholding in Aplo plc.

Note: The following mark allocation is provided as guidance for this requirement:

Pola Ltd   (4.5 marks)
Aplo plc   (3.5 marks)   (8 marks)

(10 marks)

Question 48 JEROME

Jerome made the following gifts to family members during the tax year 2017–18:

(1) On 28 May 2017, Jerome made a gift of a house valued at £187,000 to his wife. Jerome's uncle had originally purchased the house on 14 July 1998 for £45,900. The uncle died on 12 June 2007, and the house was inherited by Jerome. On that date, the house was valued at £112,800. Jerome has never occupied the house as his main residence.

(2) On 24 June 2017, Jerome made a gift of his entire 12% holding of 12,000 £1 ordinary shares in Reward Ltd, an unquoted trading company, to his son. The market value of the shares on that date was £98,400. The shares had been purchased on 15 March 2009 for £39,000. On 24 June 2017, the market value of Reward Ltd's chargeable assets was £540,000, of which £460,000 was in respect of chargeable business assets. Jerome and his son have elected to hold over the gain on this gift of a business asset.

(3) On 7 November 2017, Jerome made a gift of an antique bracelet valued at £12,200 to his granddaughter. The antique bracelet had been purchased on 1 September 2004 for £2,100.

(4) On 29 January 2018, Jerome made a gift of nine acres of land valued at £78,400 to his brother. He had originally purchased 10 acres of land on 3 November 2008 for £37,800. The market value of the unsold acre of land as at 29 January 2018 was £33,600. The land has never been used for business purposes.

Required:

(a) **Calculate Jerome's chargeable gains for the tax year 2017–18.**
    Note: You should ignore inheritance tax.   (7 marks)

(b) **For each of the four recipients of assets (1) to (4) gifted from Jerome, state their respective base cost for capital gains tax purposes.**   (3 marks)

(10 marks)

Question 49 SAM SHIRE

The following scenario relates to questions 1–5.

You should assume that today's date is 15 February 2018.

Sam Shire, aged 76, has already invested £4,000 into a cash individual savings account (ISA) during the tax year 2017–18. He now wants to invest in a stocks and shares ISA.

On 20 December 2016 he made a cash gift of £200,000 to his daughter. He is now going to make a cash gift of £450,000 to a trust on 20 February 2018. The nil rate band for the tax year 2016–17 is £325,000, and you should assume that this remains unchanged for subsequent years.

1 Identify which of the following statements is/are correct.

Since Sam has already invested £4,000 into a cash ISA, he can invest a maximum of £16,000 (20,000 – 4,000) in a stocks and shares ISA for the tax year 2017–18	CORRECT	INCORRECT
Dividend income received within a stocks and shares ISA is exempt from income tax, only chargeable gains are taxable	CORRECT	INCORRECT

2 What will be the lifetime inheritance tax that will be payable in respect of Sam's gift of £450,000 to a trust if the trust pays the tax arising from the gift?

£ ☐

3 What will be the lifetime inheritance tax that will be payable in respect of Sam's gift of £450,000 to a trust if Sam pays the tax arising from the gift?

- o £24,400
- o £25,000
- o £30,500
- o £31,250

4 If Sam were to die in the near future, how much of the nil rate band will be used by the gift to his daughter?

Select... ▼
£200,000
£197,000
£194,000
£0

5 If Sam were to die on 30 June 2022, which TWO of the following statements are correct?

- ☐ Inheritance tax will be payable at a rate of 40% on transfers above the nil rate band
- ☐ Inheritance tax will be payable at a rate of 20% on transfers above the nil rate band
- ☐ The inheritance tax liability can be reduced by 20% taper relief
- ☐ The inheritance tax liability can be reduced by 40% taper relief

(10 marks)

Question 50 PERE JONES

The following scenario relates to questions 1–5.

On 23 August 2005, Pere Jones made a gift of a house valued at £320,000 to his son, Phil Jones. This was a wedding gift when Phil got married.

On 6 September 2012 Pere transferred further property to Phil; the value of this potentially exempt transfer, after all available exemptions, was £380,000.

Pere died on 20 March 2018 aged 76, at which time his estate – consisting of cash, chattels and investments - was valued at £880,000. Under the terms of his will, Pere divided his estate equally between his wife and his son, Phil. Pere had not made any gifts during his lifetime except for the two gifts to Phil.

The nil rate band for the tax year 2005–06 is £275,000 and for 2012–13 is £325,000.

1 **What is the amount of the potentially exempt transfer (PET) of the house to Phil in 2005?**

- A £312,000
- B £317,000
- C £314,000
- D £309,000

2 **What amount of inheritance tax (IHT) will be payable in respect of the 2012 transfer as a result of Pere Jones' death?**

- A £22,000
- B £8,800
- C £4,400
- D £60,800

3 **What amount of IHT will be payable in respect of Pere's estate as a result of his death?**

- A £222,000
- B £46,000
- C £176,000
- D £352,000

4 On the occasion of his wedding, Phil also received the following gifts:

- (1) £4,000 from his grandmother
- (2) £2,000 from his fiancé
- (3) £2,000 from his fiancé's father
- (4) £2,000 from his brother

Which of these wedding gifts will be exempt from inheritance tax?

- A 1 and 2
- B 3 and 4
- C 1 and 4
- D 2 and 3

5 **What is the latest date by which the IHT liability in respect of Pere's estate will be due for payment?**

- A   20 September 2018
- B   30 September 2018
- C   20 March 2019
- D   31 March 2019

(10 marks)

Question 51 AFIYA

The following scenario relates to questions 1–5.

Afiya died on 29 November 2017. She had made the following gifts during her lifetime:

(1)   On 13 April 2016, Afiya made a cash gift of £32,000 to her husband.

(2)   On 2 May 2016, Afiya made cash gifts to her three nieces. The first niece was given £100, the second niece was given £200, and the third niece was given £400.

(3)   On 14 September 2016, Afiya made a gift of 6,500 £1 ordinary shares in Cassava Ltd, an unquoted investment company, to her daughter.

Before the transfer Afiya owned 8,000 shares out of Cassava Ltd's issued share capital of 10,000 £1 ordinary shares. On 14 September 2016, Cassava Ltd's shares were worth £3 each for a holding of 15%, £7 each for a holding of 65%, and £8 each for a holding of 80%.

(4)   On 27 January 2017, Afiya made a cash gift of £400,000 to a trust for the benefit of her son. Afiya paid the inheritance tax arising from this gift.

On 29 November 2017, Afiya's estate was valued at £620,000. Under the terms of her will Afiya left £150,000 to her husband, a specific legacy of £40,000 to her sister, and the residue of the estate to her children. Afiya had lived in her husband's house and did not own a residence of her own.

The nil rate band for the tax year 2016–17 is £325,000.

1   **How will the 2015–16 and 2016–17 annual exemptions be applied to these transfers?**

- A   £6,000 set against the gift to her husband
- B   £6,000 set against the gift to the trust
- C   £700 set against the gifts to her nieces, £5,300 against the gift to her daughter
- D   £400 set against the gifts to her nieces, £5,600 against the gift to her daughter

2   **What is the transfer value of the gift of shares to Afiya's daughter?**

- A   £52,000
- B   £19,500
- C   £59,500
- D   £45,500

3   **What amount of inheritance tax will be payable in respect of the lifetime gift to the trust on 27 January 2017?**

- A   £15,000
- B   £18,750
- C   £33,625
- D   £100,000

REVISION QUESTION BANK – TAXATION (TX-UK) (F6)

4 **What amount of inheritance tax will be payable in respect of Afiya's estate?**

- A £188,000
- B £118,000
- C £172,000
- D £58,000

5 **What will be the due date or dates for payment of IHT in respect of the gift into trust, and who will be responsible for this?**

- A 31 July 2017 only, payable by Afiya
- B 31 May 2018 only, payable by the personal representative
- C 31 July 2017 payable by Afiya and 31 May 2018 payable by the trustees
- D 31 July 2017 payable by the trustees and 31 May 2018 payable by the personal representative

(10 marks)

Question 52 KENDRA OLDER

The following scenario relates to questions 1–5.

You should assume that today's date is 1 January 2018.

Kendra Older, aged 93, is unfortunately in poor health with just a few months left to live. She has made the following gifts during her lifetime:

- Since 2007, yearly gifts to her grandchildren which exactly use her annual exemption.

- On 20 June 2010, Kendra made a cash gift of £140,000 to a trust. No inheritance tax arose in respect of this gift.

- On 5 October 2016, Kendra made a cash gift of £247,000 to her children.

Kendra owns the following assets:

- A property valued at £970,000. The property is no longer occupied by Kendra, but would qualify for the residence nil rate band. If it were disposed of during the tax year 2017–18 the disposal would result in a chargeable gain of £174,000. Kendra has made other disposals in the year utilising the annual exempt amount.

- Building society deposits of £387,000.

- Investments in individual savings accounts (ISAs) valued at £39,000 and savings certificates from NS&I (National Savings and Investments) valued at £17,000.

- A life assurance policy on her own life. The policy has an open market value of £210,000, and proceeds of £225,000 will be received following Kendra's death.

None of the above valuations are expected to change in the near future. The cost of Kendra's funeral will be £14,000.

Under the terms of her will, Kendra has left her entire estate to her children.

The nil rate band of Kendra's husband was fully utilised when he died 10 years ago.
The nil rate band for the tax years 2009–10 onwards is £325,000.

For the tax year 2017–18, Kendra will pay income tax at the higher rate.

TAXATION (TX-UK) (F6) – REVISION QUESTION BANK

1 What amount of inheritance tax (IHT) will be payable in respect of the October 2016 transfer as a result of Kendra's death?

A £0
B £12,400
C £24,800
D £42,800

2 What is the value of Kendra's chargeable estate for IHT purposes?

£ _____

3 When calculating the IHT on Kendra's chargeable estate, what deductions will be made to the nil rate band in respect of previous transfers of value?

A None
B Only the October 2016 gift to her children
C Only the June 2010 gift to a trust
D Both of these gifts, up to £325,000 in total

4 Identify, by clicking on the relevant box in the table below, what would the tax implications be if Kendra makes an immediate lifetime gift to her children of the property valued at £970,000.

The potential benefit of the residence nil rate band would be lost	YES	NO
Capital gains tax of £48,720 would be payable	YES	NO
Capital gains tax of £31,320 would be payable	YES	NO
No capital gains would be payable as a transfer on death is an exempt disposal	YES	NO

5 Kendra is considering changing her will so that part of her estate will instead be left to her grandchildren rather than her children.

Identify, by clicking on the relevant box in the table below, which of the following statements are true or false if she does so.

The IHT on her estate would be reduced	TRUE	FALSE
The IHT on her estate would be unchanged	TRUE	FALSE
There may be an IHT benefit by avoiding a further charge when the children die	TRUE	FALSE
This would only be beneficial if Kendra's children were to die within seven years of Kendra's death	TRUE	FALSE

(10 marks)

Question 53 TOBIAS

The following scenario relates to questions 1–5.

You should assume that today's date is 15 March 2018.

Tobias has recently inherited the residue of his aunt Mildred's estate. Mildred died on 8 December 2017, and her estate consisted of the following assets:

(1) A main residence valued at £660,000 with an outstanding interest-only mortgage of £14,300.
(2) A portfolio of ordinary shares valued at £92,600.
(3) A motor car valued at £21,900.

On 8 December 2017, Mildred owed £9,400 in respect of credit card debts, and she had also verbally promised to pay the £4,600 medical costs of a friend. The cost of Mildred's funeral amounted to £5,800.

Under the terms of her will, Mildred made specific legacies totalling £25,000 to her friends, with the residue of her estate being inherited by Tobias. Mildred had not made any gifts during her lifetime.

Mildred's husband had died on 19 July 2008, and 40% of his inheritance tax nil rate band of £312,000 for the tax year 2008–09 was not used.

Tobias will use some of his inheritance for the following purposes:

(1) A cash gift of £100,000 to his daughter when she gets married on 29 March 2018. He has not made any previous lifetime gifts.

(2) Tobias will make an additional personal pension contribution for the tax year 2017–18, having already made contributions of £10,000 during this tax year. He has been self-employed since 6 April 2015, and has been a member of a personal pension scheme from the tax year 2016–17 onwards. Tobias' trading profits and gross personal pension contributions since he commenced self-employment have been as follows:

Tax year	Trading profit £	Pension contribution £
2015–16	32,000	0
2016–17	34,000	26,000
2017–18	78,000	10,000

1 **Based on the information given, what is the value of Mildred's chargeable estate for IHT purposes?**

Select...
£740,400
£745,000
£750,800
£759,300

2 **If Mildred's estate also included building society savings such that the total chargeable value was actually £800,000, what amount of inheritance tax would be payable?**

£ ☐

3   What will be the amount of the potentially exempt transfer of the gift by Tobias to his daughter?

   A   £89,000
   B   £92,000
   C   £94,000
   D   £95,000

4   What is the maximum additional pension contribution which Tobias can make in 2017–18 which will fully qualify for tax relief (i.e. without incurring any restriction by way of an annual allowance charge)?

Select... ▼
£38,000
£44,000
£70,000
£84,000

5   Identify, by clicking on the relevant box in the table below, which of the following conditions must be met if Tobias wants to make gifts out of his income to his children, so that these gifts are exempt from inheritance tax.

Tobias must make the gifts as part of his normal expenditure out of income	YES	NO
The standard of living of Tobias must not be affected by the gifts	YES	NO
The pattern of making the gifts should be habitual	YES	NO
Each gift must be less than £1,000	YES	NO

(10 marks)

Question 54 ZOE

Zoe died on 17 February 2018. She had made the following gifts during her lifetime:

(1)   On 7 March 2013, Zoe made a cash gift of £270,000 to her son as a wedding gift when he got married.

(2)   On 21 June 2013, Zoe made a cash gift of £620,000 to a trust. Zoe paid the inheritance tax arising from this gift.

Zoe's husband had died on 25 July 2009, and 20% of his inheritance tax nil rate band was not used.

The nil rate band for the tax year 2009–10 onwards is £325,000.

Required:

(a)   Explain why it is important to differentiate between potentially exempt transfers and chargeable lifetime transfers for inheritance tax purposes.   (2 marks)

(b)   Calculate the additional inheritance tax which will be payable in respect of the gift made to the trust as a result of Zoe's death.   (8 marks)

(10 marks)

Question 55 MARCUS

(a) Inheritance tax legislation does not actually contain a definition of who is, and who is not, a chargeable person.

Required:

(i) **Explain whether or not a married couple is treated as a chargeable person for inheritance tax purposes.** (1 mark)

(ii) **State the special inheritance tax measures which are applicable to married couples.** (2 marks)

(b) Marcus died on 10 March 2018. He had made the following gifts during his lifetime:

(1) On 14 January 2009, Marcus made a chargeable lifetime transfer of £290,000 to a trust. The trustees paid the lifetime inheritance tax of £3,000 which arose in respect of this gift.

(2) On 3 February 2015, Marcus made a chargeable lifetime transfer of £420,000 to another trust. In addition to the gift, Marcus paid the related lifetime inheritance tax of £96,250 on this gift.

(3) On 17 March 2015, Marcus made a gift (a potentially exempt transfer) of 30,000 £1 ordinary shares in Scarum Ltd, an unquoted investment company, to his daughter.

Before the transfer, Marcus owned all of Scarum Ltd's issued share capital of 100,000 £1 ordinary shares. On 17 March 2015, Scarum Ltd's shares were worth £5 each for a holding of 30%, £9 each for a holding of 70%, and £12 each for a holding of 100%.

The nil rate band for the tax year 2008–09 is £285,000, and for the tax year 2014–15 it is £325,000.

Under the terms of his will, Marcus left his entire estate to his wife.

Required:

Calculate the inheritance tax which will be payable as a result of Marcus's death.

(7 marks)

Note: You should ignore the inheritance tax annual exemption.

(10 marks)

Question 56 JAMES

James died on 22 January 2018. He had made the following gifts during his lifetime:

(1) On 9 October 2010, a cash gift of £35,000 to a trust. No lifetime inheritance tax was payable in respect of this gift.

(2) On 14 May 2016, a cash gift of £420,000 to his daughter.

(3) On 2 August 2016, a gift of a property valued at £260,000 to a trust. No lifetime inheritance tax was payable in respect of this gift because it was covered by the nil rate band. By the time of James' death on 22 January 2018, the property had increased in value to £310,000.

On 22 January 2018, James' estate was valued at £870,000. Under the terms of his will, James left his entire estate to his children. The estate included a main residence valued at £300,000.

TAXATION (TX-UK) (F6) – REVISION QUESTION BANK

The nil rate band of James' wife was fully utilised when she died 10 years ago.

The nil rate band for the tax year 2010–11 and for the tax year 2016–17 is £325,000.

Required:

(a) **Calculate the inheritance tax which will be payable as a result of James' death, and state who will be responsible for paying the tax.** (7 marks)

(b) **Explain why it might have been beneficial for inheritance tax purposes if James had left a portion of his estate to his grandchildren rather than to his children.** (1 mark)

(c) **Explain why it might be advantageous for inheritance tax purposes for a person to make lifetime gifts even when such gifts are made within seven years of death.**

Notes:

1. Your answer should include a calculation of James' inheritance tax saving from making the gift of property to the trust on 2 August 2016 rather than retaining the property until his death.

2. You are not expected to consider lifetime exemptions in this part of the question.

(2 marks)

(10 marks)

Question 57 BLACK LTD

(a) Black Ltd owns 100% of the ordinary share capital of White Ltd. The results of Black Ltd and White Ltd for the year ended 31 March 2018 are as follows:

	Black Ltd £	White Ltd £
Trading profit/(loss)	396,800	(351,300)
Property business profit	21,100	26,700
Capital loss	–	(17,200)
Qualifying charitable donations	(4,400)	(5,600)

As at 1 April 2017 Black Ltd had unused trading losses of £57,900, and unused capital losses of £12,600, whilst White Ltd had unused trading losses of £21,800.

Required:

Advise Black Ltd as to the maximum amount of group relief that can be claimed from White Ltd in respect of its losses for the year ended 31 March 2018. Clearly identify any losses that cannot be surrendered by White Ltd as part of the group relief claim.

(4 marks)

Note: You are not expected to calculate either company's corporation tax liability.

(b) Softapp Ltd is a software developer. For the year ended 31 March 2018 the company had taxable total profits of £505,920, including chargeable gains (after indexation) of £61,300. The gain is in respect of the sale of Softapp Ltd's entire (2%) shareholding in Networked plc on 28 February 2018.

Softapp Ltd has one subsidiary company, owning 100% of the ordinary share capital of Byte-Size Ltd. On 4 March 2018, Byte-Size Ltd disposed of its entire (1%) shareholding in Cloud Ltd, and this resulted in a capital loss of £48,200. For the year ended 31 March 2018, Byte-Size Ltd made no other disposals.

Required:

(i) **Advise Softapp Ltd as to the joint election it should make with Byte-Size Ltd, regarding their respective chargeable gain and capital loss, and explain how such an election will reduce the group's overall corporation tax liability for the year ended 31 March 2018.** (1 mark)

Note: You are not expected to perform any calculations.

(ii) **State the date by which Softapp Ltd's self-assessment corporation tax return for the year ended 31 March 2018 should be submitted and explain how the company can correct the return if it is subsequently found to be incorrect.**
(2 marks)

(c) **State when an accounting period starts and when an accounting period finishes for corporation tax purposes.** (3 marks)

(10 marks)

Question 58 HEAVY LTD

Heavy Ltd runs a music publishing business. On 1 September 2016 Heavy Ltd acquired 100% of the ordinary share capital of Soft Ltd, a company that runs a music recording studio.

Heavy Ltd has prepared accounts for the year ended 31 December 2017. The following information is available:

■ The operating profit for the year ended 31 December 2017 is £140,000. Depreciation of £12,880 and amortisation of leasehold property of £9,000 (see note (2) below) have been deducted in arriving at this figure.

■ On 1 January 2017 Heavy Ltd acquired a leasehold office building, paying a premium of £90,000 for the grant of a 10-year lease. The office building was used for business purposes by Heavy Ltd throughout the year ended 31 December 2017.

■ On 1 January 2017 the tax written down values of Heavy Ltd's plant and machinery were as follows:

	£
Main pool	900
Motor car [1]	15,100
Motor car [2]	8,800
Motor car [3]	13,200
Short life assets	21,700

The following purchases and disposals of plant and machinery took place during the year ended 31 December 2017:

	Cost/(Proceeds)
	£
23 March 2017 Purchased office equipment	22,400
19 July 2017 Sold motor car [3]	(14,600)
28 July 2017 Sold all the items included in short life assets	(12,300)

All the motor cars have CO_2 emission rates of over 130 grams per kilometre. Motor car [2] is used by the managing director of Heavy Ltd, and 60% of the mileage is for private journeys. Motor car [3] sold on 19 July 2017 originally cost £19,200.

- On 18 October 2017 Heavy Ltd sold a freehold office building to Soft Ltd for £113,600. The indexed cost of the office building on that date was £102,800.

- During the year ended 31 December 2017 Heavy Ltd received the following dividends:

Company paying the dividend	£
An unconnected United Kingdom company	27,000
Soft Ltd	6,300

  These figures were the actual cash amounts received.

Required:

Calculate Heavy Ltd's corporation tax liability for the year ended 31 December 2017.

(10 marks)

Question 59 SOFT LTD AND GREENSTEW LTD

(a) **Explain how limited companies can obtain relief for capital losses.** (3 marks)

Note: You are not expected to explain how groups of companies can obtain relief for capital losses.

(b) Soft Ltd runs a music recording studio.

- The tax adjusted trading profit for the 16-month period ended 31 December 2017 is £120,200. This figure is before taking account of capital allowances.

- On 1 September 2016 the tax written down value of Soft Ltd's plant and machinery in the main pool was £24,000. On 15 December 2017 Soft Ltd sold an item of plant for £3,900. The plant had originally cost £5,200.

- On 4 August 2017 Soft Ltd disposed of some investments and this resulted in a chargeable gain of £16,650. On 3 September 2017 the company made a further disposal and this resulted in a capital loss of £2,900.

Required:

Calculate Soft Ltd's corporation tax liabilities in respect of the 16-month period ended 31 December 2017. (5 marks)

(c) Greenstew Ltd has held shares in four trading companies throughout the year ended 31 March 2018. All four companies prepare accounts to 31 March. The following information is available for the year ended 31 March 2018:

	Are Ltd	*Be Ltd*	*Can Ltd*	*Doer Co*
Residence	UK	UK	UK	Overseas
Percentage shareholding	60%	40%	90%	70%
Trading profit/(loss)	£(74,800)	£68,900	£(64,700)	£22,600

Greenstew Ltd has a tax-adjusted trading profit of £277,700 for the year ended 31 March 2018.

Required:

Calculate Greenstew Ltd's corporation tax liability for the year ended 31 March 2018.

Note: You should assume that Greenstew Ltd will claim the maximum possible amount of group relief. (2 marks)

(10 marks)

Question 60 GREENZONE LTD

Greenzone Ltd runs a business providing environmental guidance. The company's summarised statement of profit or loss for the year ended 31 March 2018 is as follows:

	Note	£	£
Gross profit			404,550
Operating expenses			
Depreciation		28,859	
Repairs and renewals	1	28,190	
Other expenses	2	107,801	
			(164,850)
Operating profit			239,700

Note 1 – Repairs and renewals

Repairs and renewals are as follows:

	£
Repainting the exterior of the company's office building	8,390
Extending the office building in order to create a new reception area	19,800
	28,190

Note 2 – Other expenses

Other expenses are as follows:

	£
Entertaining UK customers	3,600
Entertaining overseas customers	1,840
Political donations	740
Donation to a charity where Greenzone Ltd received free advertising in the charity's newsletter. This was not a qualifying charitable donation	430
Gifts to customers (pens costing £30 each, not displaying Greenzone Ltd's name)	660
Gifts to customers (clocks costing £65 each and displaying Greenzone Ltd's name)	910
Balance of expenditure (all allowable)	99,621
	107,801

Note 3 – Plant and machinery

On 1 April 2017 the tax written down values of Greenzone Ltd's plant and machinery were as follows:

	£
Main pool	48,150
Special rate pool	9,200

The following motor cars were purchased during the year ended 31 March 2018:

	Date of purchase	Cost £	CO_2 emission rate
Motor car [1]	10 April 2017	10,800	72 grams per kilometre
Motor car [2]	10 June 2017	20,400	120 grams per kilometre

The following motor cars were sold during the year ended 31 March 2018:

	Date of sale	Proceeds £	Original cost £
Motor car [3]	8 March 2018	9,100	8,500
Motor car [4]	8 March 2018	12,400	18,900

The original cost of motor car [3] has previously been added to the main pool, and the original cost of motor car [4] has previously been added to the special rate pool.

Required:

Calculate Greenzone Ltd's tax adjusted trading profit for the year ended 31 March 2018.

Note: Your computation should commence with the operating profit figure of £239,700, and should also list all of the items referred to in notes (1) and (2), indicating by the use of zero (0) any items that do not require adjustment.

(10 marks)

Question 61 OPAL LTD

(a) The managing director of Cuemore Ltd understands that the company has to file its self-assessment corporation tax return online, and that the supporting accounts and tax computations have to be filed using the inline eXtensible Business Reporting Language (iXBRL). The managing director is concerned about how the company produces documents in this format.

Required:

(i) **State the date by which Cuemore Ltd's self-assessment corporation tax return for the year ended 31 March 2018 should be filed;** (1 mark)

(ii) **Explain the options available to Cuemore Ltd regarding the production of accounts and tax computations in the iXBRL format.** (3 marks)

(b) Opal Ltd has prepared accounts for the 14-month period ended 31 May 2018, and its trading profit for this period is £868,000. This figure is before taking account of capital allowances.

The tax written down value of Opal Ltd's capital allowances main pool at 1 April 2017 was £124,000. On 10 April 2018, Opal Ltd purchased machinery for £90,000.

Required:

Calculate Opal Ltd's taxable total profits for each of the accounting periods covered by the 14-month period of account ended 31 May 2018. (6 marks)

Note: You should assume that the capital allowance rates and allowances for the financial year 2017 apply throughout.

(10 marks)

Question 62 SOFTAPP LTD

Softapp Ltd is a software developer. The company's summarised statement of profit or loss for the year ended 31 March 2018 is as follows:

	Note	£
Operating profit	1	519,300
Other income		
Income from property	2	36,700
Loan interest receivable	3	8,100
Profit on disposal of shares	4	64,900
Finance costs		
Interest payable	5	(67,200)
Profit before taxation		561,800

Note 1 – Operating profit

Depreciation of £10,170 and amortisation of leasehold property of £2,500 have been deducted in arriving at the operating profit of £519,300.

Note 2 – Income from property

Since 1 November 2017, Softapp Ltd has let out one floor of a freehold office building which is surplus to requirements. The income from property figure of £36,700 is made up of the following income and expenditure:

Date received/paid		£
23 October 2017	Advertising for tenants	(600)
25 October 2017	Security deposit of two months' rent	10,400
25 October 2017	Rent for the quarter ended 31 January 2018	15,600
1 November 2017	Insurance for the year ended 31 October 2018	(1,200)
2 February 2018	Rent for the quarter ended 30 April 2018	15,600
20 March 2018	Repairs following a flood	(12,800)
4 April 2018	Insurance claim in respect of the flood damage	9,700
		36,700

Note 3 – Loan interest receivable

The loan was made for non-trading purposes on 1 July 2017. Loan interest of £5,600 was received on 31 December 2017, and interest of £2,500 was accrued at 31 March 2018.

TAXATION (TX-UK) (F6) – REVISION QUESTION BANK

Note 4 – Profit on disposal of shares

The profit on disposal of shares is in respect of the sale of Softapp Ltd's entire (2%) shareholding in Networked plc on 28 February 2018. The disposal resulted in a chargeable gain of £61,300. This figure is after taking account of indexation.

Note 5 – Interest payable

The interest payable is in respect of the company's 4% debenture loan stock. Interest of £33,600 was paid on 30 September 2017 and again on 31 March 2018. The loan stock was used to finance the company's trading activities.

Additional information

Leasehold property

On 1 January 2018, Softapp Ltd acquired a leasehold office building, paying a premium of £100,000 for the grant of a 10-year lease. The office building was used for business purposes by Softapp Ltd throughout the period 1 January to 31 March 2018.

Plant and machinery

The tax written down value of Softapp Ltd's main plant and machinery pool as at 1 April 2017 was £50,000.

During October 2017 Softapp Ltd had an extension constructed adjacent to its existing freehold office building, which is used by the company's employees as a staff room. The total cost of £100,000 is made up as follows:

	£
Integral to the building	
Building costs of extension	61,000
Heating system	3,600
Ventilation system	4,600
Not integral to the building	
Furniture and furnishings	29,400
Refrigerator and microwave cooker	1,400
	100,000

The full annual investment allowance is available to Softapp Ltd.

Required:

Calculate Softapp Ltd's corporation tax liability for the year ended 31 March 2018.

Note: Your computation should commence with the operating profit figure of £519,300.

(15 marks)

Question 63 LONG LTD

The following scenario relates to questions 1–5.

Long Ltd owns 100% of the ordinary share capital of both Wind Ltd and Road Ltd. Road Ltd was incorporated on 15 January 2017 and commenced trading on 1 January 2018.

Long Ltd and Wind Ltd have prepared accounts for the year ended 31 March 2018, whilst Road Ltd has prepared accounts for the period 1 January 2018 to 31 March 2018.

Long Ltd

- The operating profit for the year ended 31 March 2018 is £384,400. Leasing costs of £3,600 relating to a motor car with a CO_2 emission rate of 142 grams per kilometre have been deducted in arriving at this figure.

- On 1 April 2017, the tax written down value of the plant and machinery main pool was £44,800. On 10 June 2017, Long Ltd purchased a lorry for £36,800 and a motor car for £15,700. The motor car has a CO_2 emission rate of 122 grams per kilometre. The motor car is used by the managing director of Long Ltd, and 40% of the mileage is for private journeys.

Wind Ltd

- The operating profit for the year ended 31 March 2018 is £62,900.

- On 1 April 2017, the tax written down value of the plant and machinery main pool was £900. There were no additions or disposals during the year ended 31 March 2018.

- Amortisation of £5,000 has been deducted in arriving at the operating profit. The amortisation relates to a premium which was paid in 2013 to acquire a leasehold office building on a 20-year lease. The amount of premium assessed on the landlord as income was £68,200. The building was used for business purposes.

Road Ltd

- The operating loss for the three-month period ended 31 March 2018 is £26,100. No depreciation has been charged, but donations of £2,800 have been deducted in arriving at this figure. The donations consist of political donations of £400, and qualifying charitable donations of £2,400.

- On 3 October 2017, Road Ltd purchased a motor car for £11,600. The motor car has a CO_2 emission rate of 75 grams per kilometre.

- For the three-month period ended 31 March 2018, loan interest receivable was £4,300. The loan was made for non-trading purposes.

- Road Ltd will surrender its trading loss to Long Ltd as group relief.

1 **What is the total amount of capital allowances available to Long Ltd for the year ended 31 March 2018?**

£ ☐

TAXATION (TX-UK) (F6) – REVISION QUESTION BANK

2 Complete the following sentence by matching the correct amount and adjustment to operating profit.

In respect of the leased vehicle, £ [   ] should be [   ] Long Ltd's operating profit.

Amount
£3,600
£3,060
£540

Adjustment
added to
deducted from

3 Assuming a maximum claim for capital allowances, what is the taxable total profits figure of Wind Ltd for the year ended 31 March 2018?

Select...
- £64,328
- £63,411
- £63,590
- £67,000

4 Assuming a maximum claim for capital allowances, what is the trading loss of Road Ltd for the three months ended 31 March 2018?

£ [   ]

5 What is the corporation tax payable by Road Ltd for the three months ended 31 March 2018?

A £0
B £361
C £817
D £1,900

(10 marks)

Question 64 E-COMMERCE PLC

You are a trainee Chartered Certified Accountant, and your firm has recently completed its audit of E-Commerce plc's financial statements for the year ended 31 March 2018. The company runs an internet-based retail business.

E-Commerce plc prepared its own corporation tax computations for the year ended 31 March 2018, and your colleague has completed your firm's tax audit of these figures. E-Commerce plc's original corporation tax computation, along with references to your colleague's queries, is as follows:

E-Commerce plc – Corporation tax computation for the year ended 31 March 2018

	Query	£
Operating profit	1	2,102,300
Deduction for lease premium	2	(14,400)
Capital allowances	3	(209,200)
Trading profit		1,878,700
Property business profit	4	156,700
Loan interest receivable	5	42,400
Taxable total profits		2,077,800
Corporation tax (2,077,800 at 19%)		394,782

Your colleague has raised some queries in regard to E-Commerce plc's corporation tax computation. Apart from any corrections arising from your colleague's queries, the corporation tax computation prepared by E-Commerce plc does not contain any errors.

Query 1 – Legal fees

E-Commerce plc has treated all of the company's legal expenditure as allowable when calculating its operating profit. However, legal expenses include the following amounts:

- £80,200 in connection with an issue of £1 preference shares.

- £92,800 in connection with the issue of loan notes. The loan was used to finance the company's trading activities.

- £14,900 in connection with the renewal of a 99-year lease of property.

- £4,700 in connection with an action brought against a supplier for breach of contract.

- £8,800 in connection with the registration of trade marks.

Query 2 – Deduction for lease premium

The amount assessed on the landlord has been correctly calculated, but the life of the lease should be 15 years and not the 12 years used by E-Commerce plc. The lease commenced on 1 April 2017.

Query 3 – Capital allowances

There are two issues here:

(1) E-Commerce plc purchased four motor cars during the year ended 31 March 2018, and all four motor cars have been included in the plant and machinery main pool. Details are as follows:

	Cost	CO_2 emission rate
	£	
Motor car [1]	20,300	122 grams per kilometre
Motor car [2]	24,900	114 grams per kilometre
Motor car [3]	62,100	245 grams per kilometre
Motor car [4]	19,800	72 grams per kilometre

(2) Four years ago, E-Commerce plc purchased computer equipment on which a short-life asset election has been made. For the year ended 31 March 2018, the writing down allowance claimed on this equipment was £1,512, calculated at the rate of 18%. However, the computer equipment was actually scrapped, with nil proceeds, on 10 December 2017.

TAXATION (TX-UK) (F6) – REVISION QUESTION BANK

Query 4 – Property business profit

There are two issues here:

(1) E-Commerce plc has claimed a deduction for repairs of £95,300 in respect of a warehouse which was purchased on 21 May 2017. The warehouse was purchased in a dilapidated state, and could not be let until the repairs were carried out. This fact was represented by a reduced purchase price.

(2) E-Commerce plc did not receive the rent due of £16,200 in respect of this warehouse for the quarter ended 31 May 2018 until 1 April 2018. None of this amount has been taken into account in calculating the property business profit for the year ended 31 March 2018.

Query 5 – Loan interest receivable

The accrual at 31 March 2018 has been calculated at £4,800, but because of falling interest rates the accrual should actually be £3,500.

Other information

For the year ended 31 March 2017, E-Commerce plc had profits of £1,360,000, and has forecast that its profits for the year ended 31 March 2019 will exceed £2,000,000.

E-Commerce plc does not have any group companies.

Required:

(a) **Prepare a revised version of E-Commerce plc's corporation tax computation for the year ended 31 March 2018 after making any necessary corrections arising from your colleague's queries.** (12 marks)

Note: Your calculations should commence with the operating profit figure of £2,102,300, and you should indicate by the use of zero (0) any items referred to in queries (1) to (5) which do not require adjustment.

(b) **Explain why E-Commerce plc will not have been required to make quarterly instalment payments in respect of its corporation tax liability for the year ended 31 March 2018, but will have to do so for the year ended 31 March 2019.** (3 marks)

(15 marks)

Question 65 CAIRO LTD AND KIGALI LTD

The following scenario relates to questions 1–5.

Cairo Ltd

Cairo Ltd runs a business promoting African music. The company's taxable total profits for the year ended 31 March 2018 were £87,000.

Cairo Ltd has owned 100% of the ordinary share capital of Dakar Ltd since it began trading on 1 December 2016, running a music recording studio. Dakar Ltd's results for the year ended 30 November 2017 and for the four-month period ended 31 March 2018 are as follows:

REVISION QUESTION BANK – TAXATION (TX-UK) (F6)

	Year ended 30 November 2017 £	Period ended 31 March 2018 £
Trading loss	(54,600)	(27,900)
Capital loss	0	(16,200)
Qualifying charitable donations	0	(600)

Kigali Ltd

Kigali Ltd is the holding company for a group of companies. The group structure is as follows:

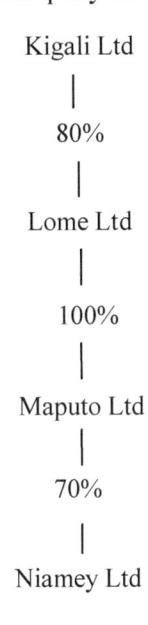

Kigali Ltd
|
80%
|
Lome Ltd
|
100%
|
Maputo Ltd
|
70%
|
Niamey Ltd

On 31 May 2017, Kigali Ltd sold a freehold office building for £310,000. The office building had been purchased on 2 October 2001 for £120,000, and during October 2001 it was extended at a cost of £42,000. The indexation factor from October 2001 to May 2017 is 0.559.

Lome Ltd, Maputo Ltd and Niamey Ltd have all recently purchased, or are planning to purchase, freehold warehouses. The directors of Kigali Ltd understand that rollover relief is available within a chargeable gains group.

1 What is the maximum amount of group relief which can be claimed by Cairo Ltd against its taxable total profits for the eight month corresponding period ended 30 November 2017?

£ ☐

2 What is the maximum amount of group relief which can be claimed by Cairo Ltd against its taxable total profits for the four month corresponding period ended 31 March 2018?

Select... ▼
£29,000
£21,750
£27,900
£28,500

3   Identify, by clicking on the relevant box in the table below, which of the following statements in relation to a group relief claim is/are correct.

It results in earlier relief, since Dakar Ltd will not make a trading profit until at least the year ended 31 March 2019	CORRECT	INCORRECT
It may allow taxation at a lower effective rate	CORRECT	INCORRECT
It allows some utilisation of the capital loss which might not otherwise be relieved	CORRECT	INCORRECT
It avoids wasting all of Dakar Ltd's qualifying charitable donations for the period ended 31 March 2017	CORRECT	INCORRECT

4   What is Kigali Ltd's chargeable gain in respect of the disposal of the freehold office building?

- £148,000
- £122,920
- £70,004
- £57,442

5   Identify by clicking on the relevant box in the table below, which of the following statements is/are correct?

Kigali Ltd's chargeable gain may be subject to a rollover claim in respect of a qualifying acquisition by Maputo Ltd	CORRECT	INCORRECT
Kigali Ltd's chargeable gain may be subject to a rollover claim in respect of a qualifying acquisition by Niamey Ltd	CORRECT	INCORRECT
An acquisition qualifying for rollover would need to be made during the period one year before the date of disposal to three years after the date of disposal	CORRECT	INCORRECT
An acquisition qualifying for rollover would need to be made during the period three years before the date of disposal to one year after the date of disposal	CORRECT	INCORRECT

(10 marks)

Question 66 RETRO LTD

Retro Ltd's summarised statement of profit or loss for the year ended 31 March 2018 is as follows:

	Note	£	£
Gross profit			127,100
Operating expenses			
Depreciation		27,240	
Gifts and donations	1	2,300	
Impairment loss	2	1,600	
Leasing costs	3	4,400	
Other expenses	4	205,160	
			(240,700)
Finance costs			
Interest payable	5		(6,400)
Loss before taxation			(120,000)

Note 1 – Gifts and donations

Gifts and donations are as follows:

	£
Gifts to employees (food hampers costing £60 each)	720
Gifts to customers	
(calendars costing £8 each and displaying Retro Ltd's name)	480
Political donations	420
Qualifying charitable donations	680
	2,300

Note 2 – Impairment loss

On 31 March 2018, Retro Ltd wrote off an impairment loss of £1,600 relating to a trade debt. This was in respect of an invoice which had been due for payment on 10 November 2017.

Note 3 – Leasing costs

The leasing costs of £4,400 are in respect of a motor car lease which commenced on 1 April 2017. The leased motor car has CO_2 emissions of 145 grams per kilometre.

Note 4 – Other expenses

The figure of £205,160 for other expenses includes a fine of £5,100 for a breach of health and safety regulations, and legal fees of £4,860 in connection with the defence of Retro Ltd's internet domain name. The remaining expenses are all fully allowable.

Note 5 – Interest payable

The interest payable is in respect of the company's 5% loan notes which were repaid on 31 July 2017. Interest of £9,600 was paid on 31 July 2017, and an accrual of £3,200 had been provided for at 1 April 2017. The loan notes were issued in order to finance the company's trading activities.

Additional information

Plant and machinery

On 1 April 2017, the tax written down value of the plant and machinery main pool was £39,300.

The following vehicles were purchased during the year ended 31 March 2018:

	Date of purchase	Cost £	CO_2 emission rate
Motor car [1]	8 June 2017	14,700	124 grams per kilometre
Delivery van	3 August 2017	28,300	162 grams per kilometre
Motor car [2]	19 October 2017	12,400	72 grams per kilometre

Previous results

Retro Ltd commenced trading on 1 September 2015. The company's results for its two previous periods of trading are as follows:

	Year ended 31 August 2016 £	Period ended 31 March 2017 £
Tax adjusted trading profit	56,600	47,900
Bank interest receivable	1,300	0
Qualifying charitable donations paid	(540)	(330)

Future results

Retro Ltd is expected to return to profitability in the year ended 31 March 2019 and to continue to be profitable in subsequent years.

Required:

(a) **Calculate Retro Ltd's tax adjusted trading loss for the year ended 31 March 2018.**

(9 marks)

Note: Your computation should commence with the loss before taxation figure of £120,000, and should also list all of the items referred to in notes (1) to (5), indicating by the use of zero (0) any items which do not require adjustment.

(b) **Assuming that Retro Ltd claims relief for its trading loss as early as possible, calculate the company's taxable total profits for the year ended 31 August 2016 and for the seven-month period ended 31 March 2017.** (4 marks)

(c) **Identify the amount of unrelieved trading loss which Retro Ltd will have at 31 March 2018, and state how this can be relieved.** (2 marks)

(15 marks)

Question 67 LUCKY LTD

Lucky Ltd was incorporated on 20 July 2017, and commenced trading on 1 December 2017. The following information is available for the four-month period 1 December 2017 to 31 March 2018:

(1) The operating profit for the four-month period ended 31 March 2018 is £432,600. Advertising expenditure of £4,700 (incurred during September 2017), depreciation of £14,700, and amortisation of £9,000 have been deducted in arriving at this figure.

The amortisation relates to a premium which was paid on 1 December 2017 to acquire a leasehold warehouse on a 12-year lease. The amount of premium assessed on the landlord as income was £46,800. The warehouse was used for business purposes by Lucky Ltd throughout the period ended 31 March 2018.

(2) Lucky Ltd purchased the following assets during the period 20 July 2017 to 31 March 2018:

		£
19 August 2017	Computer	6,300
22 January 2018	Integral features	41,200
31 January 2018	Office equipment	32,900
17 March 2018	Motor car	12,800

The integral features of £141,200 are in respect of expenditure on electrical systems and ventilation which are integral to a freehold office building owned by Lucky Ltd.

The motor car has a CO_2 emission rate of 72 grams per kilometre.

(3) Lucky Ltd made a loan to another company for non-trading purposes on 1 February 2018. Loan interest income of £700 was accrued at 31 March 2018.

Required:

(a) **State when an accounting period starts for corporation tax purposes.** (2 marks)

(b) **Calculate Lucky Ltd's corporation tax liability for the four-month period ended 31 March 2018.** (9 marks)

Note: Your computation should commence with the operating profit of £532,600, and should also indicate by the use of zero (0) any items referred to in the question for which no adjustment is required.

(c) **Advise Lucky Ltd as to how long it must retain the records used in preparing its self-assessment corporation tax return for the four-month period ended 31 March 2018, and the potential consequences of not retaining the records for the required period.** (2 marks)

(13 marks)

Question 68 JUMP LTD

Jump Ltd's summarised statement of profit or loss for the three-month period ended 31 March 2018 is as follows:

	Note	£	£
Revenue			264,900
Operating expenses			
Depreciation		8,100	
Employee costs	1	189,700	
Lease of motor car	2	1,200	
Professional fees	3	7,800	
Other expenses	4	202,800	
			(409,600)
Operating loss			(144,700)
Bank interest receivable			0
Loss before taxation			(144,700)

Note 1 – Employee costs

Employee costs are as follows:

	£
Employee training courses	3,400
Employee pension contributions paid	11,600
Cost of annual staff party (for eight employees)	1,500
Balance of expenditure (all allowable)	173,200
	189,700

Note 2 – Lease of motor car

The lease is in respect of a motor car with CO_2 emissions of 189 grams per kilometre.

Note 3 – Professional fees

Professional fees are as follows:

	£
Accountancy	2,200
Legal fees in connection with the issue of share capital	3,800
Legal fees in connection with the renewal of a 20-year property lease	1,800
	7,800

Note 4 – Other expenses

Other expenses are as follows:

	£
Entertaining UK customers	1,700
Entertaining overseas customers	790
Political donations	800
Balance of expenditure (all allowable)	199,510
	202,800

Additional information

Plant and machinery

On 1 January 2018, the tax written down values of Jump Ltd's plant and machinery were as follows:

	£
Main pool	12,100
Special rate pool	5,700

The following motor cars were sold during the three-month period ended 31 March 2018:

	Date of sale	Proceeds £	Original cost £
Motor car [1]	7 January 2018	9,700	9,300
Motor car [2]	29 March 2018	6,100	13,200

The original cost of motor car [1] was added to the special rate pool when it was purchased, and the original cost of motor car [2] was added to the main pool when it was purchased.

Previous results

Jump Ltd's results for its two previous periods of trading are as follows:

	Year ended 31 May 2017 £	Period ended 31 December 2017 £
Tax adjusted trading profit	78,600	42,400
Bank interest receivable	1,200	0

Group companies

Jump Ltd owns 80% of the ordinary share capital of Hop Ltd and 60% of the ordinary share capital of Skip Ltd.

Hop Ltd commenced trading on 1 August 2017, and for the eight-month period ended 31 March 2018 has taxable total profits of £63,000.

Skip Ltd has been trading for several years and has taxable total profits of £56,000 for the year ended 31 March 2018.

Required:

(a) **Calculate Jump Ltd's tax adjusted trading loss for the three-month period ended 31 March 2018.**

Notes:

1. Your computation should commence with the operating loss figure of £144,700, and should list all of the items referred to in notes (1) to (4), indicating by the use of zero (0) any items which do not require adjustment.

2. You should assume that the company claims the maximum available capital allowances. **(10 marks)**

(b) (i) **State the main factor which will influence Jump Ltd's choice of loss relief or group relief claims.** (1 mark)

(ii) **Advise Jump Ltd as to the maximum amount of its trading loss which can be relieved against its total profits for the year ended 31 May 2017 and the seven-month period ended 31 December 2017.** (2 marks)

(iii) **Advise Jump Ltd as to the maximum amount of its trading loss which can be surrendered as group relief.** (2 marks)

(15 marks)

Question 69 WIKI LTD

The following scenario relates to questions 1–5.

Wiki Ltd sold a freehold warehouse on 3 February 2018 for £308,600. The warehouse had been purchased on 12 November 2007 for £171,000. Wiki Ltd incurred legal fees of £2,200 in connection with the purchase of the warehouse. The relevant retail price indexes (RPIs) are as follows:

November 2007	209.7
February 2018 (notional)	278.9

Wiki Ltd is unsure as to how to reinvest the proceeds from the sale of the warehouse. The company can either purchase a freehold factory for £166,000, or it can purchase a freehold office building for £296,000. The reinvestment will take place during July 2018.

All of the above buildings have been, or will be, used for business purposes by Wiki Ltd.

1 What was the chargeable gain in respect of the disposal of the warehouse before taking account of any available rollover relief?

- A £76,444
- B £78,244
- C £78,970
- D £81,170

2 Assuming Wiki Ltd reinvests part of the proceeds to purchase the freehold factory, what will be the base cost of the new asset?

- A £166,000
- B £142,000
- C £87,756
- D £30,600

3 Assuming Wiki Ltd instead reinvests part of the proceeds to purchase the freehold office building and claims the maximum rollover relief, what now will be the chargeable gain?

- A £0
- B £12,600
- C £39,600
- D £65,664

4 Which of the following statements is/are correct?

(1) Indexation allowance applies only to corporate taxpayers

(2) Indexation allowance is based on the monthly consumer price index

(3) In times of rising prices indexation allowance will act to reduce a chargeable gain or increase a chargeable loss

(4) If prices fall over the relevant period of ownership then indexation allowance is ignored

- A 2 and 3 only
- B 1, 2 and 3
- C 1, 3 and 4
- D 1 and 4

5 What is the latest date for Wiki Ltd to make a claim for rollover relief in respect of these transactions?

- A Three years after the date of disposal
- B Four years after the date of disposal
- C Four years after the end of the accounting period in which the disposal is made
- D One year after the end of the accounting period in which the qualifying reinvestment is made

(10 marks)

REVISION QUESTION BANK – TAXATION (TX-UK) (F6)

Question 70 ACEBOOK LTD

The following scenario relates to questions 1–5.

Acebook Ltd sold the following assets during the year ended 31 December 2017:

- On 10 March 2017 Acebook Ltd sold its entire shareholding of £0.50 ordinary shares in Oogle plc for £3·20 per share. The company had originally purchased 24,000 shares in Oogle plc on 28 June 2008 for £25,200. On 14 February 2013, Oogle plc made a 1 for 5 rights issue. Acebook Ltd took up its allocation under the rights issue in full, paying £4·30 for each new share issued.

- Also on 10 March 2017 Acebook Ltd sold its entire shareholding of £0.50 ordinary shares in Pogle plc for £1·30 per share. The company had originally purchased 50,000 shares in Pogle plc on 8 June 2008 at par value.

- Indexation factors are as follows:

June 2008 to February 2013	0.142
June 2008 to March 2017	0.242
October 2011 to February 2013	0.040
October 2011 to March 2017	0.132
February 2013 to March 2017	0.088

- On 30 June 2017 three acres of land were sold for £192,000. Acebook Ltd had originally purchased four acres of land, and the indexed cost of the four acres on 30 June 2017 was £196,000. The market value of the unsold acre of land as at 30 June 2017 was £53,000. During June 2017 Acebook Ltd spent £29,400 clearing and levelling all four acres of land. The land has never been used for business purposes.

- On 1 October 2017 an investment property owned by Acebook Ltd was destroyed in a fire. The indexed cost of the property on that date was £138,400. Acebook Ltd received insurance proceeds of £189,000 on 20 October 2017, and on 31 October 2017 the company paid £172,400 for a replacement investment property. Acebook Ltd has made a claim to defer the gain arising from the receipt of the insurance proceeds.

1   What was the indexed cost of Acebook Ltd's shareholding in Oogle Ltd as at February 2013 after the rights issue was taken up?

    A   £48,048
    B   £49,418
    C   £51,938
    D   £52,349

2   What is Acebook Ltd's chargeable gain in respect of the disposal of its shareholding in Pogle?

Select... ▼
£40,000
£37,800
£33,950
£2,900

TAXATION (TX-UK) (F6) – REVISION QUESTION BANK

3 What is Acebook Ltd's chargeable gain in respect of the disposal of the three acres of land?

£ ☐

4 What is Acebook Ltd's chargeable gain in respect of the insurance proceeds for the investment property?

- A £0
- B £16,600
- C £34,000
- D £50,600

5 Identify, by clicking on the relevant box in the table below, which of the following statements are true or false in respect of damage to non-wasting assets.

If no insurance proceeds or other compensation is received there is no disposal for tax purposes	TRUE	FALSE
If compensation is received, a chargeable disposal arises on the date the damage occurred	TRUE	FALSE
If compensation is received, a chargeable disposal arises on the date of receipt	TRUE	FALSE
If at least 90% of proceeds are applied to restoration of the damaged asset, then a no gain/no loss disposal arises	TRUE	FALSE

(10 marks)

Question 71 LUNA LTD

Luna Ltd had the following transactions in shares during the year ended 31 March 2018:

(1) On 29 October 2017, Luna Ltd sold its entire shareholding of £1 ordinary shares in Pluto plc for £53,400. Luna Ltd had originally purchased 16,000 shares in Pluto plc on 14 June 2011 for £36,800. On 22 May 2013, Luna Ltd sold 10,000 of the shares for £46,200.

Retail price indices (RPIs) are as follows:

June 2011	235.2
May 2013	250.0
October 2017 (notional)	275.9

(2) On 12 February 2018, Luna Ltd's shareholding in Asteroid plc was taken over by Comet plc. Luna Ltd had originally purchased 10,000 £1 ordinary shares in Asteroid plc, and their indexed cost on 12 February 2018 was £33,000.

Under the terms of the takeover, for each of its £1 ordinary shares in Asteroid plc, Luna Ltd received £6·50 in cash plus one £1 ordinary share in Comet plc. Immediately after the takeover, Comet plc's £1 ordinary shares were quoted at £4·50.

Required:

(a) Explain how the indexation allowance can be used when a company makes a capital loss, or where the indexation allowance is greater than a company's unindexed gain. **(2 marks)**

(b) **Calculate the chargeable gain arising from each of Luna Ltd's transactions in shares during the year ended 31 March 2018.** (8 marks)

Note: When calculating the chargeable gain arising from the disposal of the shareholding in Pluto plc, you should show full workings for the share pool.

(10 marks)

Question 72 FLICK PICK

The following scenario relates to questions 1–5.

On 1 January 2018 Flick Pick commenced in partnership with Art Reel running a small cinema, preparing accounts to 30 April.

Value added tax (VAT)

- The partnership voluntarily registered for VAT on 1 January 2018, and immediately began using the flat rate scheme to calculate the amount of VAT payable. The relevant flat rate scheme percentage applicable in 2018 for the partnership's trade is 12%.

- For the quarter ended 31 March 2018 the partnership had standard rated sales of £59,700, and these were all made to members of the general public. For the same period standard rated expenses amounted to £27,300. Both figures are stated inclusive of VAT.

- The partnership has two private boxes in its cinema that can be booked on a special basis by privileged customers. Such customers can book the boxes up to two months in advance, at which time they have to pay a 25% deposit. An invoice is then given to the customer on the day of the screening of the film, with payment of the balance of 75% required within seven days. For VAT purposes, the renting out of the cinema boxes is a supply of services.

1   How much VAT is payable for the quarter ended 31 March 2018?

   A   £3,888
   B   £3,240
   C   £7,164
   D   £5,970

2   How much VAT would be payable for the quarter ended 31 March 2018 if the partnership had not used the flat rate basis?

   A   £6,111
   B   £5,400
   C   £6,480
   D   £4,500

3   Which of the following statements is/are correct?

   (1)   To the extent it is not possible to pass the output VAT on to customers the partnership would have had to absorb this as a cost

   (2)   It was probably not beneficial for the partnership to have voluntarily registered for VAT from 1 January 2018

   (3)   Voluntary registration allows the partnership to recover VAT on its purchases

   (4)   It was probably beneficial for the partnership to have voluntarily registered for VAT from 1 January 2018

A	1, 2 and 3
B	1, 3 and 4
C	1 and 2 only
D	3 and 4 only

4 **When will the VAT liability arise in respect of rentals of the private boxes?**

A	100% at the time the booking is made
B	25% at the time of booking, 75% at the time of screening
C	25% at the time of booking, 75% on receipt of balance
D	100% on invoice date

5 **Which of the following statements is/are correct?**

(1) The flat rate scheme can be used in association with the annual accounting scheme

(2) It would have been beneficial for the partnership to have joined the annual accounting scheme from 1 January 2018 as it would delay payment until 2019

(3) If the partnership leaves the flat rate scheme it would be unable to re-join for at least 12 months

(4) If the cash accounting scheme is used it is applied for outputs but not necessarily for inputs

A	1 and 2 only
B	1, 3 and 4
C	3 and 4 only
D	1 and 3 only

(10 marks)

Question 73 CLUELESS LTD

The following scenario relates to questions 1–5.

Clueless Ltd is registered for value added tax (VAT), but currently does not use any of the special VAT schemes. The company has annual standard rated sales of £1,200,000 and annual standard rated expenses of £550,000. Both these figures are exclusive of VAT and are likely to remain the same for the foreseeable future. Clueless Ltd is up to date with all of its tax returns, including those for corporation tax, PAYE and VAT. It is also up to date with its corporation tax, PAYE and VAT payments. However, the company often incurs considerable overtime costs due to its employees working late in order to meet tax return filing deadlines.

Clueless Ltd pays its expenses on a cash basis, but allows customers two months credit when paying for sales. The company does not have any impairment losses.

Clueless Ltd is planning to purchase some new machinery at a cost of £22,000 (exclusive of VAT). The machinery can either be purchased from an overseas supplier situated outside the European Union, or from a VAT registered supplier situated in the European Union. Clueless Ltd is not a regular importer and so is unsure of the VAT treatment for this purchase.

1 **Which of the following statements is/are correct?**

(1) Clueless Ltd could join the annual or cash accounting schemes as its expected turnover is below the threshold of £1,350,000

(2) Clueless Ltd could join the annual or cash accounting schemes as its expected turnover is below the threshold of £1,500,000

(3) A company is required to have a good track record of both filing and payment in order to apply to join annual or cash accounting schemes

(4) A company is not required to have a good track record of both filing and payment in order to apply to join annual or cash accounting schemes

A 1 and 3
B 1 and 4
C 2 and 3
D 2 and 4

2 **Which of the following statements is/are correct?**

(1) Clueless Ltd could benefit under the annual accounting scheme as it should save overtime costs incurred in meeting filing requirements

(2) Clueless Ltd would receive an ongoing benefit under the cash accounting scheme as VAT on sales will arise two months later

(3) Clueless Ltd would receive a one-off cash flow benefit on joining the cash accounting scheme

(4) Clueless Ltd would not be allowed to join both the annual accounting scheme and the cash accounting scheme

A 1 and 2
B 1 and 3
C 2 and 4
D 1, 3 and 4

3 **If Clueless purchases the machinery from a supplier situated outside the European Union, which of the following statements is/are correct about how VAT will be accounted?**

(1) Clueless Ltd will have to pay VAT to HMRC at the time of physical importation

(2) Clueless Ltd will have to account for output VAT as a self-supply based on the acquisition date as per the supplier's invoice

(3) Clueless Ltd can reclaim the equivalent input VAT in its VAT return

(4) The supplier's invoice will show the sale of machinery as zero-rated

A 1 and 3
B 2 and 3
C 1 and 4
D 2 and 4

TAXATION (TX-UK) (F6) – REVISION QUESTION BANK

4   If Clueless Ltd purchases the machinery from a supplier situated within the European Union, which of the following statements is/are correct about how VAT will be accounted?

   (1)   Clueless Ltd will have to pay VAT to HMRC at the time of physical importation

   (2)   Clueless Ltd will have to account for output VAT as a self-supply based on the acquisition date as per the supplier's invoice

   (3)   Clueless Ltd can reclaim the equivalent input VAT in its VAT return

   (4)   The supplier's invoice will show the sale of machinery as zero-rated

   A   1 and 3
   B   2 and 3 only
   C   1, 2 and 4
   D   2, 3 and 4

5   The purchase by Clueless of goods from a VAT registered supplier within the European Union is referred to by which of the following terms?

   A   An import
   B   An export
   C   An acquisition
   D   A dispatch

(10 marks)

Question 74 RICHARD FAMINE

The following scenario relates to questions 1–5.

Richard's sales since the commencement of trading on 6 April 2017 have been as follows:

April to July 2017	£11,000 per month
August to November 2017	£14,000 per month
December 2017 to March 2018	£21,500 per month

These figures are stated exclusive of value added tax (VAT). Richard's sales are all standard rated.

As a trainee in Inspire Co, a firm of Chartered Certified Accountants, you have advised Richard in writing that he should be registered for VAT. However, he has refused to register because he thinks his net profit is insufficient to cover the additional cost which would be incurred.

While complaining about the costs of administration and compliance, Richard has also asked for information about the use of simplified invoices.

1   **From what date was Richard Famine required to be compulsorily registered for VAT?**

   Select...
   - 31 October 2017
   - 1 November 2017
   - 30 November 2017
   - 1 December 2017

2 **Which of the following statements is/are correct?**

(1) If Richard continued to trade after the compulsory registration date without registering for VAT, he would still have to pay the VAT due from the time he should have been registered

(2) If Richard registers for VAT he will have to file his VAT returns online and pay the VAT which is due electronically

- A   1 only
- B   1 and 2
- C   2 only
- D   Neither 1 nor 2

3 **From an ethical viewpoint, if Richard Famine continues to refuse to register for VAT, which of the following actions could be expected of your firm?**

Ceasing to act for Richard	YES	NO
Reporting under the money laundering regulations	YES	NO
Notifying HM Revenue and Customs that Inspire Co no longer acts for Richard and the reason for this	YES	NO
Disclosing the matter fully to Richard's successor advisors when replying to their professional clearance letter	YES	NO

4 **Which of the following statements is/are correct?**

(1) A simplified VAT invoice may be issued for a VAT inclusive sale not exceeding £250, but this only applies to retailers

(2) A simplified VAT invoice may be issued for a VAT inclusive sale not exceeding £250, whether the supplier is a retailer or not

(3) Retailers need only issue a VAT invoice if the customer requests one

- A   1 only
- B   2 only
- C   1 and 3
- D   2 and 3

5 **Which TWO of the following need to be included in a simplified VAT invoice?**

- ☐ A description of the goods or services supplied
- ☐ The VAT exclusive and VAT inclusive totals
- ☐ The supplier's name, address and VAT registration number
- ☐ The rate of VAT and the total amount of VAT

(10 marks)

Question 75 WRONG LTD

The following scenario relates to questions 1–5.

Wrong Ltd owns 100% of the ordinary share capital of both Wind Ltd and Road Ltd. Wrong Ltd, Wind Ltd and Road Ltd are not registered as a group for value added tax (VAT) purposes. The following VAT information is available for the quarter ended 31 March 2018:

Wrong Ltd

- All of Wrong Ltd's sales are standard rated for VAT.

- Output VAT of £52,640 was charged in respect of sales. This figure includes output VAT of £1,760 on a deposit received on 28 December 2017. The deposit was in respect of a contract which was completed on 6 January 2018, with a sales invoice being issued on 20 January 2018.

- In addition to the above, Wrong Ltd also charged output VAT of £1,940 on sales to Wind Ltd and output VAT of £960 on sales to Road Ltd.

- The managing director of Wrong Ltd is provided with a company motor car which is used for both business and private mileage. The director reimburses Wrong Ltd for the 40% private use element. For the quarter ended 31 March 2018, input VAT of £140 was incurred in respect of the total cost of fuel, and £560 in respect of repairs to the managing director's motor car.

- Wrong Ltd has discovered that it has not been claiming for the input VAT of £18 which it has paid each month since 1 January 2012 for the hire of a photocopier.

Wind Ltd

- All of Wind Ltd's sales are exempt from VAT.

- Input VAT of £7,330 was incurred in respect of expenses. This includes input VAT of £1,940 incurred on purchases from Long Ltd.

Road Ltd

- All of Road Ltd's sales are zero rated for VAT.

- Road Ltd registered for VAT on 1 January 2018, when it commenced trading, and this is the company's first VAT return.

- Input VAT of £3,120 was incurred in respect of expenses. This includes input VAT of £960 incurred on purchases from Wrong Ltd.

- In addition to the above, Road Ltd incurred input VAT in respect of advertising expenditure as follows:

	£
April 2017	640
November 2017	380
	1,020

REVISION QUESTION BANK – TAXATION (TX-UK) (F6)

1. Drag and drop the amounts that will be included in Wrong Ltd's VAT return for the quarter ended 31 March 2018 in respect of fuel for the managing director's car.

Amount
£0
£56
£84
£140
£280
£700

Output VAT	Input VAT

2. Apart from any amount in respect of fuel, what will be the total output VAT included in Wrong Ltd's VAT return for the quarter ended 31 March 2018?

£ ☐

3. What amounts will be included in Wrong Ltd's VAT return for the quarter ended 31 March 2018 in respect of the photocopier hire?

A   £54
B   £1,350
C   £864
D   £918

4. How much VAT will be payable or recoverable by Wind Ltd for the quarter ended 31 March 2018?

Select... ▼
£0
£1,940
£5,390
£7,330

5. How much VAT will be payable or recoverable by Road Ltd for the quarter ended 31 March 2018?

A   £2,160
B   £3,180
C   £3,500
D   £4,140

(10 marks)

Question 76 DEE-COMMERCE PLC

The following scenario relates to questions 1–5.

For the previous three value added tax (VAT) quarters, DEE-Commerce plc has been late in submitting its VAT returns and in paying the related VAT liabilities. The company is therefore currently serving a default surcharge period.

As part of your firm's tax audit for the year ended 31 March 2018, you have discovered that DEE-Commerce plc has been careless in incorrectly treating the supply of standard rated services received from VAT registered businesses situated elsewhere within the European Union. This careless incorrect treatment has resulted in an underpayment of VAT to HM Revenue and Customs (HMRC) of £8,200 for the year ended 31 March 2018.

1   During the current default surcharge period DEE-Commerce plc is late in paying a further VAT liability.

       Which TWO of the following statements is/are correct?

- ☐ The further default will result in a surcharge of 10% of the amount of VAT outstanding
- ☐ The further default will result in a surcharge of 15% of the amount of VAT outstanding
- ☐ The default surcharge period will be extended to the 12-month anniversary of the due date for payment of the VAT quarter to which the default relates
- ☐ The default surcharge period will be extended to the 12-month anniversary of the VAT quarter to which the default relates

2   **What will DEE-Commerce plc need to do in order to regain a clean default surcharge position?**

- ○ Submit four consecutive VAT returns on time only
- ○ Make four consecutive VAT payments on time only
- ○ Submit four consecutive VAT returns on time and pay the related VAT
- ○ Submit four consecutive VAT returns on time and pay the related VAT on time

3   **Identify, Which of the following statements is/are correct regarding the VAT treatment of services received from a VAT registered EU supplier?**

DEE-Commerce plc should account for VAT on the earlier of the date when the service is completed and the date the service is paid for	CORRECT	INCORRECT
DEE-Commerce plc should account for VAT according to the date on the suppliers invoice showing the VAT charged	CORRECT	INCORRECT
Input VAT will be claimed on the same VAT return as the output VAT	CORRECT	INCORRECT
No input VAT can be claimed as the supplier will not have charged VAT	CORRECT	INCORRECT

4   **Which of the following statements is/are correct regarding the correction by DEE-Commerce plc of the £8,200 VAT underpayment?**

   (1)   The underpayment of VAT may be corrected simply by entering this amount on its next VAT return

   (2)   As well as including the underpayment in its VAT return, DEE-Commerce should separately notify HMRC

   (3)   Default interest may be charged

   (4)   No default interest will arise

   A   1 and 3
   B   1 and 4
   C   2 and 3
   D   2 and 4

5   **Which TWO of the following statements is/are correct regarding the maximum penalty for the incorrect returns?**

   ☐   It would be 100% of the VAT underpaid

   ☐   It would be 30% of the VAT underpaid

   ☐   It would be reduced to nil as a result of unprompted disclosure

   ☐   It could be reduced to nil as a result of unprompted disclosure at HMRC's discretion

(10 marks)

Question 77 ZIM

Zim has been registered for value added tax (VAT) since 1 April 2008. The following information is available for the year ended 31 March 2018:

(1)   Sales invoices totalling £126,000 were issued, of which £115,200 were in respect of standard rated sales and £10,800 were in respect of zero rated sales. Zim's customers are all members of the general public.

(2)   On 31 March 2018, Zim wrote off two impairment losses which were in respect of standard rated sales. The first impairment loss was for £780, and was in respect of a sales invoice which had been due for payment on 15 August 2017. The second impairment loss was for £660, and was in respect of a sales invoice which had been due for payment on 15 September 2017.

(3)   Purchase invoices totalling £49,200 were received, of which £43,200 were in respect of standard rated purchases and £6,000 were in respect of zero rated purchases.

(4)   Rent of £1,200 is paid each month. During the year ended 31 March 2018, Zim made 13 rental payments because the invoice dated 1 April 2018 was paid early on 31 March 2018. This invoice was in respect of the rent for April 2018.

(5)   During the year ended 31 March 2018, Zim spent £2,600 on mobile telephone calls, of which 40% related to private calls.

(6)   During the year ended 31 March 2018, Zim spent £1,560 on entertaining customers, of which £240 was in respect of overseas customers.

TAXATION (TX-UK) (F6) – REVISION QUESTION BANK

All of the above figures are inclusive of VAT where applicable. The expenses referred to in notes (4), (5) and (6) are all standard rated.

Zim does not use either the cash accounting scheme or the flat rate scheme. He has forecast that for the year ended 31 March 2019, his total sales will be the same as for the year ended 31 March 2018.

Required:

(a) **Calculate the amount of value added tax (VAT) payable by Zim for the year ended 31 March 2017.** (6 marks)

Note: You should indicate by the use of zero any items referred to in notes (1) to (6) where there is no VAT impact.

(b) **Explain why Zim will be permitted to use the VAT flat rate scheme from 1 April 2017, and state the circumstances in which he will have to leave the scheme.** (2 marks)

(c) **Explain whether or not it would have been beneficial for Zim to have used the VAT flat rate scheme for the year ended 31 March 2017.** (2 marks)

Notes:

1. You should assume that the relevant flat rate scheme percentage for Zim's trade would have been 12% throughout the whole of the year ended 31 March 2017.

2. Your answer for this part of the question should be supported by appropriate calculations.

(10 marks)

Question 78 SMART LTD

Smart Ltd commenced trading on 1 September 2017. The company's sales for the first four months of trading were as follows:

2017	£
September	26,000
October	47,000
November	134,000
December	113,000

On 1 November 2017, the company signed a contract valued at £86,000 for completion during November 2017.

All of the above figures are stated exclusive of value added tax (VAT). Smart Ltd only supplies services and all of the company's supplies are standard rated.

Smart Ltd allows its customers 60 days credit when paying for services, and it is concerned that some customers will default on the payment of their debts. The company pays its purchase invoices as soon as they are received.

Smart Ltd does not use either the VAT cash accounting scheme or the annual accounting scheme.

Required:

(a) **State, giving reasons, the date from which Smart Ltd was required to register for value added tax (VAT), and by when it was required to notify HM Revenue and Customs (HMRC) of the registration.** (3 marks)

(b) State how and when Smart Ltd will have to submit its quarterly VAT returns and pay any related VAT liability. **(2 marks)**

Note: You are not expected to cover substantial traders or the election for monthly returns.

(c) State the circumstances when a VAT registered business like Smart Ltd, which is not using the VAT cash accounting scheme, would still have to account for output VAT at the time that payment is received from a customer. **(2 marks)**

(d) Advise Smart Ltd as to why it should be beneficial for the company to use the VAT cash accounting scheme. **(3 marks)**

(10 marks)

Question 79 GARFIELD

Garfield has been registered for valued added tax (VAT) since 1 April 2011. Garfield has previously completed his VAT returns himself, but for the quarter ended 31 March 2018 there are some items for which he is unsure of the correct VAT treatment.

Garfield's partly completed VAT computation for the quarter ended 31 March 2018 is shown below. All of the completed sections of the computation are correct, with the omissions marked as outstanding (O/S).

	Note	£
Output VAT		
Sales (all standard rated)		22,500
Discounted sale	1	O/S
Equipment	2	O/S
Fuel scale charge		60
Input VAT		
Purchases (all standard rated)		(11,200)
Motor car (purchased on 1 January 2018)		0
Equipment	2	O/S
Impairment losses	3	O/S
Entertaining – UK customers		0
– Overseas customers	4	O/S
Motor expenses	5	O/S
VAT payable		O/S

Unless otherwise stated, all of the figures in the following notes are stated exclusive of VAT.

Note 1 – Discounted sale

On 10 February 2018, a sales invoice for £4,300 was issued by Garfield in respect of a standard rated supply. To encourage this previously late paying customer to pay promptly, Garfield offered a 10% discount for payment within 14 days of the date of the sales invoice. The customer paid within the 14-day period.

This invoice has not been taken into account in calculating the output VAT figure of £22,500, and this is the only sale for which Garfield has offered a prompt payment discount.

Note 2 – Equipment

During the quarter ended 31 March 2018, Garfield acquired some new equipment at a cost of £12,400 from a VAT registered supplier situated in the European Union.

Note 3 – Impairment losses

On 31 March 2018, Garfield wrote off three impairment losses. Details are as follows:

Amount	Invoice date	Payment due date
£1,400	30 July 2017	29 August 2017
£2,700	12 September 2017	12 October 2017
£1,900	4 October 2017	3 November 2017

Note 4 – Entertaining

During the quarter ended 31 March 2018, Garfield spent £960 on entertaining overseas customers. This figure is inclusive of VAT.

Note 5 – Motor expenses

The motor car purchased on 1 January 2018 is used by Garfield 60% for business mileage. During the quarter ended 31 March 2018, Garfield spent £1,008 on repairs to the motor car and £660 on fuel for both his business and private mileage. Both of these figures are inclusive of VAT.

Additional information

Garfield does not use the cash accounting scheme, the annual accounting scheme or the flat rate scheme, but has read that the use of these schemes can be beneficial for small businesses such as his.

Garfield's VAT exclusive annual turnover is currently £450,000, and this is expected to steadily decrease over the coming years. He pays for most of his purchases and expenses on a cash basis, but allows many of his customers 30 days credit when paying for sales.

Required:

(a) Calculate the amount of value added tax (VAT) payable by Garfield for the quarter ended 31 March 2018. (7 marks)

(b) State which VAT schemes Garfield is currently permitted to use, and explain, with supporting reasons, which ONE of the available schemes would appear to be the most beneficial for him to use.

Notes:
1. Your answer should be confined to the information given in the question.
2. You are not expected to explain how any of the schemes operate. (3 marks)

(10 marks)

REVISION QUESTION BANK – TAXATION (TX-UK) (F6)

SPECIMEN EXAM

Section A

This section of the exam contains **15 objective test (OT) questions**.
Each question is worth **2 marks** and is compulsory.

1 William is self-employed, and his tax adjusted trading profit for the year ended 5 April 2018 was £82,700. During the tax year 2017–18, William contributed £5,400 (gross) into a personal pension scheme.

   What amount of class 4 national insurance contributions (NIC) will William pay for the tax year 2017–18?

   A   £3,961
   B   £6,708
   C   £4,069
   D   £3,315

2 You are a trainee Chartered Certified Accountant and your firm has a client who has refused to disclose a chargeable gain to HM Revenue and Customs (HMRC).

   From an ethical viewpoint, which TWO of the following actions could be expected of your firm?

   ☐ Reporting under the money laundering regulations

   ☐ Advising the client to make disclosure

   ☐ Informing HMRC of the non-disclosure

   ☐ Warning the client that your firm will be reporting the non-disclosure

3 Martin is self-employed, and for the year ended 5 April 2018 his trading profit was £109,400. During the tax year 2017–18, Martin made a gift aid donation of £800 (gross) to a national charity.

   What amount of personal allowance will Martin be entitled to for the tax year 2017–18?

   £ ☐

4 For the year ended 31 March 2018, Halo Ltd made a trading loss of £180,000.

   Halo Ltd has owned 100% of the ordinary share capital of Shallow Ltd since it began trading on 1 July 2017. For the year ended 30 June 2018, Shallow Ltd will make a trading profit of £224,000.

   Neither company has any other taxable profits or allowable losses.

   What is the maximum amount of group relief which Shallow Ltd can claim from Halo Ltd in respect of the trading loss of £180,000 for the year ended 31 March 2018?

   A   £180,000
   B   £168,000
   C   £45,000
   D   £135,000

5   For the year ended 31 March 2017, Sizeable Ltd had taxable total profits of £820,000, and for the year ended 31 March 2018 had taxable total profits of £970,000. The profits accrue evenly throughout the year.

Sizeable Ltd has had one 51% group company for many years.

How will Sizeable Ltd pay its corporation tax liability for the year ended 31 March 2018?

A   Nine instalments of £15,580 and a balancing payment of £44,080
B   Four instalments of £46,075
C   Four instalments of £38,950 and a balancing payment of £28,500
D   One payment of £184,300

6   For the year ended 31 December 2017, Lateness Ltd had a corporation tax liability of £60,000, which it did not pay until 31 March 2019. Lateness Ltd is not a large company.

How much interest will Lateness Ltd be charged by HM Revenue and Customs (HMRC) in respect of the late payment of its corporation tax liability for the year ended 31 December 2017?

Select... ▼
£825
£2,062
£300
£412

7   On 26 November 2017, Alice sold an antique table for £8,700. The antique table had been purchased on 16 May 2014 for £3,800.

What is Alice's chargeable gain in respect of the disposal of the antique table?

A   £4,500
B   £1,620
C   £4,900
D   £0

8   On 14 November 2017, Jane made a cash gift to a trust of £800,000 (after deducting all available exemptions). Jane paid the inheritance tax arising from this gift. Jane has not made any other lifetime gifts.

What amount of lifetime inheritance tax would have been payable in respect of Jane's gift to the trust?

£ [   ]

9 During the tax year 2017–18, Mildred made four cash gifts to her grandchildren.

For each of the gifts listed below, click in the box to indicated whether the gift will be exempt or not exempt from inheritance tax under the small gifts exemption.

£400 to Alfred	EXEMPT	NOT EXEMPT
£140 to Minnie	EXEMPT	NOT EXEMPT
A further £280 to Minnie	EXEMPT	NOT EXEMPT
£175 to Winifred	EXEMPT	NOT EXEMPT

10 For the quarter ended 31 March 2018, Zim had standard rated sales of £49,750 and standard rated expenses of £22,750. Both figures are exclusive of value added tax (VAT).

Zim uses the flat rate scheme to calculate the amount of VAT payable, with the relevant scheme percentage for her trade being 12%. The percentage reduction for the first year of VAT registration is not available.

How much VAT will Zim have to pay to HM Revenue and Customs (HMRC) for the quarter ended 31 March 2018?

- A £5,970
- B £3,888
- C £5,400
- D £7,164

11 **Which TWO of the following assets will ALWAYS be exempt from capital gains tax?**

- ☐ A motor car suitable for private use
- ☐ A chattel
- ☐ A UK Government security (gilt)
- ☐ A house

12 Winston has already invested £8,000 into a cash individual savings account (ISA) during the tax year 2017–18. He now wants to invest into a stocks and shares ISA.

What is the maximum possible amount which Winston can invest into a stocks and shares ISA for the tax year 2017–18?

- A £20,000
- B £12,000
- C £0
- D £10,000

13 Ming is self-employed.

For each of the types of records listed below, click in the box to indicate the date until which Ming must retain the records used in preparing her self-assessment tax return for the tax year 2017–18.

Business records	31 January 2020	31 January 2024
Non-business records	31 January 2020	31 January 2024

14 Moon Ltd has had the following results:

Period	Profit/(loss)
	£
Year ended 31 December 2017	(105,000)
Four-month period ended 31 December 2016	43,000
Year ended 31 August 2016	96,000

The company does not have any other income.

How much of Moon Ltd's trading loss for the year ended 31 December 2017 can be relieved against its total profits of £96,000 for the year ended 31 August 2016?

- A £64,000
- B £96,000
- C £70,000
- D £62,000

15 Nigel has not previously been resident in the UK, being in the UK for less than 20 days each tax year. For the tax year 2017–18, he has three ties with the UK.

What is the maximum number of days which Nigel could spend in the UK during the tax year 2017–18 without being treated as resident in the UK for that year?

- A 90 days
- B 182 days
- C 45 days
- D 120 days

(30 marks)

Section B

This section of the exam contains **three OT cases**.
Each OT case contains a scenario which relates to **five OT questions**.
Each question is worth **2 marks** and is compulsory.

The following scenario relates to questions 16 – 20.

Delroy and Grant

On 10 January 2018, Delroy made a gift of 25,000 £1 ordinary shares in Dub Ltd, an unquoted trading company, to his son, Grant. The market value of the shares on that date was £240,000. Delroy had subscribed for the 25,000 shares in Dub Ltd at par on 1 July 2006. Delroy and Grant have elected to hold over the gain as a gift of a business asset.

Grant sold the 25,000 shares in Dub Ltd on 18 March 2018 for £240,000.

Dub Ltd has a share capital of 100,000 £1 ordinary shares. Delroy was the sales director of the company from its incorporation on 1 July 2006 until 10 January 2018. Grant has never been an employee or a director of Dub Ltd.

For the tax year 2017–18, Delroy and Grant are both higher rate taxpayers. They have each made other disposals of assets during the tax year 2017–18, and therefore they have both already utilised their annual exempt amount for this year.

Marlon and Alvita

On 28 March 2018, Marlon sold a house for £497,000, which he had owned individually. The house had been purchased on 22 October 2000 for £152,600.

Throughout the period of ownership, the house was occupied by Marlon and his wife, Alvita, as their main residence.

One-third of the house was always used exclusively for business purposes by the couple. Entrepreneurs' relief is not available in respect of this disposal.

For the tax year 2017–18, Marlon is a higher rate taxpayer, but Alvita did not have any taxable income. This will remain the case for the tax year 2018–19. Neither of them has made any other disposals of assets during the year.

16   What is Grant's capital gains tax (CGT) liability for the tax year 2017–18 in respect of the disposal of the shares in Dub Ltd?

        A   £43,000
        B   £21,500
        C   £0
        D   £40,740

17 Which TWO of the following statements would have been true in relation to the CGT implications if Delroy had instead sold the 25,000 shares in Dub Ltd himself for £240,000 on 10 January 2018, and then gifted the cash proceeds to Grant?

☐ Entrepreneurs' relief would have been available

☐ The CGT liability would have been paid later

☐ The cash gift would not have been a chargeable disposal

☐ The cash gift would have qualified for holdover relief

18 What is Marlon's chargeable gain for the tax year 2017–18?

    A   £229,600
    B   £0
    C   £114,800
    D   £344,400

19 What is the amount of CGT which could have been saved if Marlon had transferred 50% ownership of the house to Alvita prior to its disposal?

    A   £3,164
    B   £6,514
    C   £3,350
    D   £12,544

20 Why would it have been beneficial if Marlon had delayed the sale of the house until 6 April 2018?

Select... ▼
A lower rate of CGT would have been applicable
Two annual exempt amounts would have been available
Principal private residence relief would have been greater
The CGT liability would have been paid later

The following scenario relates to questions 21 – 25.

You should assume that today's date is 15 March 2018.

Opal is aged 71, and has a chargeable estate for inheritance tax (IHT) purposes valued at £950,000.

She owns two properties, respectively valued at £374,000 and £442,000. The first property has an outstanding repayment mortgage of £160,000, and the second property has an outstanding endowment mortgage of £92,000. Neither property qualifies for the additional residence nil rate band.

Opal owes £22,400 in respect of a personal loan from a bank, and she has also verbally promised to pay legal fees of £4,600 incurred by her nephew. Opal expects the cost of her funeral to be £5,200, and this cost will be covered by the £6,000 which she has invested in an individual savings account (ISA).

Under the terms of her will, Opal has left all of her estate to her children. Opal's husband is still alive.

On 14 August 2007, Opal had made a gift of £100,000 to her daughter, and on 7 November 2017, she made a gift of £220,000 to her son. Both these figures are after deducting all available exemptions.

REVISION QUESTION BANK – TAXATION (TX-UK) (F6)

The nil rate band for the tax year 2007–08 is £285,000.

You should assume that both the value of Opal's estate and the nil rate band will remain unchanged for future years.

21 What is the net value for the two properties, and related mortgages, which will have been included in the calculation of Opal's chargeable estate of £950,000?

    A   £816,000
    B   £564,000
    C   £656,000
    D   £724,000

22 Which TWO of the following amounts will have been deducted in calculating Opal's chargeable estate of £950,000?

- [ ] Personal loan from a bank of £22,400
- [ ] Promise to pay legal fees of £4,600
- [ ] Funeral cost of £5,200
- [ ] ISA investment of £6,000

23 What amount of IHT will be payable in respect of Opal's chargeable estate valued at £950,000 were she to die on 20 March 2018?

    A   £250,000
    B   £338,000
    C   £378,000
    D   £335,600

24 By how much would the IHT payable on Opal's death be reduced if she were to live for another seven years until 20 March 2025, compared to if she were to die on 20 March 2018?

Select... ▼
£88,000
£40,000
£128,000
£0

25 Which TWO of the following conditions must be met if Opal wants to make gifts out of her income, so that these gifts are exempt from IHT?

- [ ] The gifts cannot exceed 10% of income
- [ ] The gifts must be habitual
- [ ] Opal must have enough remaining income to maintain her normal standard of living
- [ ] Opal must make the gifts monthly or quarterly

The following scenario relates to questions 26 – 30.

The following information is available in respect of Glacier Ltd's value added tax (VAT) for the quarter ended 31 March 2018:

(1) Invoices were issued for sales of £44,600 to VAT registered customers. Of this figure, £35,200 was in respect of exempt sales and the balance in respect of standard rated sales. The standard rated sales figure is exclusive of VAT.

(2) In addition to the above, on 1 March 2018 Glacier Ltd issued a VAT invoice for £8,000 plus VAT of £1,600 to a VAT registered customer in respect of a contract which will be completed on 15 April 2018. The customer paid for the contract in two instalments of £4,800 on 31 March 2018 and 30 April 2018.

(3) The managing director of Glacier Ltd is provided with free fuel for private mileage driven in her company motor car. During the quarter ended 31 March 2018, the total cost of fuel for business and private mileage was £720, of which £270 was for private mileage. The relevant quarterly scale charge is £415. All of these figures are inclusive of VAT.

For the quarters ended 30 September 2016 and 30 June 2017, Glacier Ltd was one month late in submitting its VAT returns and in paying the related VAT liabilities. All of the company's other VAT returns have been submitted on time.

26 What is the amount of output VAT payable by Glacier Ltd in respect of its sales for the quarter ended 31 March 2018?

Select... ▼
£2,680
£3,480
£10,520
£1,880

27 Calculate the amounts required to complete the following sentence:

Glacier Ltd will include output VAT of £ [   ] and input VAT of £ [   ] on its VAT return for the quarter ended 31 March 2018 in respect of the managing director's company motor car.

28 What surcharge penalty could Glacier Ltd be charged if the company is one month late in paying its VAT liability for the quarter ended 31 March 2018?

    A   5% of the VAT liability
    B   2% of the VAT liability
    C   There will be no penalty
    D   10% of the VAT liability

29 What is the minimum requirement which Glacier Ltd needs to meet in order to revert to a clean default surcharge record?

    A   Submit four consecutive VAT returns on time
    B   Submit any four VAT returns on time and also pay the related VAT liabilities on time
    C   Pay four consecutive VAT liabilities on time
    D   Submit four consecutive VAT returns on time and also pay the related VAT liabilities on time

30 Glacier Ltd will be required to issue a VAT invoice in certain circumstances.

Complete the following sentence by matching one of the "types of supply" and one of the "types of customer" into each target area.

Glacier Ltd will be required to issue a VAT invoice when [   ] is made to [   ]

Types of supply
a standard rated supply
any type of supply

Types of customer
a VAT registered customer
any customer

(30 marks)

Section C

This section of the exam contains **three constructed response** questions, each containing a scenario which relates to one or more requirement(s).
Each constructed response question is worth **10** or **15 marks**
All questions are compulsory.

31 **You should assume that today's date is 1 March 2017.**

Sarah is currently self-employed. If she continues to trade on a self-employed basis, her total income tax liability and national insurance contributions (NIC) for the tax year 2017–18 will be £12,263.

Sarah does not have any employees and therefore cannot currently make use of the £3,000 employment allowance.

However, Sarah is considering incorporating her business on 6 April 2017. The forecast taxable total profits of the new limited company for the year ended 5 April 2018 will be £50,000 (before taking account of any director's remuneration). Sarah will pay herself gross director's remuneration of £30,000 and dividends of £10,000. The balance of the profits will remain undrawn within the new company.

Required:

(a) **Determine whether or not there will be an overall saving of tax and national insurance contributions (NIC) for the year ended 5 April 2018 if Sarah incorporates her business on 6 April 2017.** [1]

Notes:

1. You are expected to calculate the income tax payable by Sarah, the class 1 NIC payable by Sarah and the new limited company, and the corporation tax liability of the new limited company for the year ended 5 April 2018.

2. You should assume that the rates of corporation tax remain unchanged.

(8 marks)

---

[1] The answer layout provided in the exam for this part of the question is a blank spreadsheet. The answer layout for other parts is a blank word processing page.

(b) **Advise Sarah as to why her proposed basis of extracting profits from the new limited company is not optimum for tax purposes, and suggest how the mix of director's remuneration and dividends could therefore be improved.**

Note: You are not expected to calculate any revised tax or NIC figures. (2 marks)

(10 marks)

32 On 6 April 2017, Simon commenced employment with Echo Ltd. On 1 January 2018, he commenced in partnership with Art running a small music venue, preparing accounts to 30 April. The following information is available for the tax year 2017–18:

Employment

(1) During the tax year 2017–18, Simon was paid a gross annual salary of £23,700.

(2) Throughout the tax year 2017–18, Echo Ltd provided Simon with living accommodation. The company had purchased the property in 2006 for £89,000, and it was valued at £143,000 on 6 April 2017. The annual value of the property is £4,600. The property was furnished by Echo Ltd during March 2017 at a cost of £9,400. The living accommodation is not job related.

(3) On 1 December 2017, Echo Ltd provided Simon with an interest-free loan of £84,000, which he used to purchase a holiday cottage.

Partnership

(1) The partnership's tax adjusted trading profit for the four-month period ended 30 April 2018 is £29,700. This figure is before taking account of capital allowances.

(2) The only item of plant and machinery owned by the partnership is a motor car which cost £18,750 on 1 February 2018. The motor car has a CO_2 emission rate of 155 grams per kilometre. It is used by Art, and 40% of the mileage is for private journeys.

(3) Profits are shared 40% to Simon and 60% to Art. This is after paying an annual salary of £6,000 to Art.

Property income

(1) Simon owns a freehold house which is let out furnished. The property was let throughout the tax year 2017–18 at a monthly rent of £660.

(2) During the tax year 2017–18, Simon paid council tax of £1,320 in respect of the property, and also spent £2,560 on purchasing replacement furniture.

Required:

(a) **Calculate Simon's taxable income for the tax year 2017–18.** (13 marks)

(b) **State TWO advantages for the partnership of choosing 30 April as its accounting date rather than 5 April.** (2 marks)

(15 marks)

33 You are a trainee accountant and your manager has asked you to correct a corporation tax computation which has been prepared by the managing director of Naive Ltd. The corporation tax computation is for the year ended 31 March 2018 and contains a significant number of errors:

Naive Ltd – Corporation tax computation for the year ended 31 March 2018

	£
Trading profit (W1)	372,900
Loan interest received (W2)	32,100
	405,000
Corporation tax (405,000 at 19%)	76,950

WORKINGS

(1)　Trading profit

	£
Profit before taxation	274,530
Depreciation	15,740
Donations to political parties	400
Qualifying charitable donations	900
Accountancy	2,300
Legal fees in connection with the issue of loan notes (the loan was used to finance the company's trading activities)	5,700
Entertaining suppliers	3,600
Entertaining employees	1,700
Gifts to customers (£40 pens displaying Naive Ltd's name)	920
Gifts to customers (£45 food hampers displaying Naive Ltd's name)	1,650
Capital allowances (W3)	65,460
Trading profit	372,900

(2)　Loan interest received

	£
Loan interest receivable	32,800
Accrued at 1 April 2017	10,600
Accrued at 31 March 2018	(11,300)
Loan interest received	32,100

The loan was made for non-trading purposes.

(3) Capital allowances

	Main pool £	Motor car £	Special rate pool £	Allowances £
Written down value (WDV) brought forward	12,400		13,600	
Additions				
Machinery	42,300			
Motor car [1]	13,800			
Motor car [2]		14,000		
	68,500			
Annual investment allowance (AIA)	(68,500)			68,500
Disposal proceeds			(9,300)	
			4,300	
Balancing allowance			(4,300)	(4,300)
Writing down allowance (WDA) – 18%		(2,520) × 50%		1,260
WDV carried forward	0	11,480		
Total allowances				65,460

(1) Motor car [1] has a CO_2 emission rate of 110 grams per kilometre.

(2) Motor car [2] has a CO_2 emission rate of 155 grams per kilometre. This motor car is used by the sales manager and 50% of the mileage is for private journeys.

(3) All of the items included in the special rate pool at 1 April 2017 were sold for £9,300 during the year ended 31 March 2018. The original cost of these items was £16,200.

Required:

(a) **Prepare a revised version of Naive Ltd's corporation tax computation for the year ended 31 March 2018.**

Note: Your calculations should commence with the profit before taxation figure of £274,530, and you should indicate by the use of zero (0) any items in the computation of the trading profit for which no adjustment is required. (12 marks)

(b) The managing director of Naive Ltd understands that the company will have to file its self-assessment corporation tax returns online, and that the supporting accounts and tax computations will have to be filed using the inline eXtensible Business Reporting Language (iXBRL). The managing director is concerned about how the company will be able to produce documents in this format.

Required:

Explain the options available to Naive Ltd regarding the production of accounts and tax computations in the iXBRL format. (3 marks)

(15 marks)

REVISION QUESTION BANK – TAXATION (TX-UK) (F6)

SEPTEMBER 2016 EXAM

Section A

This section of the exam contains **15 objective test (OT) questions.**
Each question is worth **2 marks** and is compulsory.

1 On 1 July 2016, Sameer made a cash gift of £2,500 to his sister.
   On 1 May 2017, he made a cash gift of £2,000 to a friend.
   On 1 June 2017, he made a cash gift of £50,000 to a trust.

   Sameer has not made any other lifetime gifts.

   In respect of Sameer's cash gift of £50,000 to the trust, what is the lifetime transfer of value for inheritance tax purposes after taking account of all available exemptions?

   A   £48,500
   B   £44,000
   C   £46,000
   D   £46,500

2 On 31 March 2018, Angus sold a house, which he had bought on 31 March 2004.

   Angus occupied the house as his main residence until 31 March 2009, when he left for employment abroad.

   Angus returned to the UK on 1 April 2011 and lived in the house until 31 March 2012, when he bought a flat in a neighbouring town and made that his principal private residence.

   What is Angus' total number of qualifying months of occupation for principal private residence relief on the sale of the house?

   A   72 months
   B   54 months
   C   114 months
   D   96 months

3 Abena has made the following gross contributions to her personal pension scheme over the past three tax years:

	£
2014–15	52,000
2015–16	37,000
2016–17	28,000

   What is the maximum gross contribution which Abena can make to her personal pension scheme for the tax year 2017–18 without giving rise to an annual allowance charge?

   A   £43,000
   B   £40,000
   C   £55,000
   D   £52,000

TAXATION (TX-UK) (F6) – REVISION QUESTION BANK

4 Triangle Ltd is registered for value added tax (VAT) and uses the annual accounting scheme.

For the year ended 31 December 2017, the net VAT payable by Triangle Ltd was £73,500.
For the year ended 31 December 2016, the net VAT payable by Triangle Ltd was £47,700.

Indicate, by clicking on the relevant boxes in the table below, the number and amount of the monthly payments on account of VAT which Triangle Ltd must make in respect of the year ended 31 December 2017 prior to submitting its VAT return for that year.

Number of monthly payments	NINE	TEN
Monthly payment amount	£4,770	£7,350

5 Lili Ltd commenced trading on 1 January 2017. The company incurred the following expenditure prior to 1 January 2017:

		£
30 November 2009	Initial market research	15,000
6 June 2012	Research into competitors	12,000
31 July 2016	Entertaining potential customers and suppliers	8,000
15 December 2016	Donation to local school fair in exchange for advertising	2,000

What is the amount of Lili Ltd's deductible pre-trading expenditure in respect of the year ended 31 December 2017?

£ _____

6 Paloma has been trading for a number of years. Her tax adjusted trading profit for the year ended 31 May 2017 was £48,000 and for the year ended 31 May 2018 was £43,200.

What is the amount of class 4 national insurance contributions (NIC) payable by Paloma for the tax year 2017–18?

- A £3,225
- B £3,585
- C £3,153
- D £3,375

7 **Identify, by clicking on the relevant boxes in the table below, whether the following statements are true or false.**

	TRUE	FALSE
Corporation tax is a direct tax on the turnover of companies	TRUE	FALSE
National insurance is a direct tax suffered by employees, employers and the self-employed on earnings	TRUE	FALSE
Inheritance tax is a direct tax on transfers of income by individuals	TRUE	FALSE
Value added tax is a direct tax on the supply of goods and services by businesses	TRUE	FALSE

8 Which of the following statements concerning self-assessment tax returns for individuals is true?

   A   Individuals with tax payable of less than £1,000 for a tax year are not required to file a tax return

   B   Individuals are only required to file a tax return for a tax year if they receive a notice to deliver from HM Revenue and Customs

   C   All individuals who submit a tax return on time are able to have their tax payable calculated by HM Revenue and Customs

   D   The tax return for an individual covers income tax, class 1, class 2 and class 4 national insurance contributions and capital gains tax liabilities

9 In certain circumstances an individual is automatically not resident in the UK.

   Indicate, by clicking on the relevant boxes in the table below, whether the following two individuals satisfy or do not satisfy the tests to be treated as automatically not resident in the UK for the tax year 2017–18.

   Eric, who has never previously been resident in the UK. In the tax year 2017–18, he was in the UK for 40 days.

   Fran, who was resident in the UK for the two tax years prior to the tax year 2017–18. In the tax year 2017–18, she was in the UK for 18 days.

Eric	SATISFIES	DOES NOT SATISFY
Fran	SATISFIES	DOES NOT SATISFY

10 Max is employed by Star Ltd. On 6 April 2016, Star Ltd provided Max with a camera for his personal use. The camera had a market value of £2,000 on 6 April 2016.

   On 6 April 2017, Star Ltd gave the camera to Max for free. The camera had a market value of £1,400 on 6 April 2017.

   What is Max's taxable benefit in respect of the camera for the tax year 2017–18?

Select... ▼
£1,000
£1,400
£2,000
£1,600

11 Cora made a cash gift of £300,000 to her niece on 30 April 2012.

   She then made a cash gift of £500,000 to her nephew on 31 May 2013.

   Both of these amounts are stated after deducting available exemptions.

   Cora subsequently died on 31 October 2017.

What amount of inheritance tax was payable as a result of Cora's death in respect of the cash gift of £500,000 to her nephew?

A £190,000
B £110,000
C £114,000
D £105,000

12 Rajesh is a sole trader. He correctly calculated his self-assessment payments on account for the tax year 2017–18 and paid these on the due dates.

Rajesh paid the correct balancing payment of £1,200 for the tax year 2017–18 on 30 June 2019.

Indicate, by clicking on the relevant boxes in the table below, what penalty and interest Rajesh may be charged as a result of his late balancing payment for the tax year 2017–18.

Penalty	£0	£60
Interest	£14	£33

13 Oblong Ltd has had the following results:

	Year ended 31 March 2017 £	Year ended 31 March 2018 £
Trading profit/(loss)	79,400	(102,800)
Property business income	6,800	10,100
Qualifying charitable donations	(1,600)	(1,300)

If Oblong Ltd makes a claim to relieve its trading loss of £102,800 for the year ended 31 March 2018 against total profits for the year ended 31 March 2017, how much of this loss will remain unrelieved?

A £6,500
B £16,600
C £9,400
D £23,400

14 Putting an asset into joint names with a spouse (or a partner in a registered civil partnership) prior to the asset's disposal can be sensible capital gains tax (CGT) planning.

Which of the following CANNOT be achieved as a direct result of using this type of tax planning?

Select... ▼
Making the best use of annual exempt amounts
Deferring the CGT due date
Reducing the amount of CGT payable
Making the best use of capital losses

15 Eva's income tax liability and class 4 national insurance contributions (NIC) for the tax year 2017–18 are £4,840.

Her income tax liability and class 4 NICs for the tax year 2016–17 were £6,360.

What is the lowest amount to which Eva could make a claim to reduce each of her payments on account for the tax year 2017–18 without being charged interest?

Select... ▼
£4,840
£0
£3,180
£2,420

(30 marks)

Section B

This section of the exam contains **three OT cases**.
Each OT case contains a scenario which relates to **five OT questions**.
Each question is worth **2 marks** and is compulsory.

The following scenario relates to questions 16–20.

Adana died on 17 March 2018, and inheritance tax (IHT) of £566,000 is payable in respect of her chargeable estate. Under the terms of her will, Adana left her entire estate to her children. Adana's estate included a mixture of chattels, cash, ISAs and other investments, but no residential property.

At the date of her death, Adana had the following debts and liabilities:

(1) An outstanding interest-only mortgage of £220,000.
(2) Income tax of £43,700 payable in respect of the tax year 2017–18.
(3) Legal fees of £4,600 incurred by Adana's sister which Adana had verbally promised to pay.

Adana's husband had died on 28 May 2006, and only 20% of his inheritance tax nil rate band was used on his death. The nil rate band for the tax year 2006–07 was £285,000.

On 22 April 2008, Adana had made a chargeable lifetime transfer of shares valued at £500,000 to a trust. Adana paid the lifetime IHT of £52,250 arising from this gift. If Adana had not made this gift, her chargeable estate at the time of her death would have been £650,000 higher than it otherwise was. This was because of the subsequent increase in the value of the gifted shares.

16   **What is the maximum nil rate band which will have been available when calculating the IHT of £566,000 payable in respect of Adana's chargeable estate?**

Select... ▼
£325,000
£553,000
£390,000
£585,000

17   **What is the total amount of deductions which would have been permitted in calculating Adana's chargeable estate for IHT purposes?**

£ _____

18 Indicate, by clicking on the relevant boxes in the table below, who will be responsible for paying the IHT of £566,000 in respect of Adana's chargeable estate, and what is the due date for the payment of this liability.

Responsible persons	Beneficiaries of Adana's estate (her children)	Personal representatives of Adana's estate
Due date for payment	17 September 2018	30 September 2018

19 How much of the IHT payable in respect of Adana's estate would have been saved if, under the terms of her will, Adana had made specific gifts of £400,000 to a trust and £200,000 to her grandchildren, instead of leaving her entire estate to her children?

    A   £240,000
    B   £160,000
    C   £0
    D   £80,000

20 How much IHT did Adana save by making the chargeable lifetime transfer of £500,000 to a trust on 22 April 2008, rather than retaining the gifted investments until her death?

    A   £260,000
    B   £207,750
    C   £147,750
    D   £200,000

The following scenario relates to questions 21–25.

Kitten is the controlling shareholder in Kat Ltd, an unquoted trading company.

Kat Ltd

Kat Ltd sold a freehold factory on 31 May 2017 for £364,000, which resulted in a chargeable gain of £120,700. The factory was purchased on 1 October 2005 for £138,600, and further capital improvements were immediately made at a cost of £23,400 during the month of purchase. Further improvements to the factory were made during the month of disposal. The relevant retail prices indexes (RPIs) are as follows:

    October 2005   193.3
    May 2017   271.7

Kat Ltd is unsure how to reinvest the proceeds from the sale of the factory. The company is considering either purchasing a freehold warehouse for £272,000, or acquiring a leasehold office building on a 40-year lease for a premium of £370,000. If either reinvestment is made, it will take place on 30 September 2018.

All of the above buildings have been, or will be, used for the purposes of Kat Ltd's trade.

REVISION QUESTION BANK – TAXATION (TX-UK) (F6)

Kitten

Kitten sold 20,000 £1 ordinary shares in Kat Ltd on 5 October 2017, which resulted in a chargeable gain of £142,200. This disposal qualified for entrepreneurs' relief.

Kitten had originally subscribed for 90,000 shares in Kat Ltd on 7 July 2010 at their par value. On 22 September 2013, Kat Ltd made a 2 for 3 rights issue. Kitten took up her allocation under the rights issue in full, paying £6.40 for each new share issued.

Kitten also sold an antique vase on 16 January 2018, which resulted in a chargeable gain of £27,900.

For the tax year 2017–18, Kitten had taxable income of £12,000.

21 What amount of indexation allowance will have been deducted in calculating the chargeable gain of £120,700 on the disposal of Kat Ltd's factory?

- A   £46,818
- B   £40,055
- C   £65,772
- D   £56,272

22 If Kat Ltd decides to purchase the freehold warehouse and makes a claim to roll over the chargeable gain on the factory under the rollover relief rules, what will be the base cost of the warehouse for chargeable gains purposes?

- A   £243,300
- B   £272,000
- C   £180,000
- D   £151,300

23 If Kat Ltd decides to acquire the leasehold office building and makes a claim to hold over the chargeable gain on the factory under the rollover relief rules, what is the latest date by which the held-over gain will crystallise?

- A   10 years from 31 May 2017
- B   The date when the office building is sold
- C   40 years from 30 September 2018
- D   10 years from 30 September 2018

24 What cost figure will have been used in calculating the chargeable gain on Kitten's disposal of 20,000 ordinary shares in Kat Ltd?

- A   £12,000
- B   £63,200
- C   £84,800
- D   £20,000

25 What is Kitten's capital gains tax (CGT) liability for the tax year 2017–18?

- A   £15,880
- B   £19,800
- C   £17,650
- D   £17,540

TAXATION (TX-UK) (F6) – REVISION QUESTION BANK

The following scenario relates to questions 26–30.

Alisa commenced trading on 1 January 2017. Her sales since commencement have been as follows:

January to April 2017	£8,000 per month
May to August 2017	£10,000 per month
September to December 2017	£13,500 per month

The above figures are stated exclusive of value added tax (VAT). Alisa only supplies services, and these are all standard rated for VAT purposes. Alisa notified her liability to compulsorily register for VAT by the appropriate deadline.

For each of the eight months prior to the date on which she registered for VAT, Alisa paid £240 per month (inclusive of VAT) for website design services and £180 per month (exclusive of VAT) for advertising. Both of these supplies are standard rated for VAT purposes and relate to Alisa's business activity after the date from when she registered for VAT.

After registering for VAT, Alisa purchased a motor car on 1 January 2018. The motor car is used 60% for business mileage. During the quarter ended 31 March 2018, Alisa spent £456 on repairs to the motor car and £624 on fuel for both her business and private mileage. The relevant quarterly scale charge is £294. All of these figures are inclusive of VAT.

All of Alisa's customers are registered for VAT, so she appreciates that she has to issue VAT invoices when services are supplied.

26 **From what date would Alisa have been required to be compulsorily registered for VAT and therefore have had to charge output VAT on her supplies of services?**

Select...
- 30 September 2017
- 1 November 2017
- 1 October 2017
- 30 October 2017

27 **What amount of pre-registration input VAT would Alisa have been able to recover in respect of inputs incurred prior to the date on which she registered for VAT?**

- A £468
- B £608
- C £536
- D £456

28 **What is the maximum amount of input VAT which Alisa can reclaim in respect of her motor expenses for the quarter ended 31 March 2018?**

- A £108
- B £138
- C £180
- D £125

29 Complete the following sentence by matching the correct due date and payment method into the relevant target area.

Alisa has to pay any VAT liability for the quarter ended 31 March 2018 by ☐ using ☐ method

Due date
30 April 2018
7 May 2018

Payment method
An electronic payment
Any payment

30 Identify, by clicking on the relevant box in the table below, which of the following items of information is Alisa NOT required to be included by Alisa on a valid VAT invoice.

The customer's VAT registration number
An invoice number
The customer's address
A description of the services supplied

Section C

This section of the exam contains **three constructed response** questions, each containing a scenario which relates to one or more requirement(s).
Each constructed response question is worth **10 or 15 marks**
All questions are compulsory.

31 Joe is the managing director, sole employee and 100% shareholder of OK-Joe Ltd. He has always withdrawn the entire profits of the company as director's remuneration, but given a recent increase in profitability he wants to know whether this basis of extracting the profits is beneficial.

For the year ended 5 April 2018, OK-Joe Ltd's taxable total profits, before taking account of director's remuneration, are £65,000. After allowing for employer's class 1 national insurance contributions (NIC) of £6,892, Joe's gross director's remuneration is £58,108.

Required:

Calculate the overall saving of tax and NIC for the year ended 5 April 2018 if Joe had instead paid himself gross director's remuneration of £8,000 and dividends of £46,170.

Notes:

1. You are expected to calculate the income tax payable by Joe, the class 1 NIC payable by both Joe and OK-Joe Ltd, and the corporation tax liability of OK-Joe Ltd for the year ended 5 April 2018.

2. You should assume that the rate of corporation tax remains unchanged.

(10 marks)

32 Ashura has been employed by Rift plc since 1 January 2015. She has also been self-employed since 1 July 2017, preparing her first accounts for the nine-month period ended 5 April 2018. The following information is available for the tax year 2017–18:

Employment

(1) During the tax year 2017–18, Ashura was paid a gross annual salary of £56,200.

(2) On 1 January 2018, Ashura personally paid two subscriptions. The first was a professional subscription of £320 paid to an HM Revenue and Customs' (HMRC's) approved professional body. The second was a subscription of £680 to a health club which Ashura regularly uses to meet Rift plc's clients. Ashura was not reimbursed for the costs of either of these subscriptions by Rift plc.

(3) During the tax year 2017–18, Ashura used her private motor car for business purposes. She drove 3,400 miles in the performance of her duties for Rift plc, for which the company paid her an allowance of 55 pence per mile.

(4) During the tax year 2017–18, Ashura contributed £2,800 into Rift plc's HMRC registered occupational pension scheme and £3,400 (gross) into a personal pension scheme.

Self-employment

(1) Ashura's tax adjusted trading loss based on her draft accounts for the nine-month period ended 5 April 2018 is £3,300. This figure is before making any adjustments required for:

  (i) Advertising expenditure of £800 incurred during January 2017. This expenditure has not been deducted in calculating the loss of £3,300.

  (ii) The cost of Ashura's office (see note (2) below).

  (iii) Capital allowances.

(2) Ashura runs her business using one of the five rooms in her private house as an office. The total running costs of the house for the nine-month period ended 5 April 2018 were £4,350. No deduction has been made for the cost of the office in calculating the loss of £3,300.

(3) On 10 June 2017, Ashura purchased a laptop computer for £2,600.

On 1 July 2017, Ashura purchased a motor car for £19,200. The motor car has a CO_2 emission rate of 137 grams per kilometre. During the nine-month period ended 5 April 2018, Ashura drove a total of 8,000 miles, of which 2,500 were for self-employed business journeys.

Other information

Ashura's total income for the previous four tax years is as follows:

Tax year	Total income £
2013–14	10,700
2014–15	10,400
2015–16	48,800
2016–17	54,300

Required:

(a) State TWO advantages for Ashura of choosing 5 April as her accounting date rather than a date early in the tax year such as 30 April. (2 marks)

(b) Calculate Ashura's revised tax adjusted trading loss for the nine-month period ended 5 April 2018. (6 marks)

(c) Explain why it would not be beneficial for Ashura to claim loss relief under the provisions giving relief to a loss incurred in the early years of trade.

Note: You should assume that the tax rates and allowances for the tax year 2017–18 also applied in all previous tax years. (2 marks)

(d) Assuming that Ashura claims loss relief against her total income for the tax year 2017–18, calculate her taxable income for this tax year. (5 marks)

(15 marks)

33 Mable is a serial entrepreneur, regularly starting and disposing of businesses. On 31 July 2017, Tenth Ltd, a company owned by Mable, ceased trading. On 1 October 2017, Eleventh Ltd, another company owned by Mable, commenced trading. The following information is available:

Tenth Ltd

(1) For the final four-month period of trading ended 31 July 2017, Tenth Ltd had a tax adjusted trading profit of £52,400. This figure is **before** taking account of capital allowances.

(2) On 1 April 2017, the tax written down value of the company's main pool was £12,400. On 3 June 2017, Tenth Ltd purchased a laptop computer for £1,800.

On 31 July 2017, the company sold all of the items included in the main pool at the start of the period for £28,200 and the laptop computer for £1,300. None of the items included in the main pool was sold for more than its original cost.

(3) On 31 July 2017, Tenth Ltd sold the company's freehold office building for £180,300. The building was purchased on 3 May 2013 for £150,700, and its indexed cost on 31 July 2017 was £164,500.

(4) During the four-month period ended 31 July 2017, Tenth Ltd let out one floor of its freehold office building which was always surplus to requirements. The floor was rented at £1,200 per month, but the tenant left owing the rent for July 2017 which Tenth Ltd was unable to recover. The total running costs of the office building for the four-month period ended 31 July 2017 were £6,300, of which one-third related to the let floor. The other two-thirds of the running costs have been deducted in calculating Tenth Ltd's tax-adjusted trading profit of £52,400.

(5) During the four-month period ended 31 July 2017, Tenth Ltd made qualifying charitable donations of £800.

Eleventh Ltd

(1) Eleventh Ltd's operating profit for the six-month period ended 31 March 2018 is £122,900. Depreciation of £2,580 and amortisation of leasehold property of £2,000 (see note (2) below) have been deducted in arriving at this figure.

(2) On 1 October 2017, Eleventh Ltd acquired a leasehold office building, paying a premium of £60,000 for the grant of a 15-year lease. The office building was used for business purposes by Eleventh Ltd throughout the six-month period ended 31 March 2018.

(3) On 1 October 2017, Eleventh Ltd purchased two motor cars. The first motor car cost £12,600, and has a CO_2 emission rate of 110 grams per kilometre. This motor car is used as a pool car by the company's employees. The second motor car cost £13,200, and has a CO_2 emission rate of 60 grams per kilometre. This motor car is used by Mable, and 45% of the mileage is for private journeys.

(4) On 1 October 2017, Mable made a loan of £100,000 to Eleventh Ltd at an annual interest rate of 5%. This is a commercial rate of interest, and no loan repayments were made during the period ended 31 March 2018. The loan was used to finance the company's trading activities.

Required:

(a) **Calculate Tenth Ltd's taxable total profits for the four-month period ended 31 July 2017.** (7 marks)

(b) **Calculate Eleventh Ltd's tax adjusted trading profit for the six-month period ended 31 March 2018.** (8 marks)

(15 marks)

DECEMBER 2016 EXAM

Section A

This section of the exam contains **15 objective test (OT) questions**.
Each question is worth **2 marks** and is compulsory.

1. Emil is registered for value added tax (VAT). For the quarter ended 31 March 2018, the input VAT incurred on his purchases and expenses included the following:

	£
Entertaining overseas customers	320
Purchase of new office equipment	1,250
Purchase of a new motor car for business and private use by one of Emil's employees	3,000

   What is the amount of input VAT recoverable by Emil in the quarter ended 31 March 2018 in respect of the entertaining, office equipment and motor car?

   £ ☐

2. Acasta Ltd owns 75% of the ordinary share capital of Barge Ltd and 100% of the ordinary share capital of Coracle Ltd. Barge Ltd owns 75% of the ordinary share capital of Dhow Ltd. Coracle Ltd owns 51% of the ordinary share capital of Eight Ltd.

   Which companies, along with Coracle Ltd, are within Acasta Ltd's chargeable gains group?

   A   Barge Ltd, Dhow Ltd and Eight Ltd
   B   Barge Ltd only
   C   Barge Ltd and Dhow Ltd only
   D   None of the other companies

3. Nadia died on 13 February 2004, leaving an estate valued at £275,400 for inheritance tax purposes. Nadia left 50% of her estate to her son and 50% to her husband, Tareq.

   Tareq subsequently died on 17 January 2018.

   Neither Nadia nor Tareq made any lifetime gifts.

   The inheritance nil rate band for the tax year 2003–04 was £255,000.

   What is the maximum available nil rate band which can be used when calculating the inheritance tax payable in respect of Tareq's estate?

   A   £500,500
   B   £474,500
   C   £442,300
   D   £462,700

4 Habib purchased a copyright on 30 April 2001 for £31,320. The remaining life of the copyright at the date of purchase was 30 years. On 30 April 2017, Habib sold the copyright for £27,900.

What is Habib's chargeable gain or allowable loss for the tax year 2017–18 in respect of the disposal of the copyright?

A   (£3,420)
B   £11,196
C   £0
D   £13,284

5   **Which of the following is the correct definition of an extra-statutory concession?**

A   A provision for the relaxation of the strict application of the law where it would lead to anomalies or cause hardship

B   Supplementary information providing additional detail in relation to the general principles set out in legislation

C   HM Revenue and Customs' interpretation of tax legislation

D   Guidance provided to HM Revenue and Customs' staff in interpreting and applying tax legislation

6   **Complete the following sentence relating to the length of time a sole trader is required to keep their accounting records after the end of a tax year in which a self-assessment tax return has been completed.**

A sole trader required to keep their accounting records ☐ months after the ☐.

Number of months
12
30

Period
end of the tax year
31 January which follows the end of the tax year

7 Sanjay commenced trading on 1 January 2017 and prepared his first set of accounts for the six-month period ended 30 June 2017. His second set of accounts were prepared for the year ended 30 June 2018.

Sanjay's tax-adjusted trading profits were:
Six-month period ended 30 June 2017   £8,800
Year ended 30 June 2018   £24,400

What are the class 4 national insurance contributions (NICs) which Sanjay should pay in respect of the tax year 2017–18?

A   £57
B   £0
C   £1,155
D   £1,461

8   Modal Ltd lets out an unfurnished investment property.

During the year ended 31 December 2017, the company received rental income of £3,000 per month and paid electricity (relating to the rental property) of £200 per month. The electricity payment for December 2017 was not paid until 30 January 2018.

Modal Ltd also paid interest of £1,200 per month on a loan taken out to finance the purchase of the rental property.

What amount of property business income will be included in Modal Ltd's corporation tax computation for the year ended 31 December 2017?

A   £33,600
B   £19,200
C   £33,800
D   £19,400

9   **Which of the following will NOT cause Harper to be treated as automatically UK resident for the tax year 2017–18?**

A   Harper spending 192 days in the UK during the tax year 2017–18

B   Harper renting a house in the UK to live in and then occupying it (as her only home) throughout the tax year 2017–18

C   Harper accepting a 15-month contract for a full-time job in the UK on 6 April 2017

D   Harper's husband living in the UK throughout the tax year 2017–18 and Harper staying with him when she visits the UK

10 Somily Ltd filed its self-assessment corporation tax return for the year ended 31 December 2017 on 15 March 2019.

Identify, by clicking on the correct date on the timeline below, what the deadline is for HM Revenue and Customs (HMRC) to start a compliance check enquiry into Somily Ltd's corporation tax return for the year ended 31 December 2017.

31 December 2019   31 January 2020   15 March 2020   30 April 2020

11 On 6 April 2017, Melinda rented out a furnished room in her house to Jenny at a rent of £650 a month. Jenny continued to rent the room on the same terms until 5 July 2018.

Melinda continued to live in the house and paid for all of the living expenses, of which £275 a month related to the room rented out to Jenny.

What is Melinda's property income for the tax year 2017–18, assuming that any beneficial elections are made?

A   £300
B   £0
C   £4,500
D   £3,720

12 Three unconnected companies have the following results for corporation tax purposes:

Company	Current accounting period	Number of 51% group companies	Taxable total profits (TTP) £	TTP for previous 12-month period £
Asher Ltd	Year ended 31 March 2018	3	700,000	600,000
Barton Ltd	Four-month period ended 31 December 2017	0	600,000	1,600,000
Chelfry Ltd	Year ended 30 November 2017	0	1,600,000	1,400,000

All the companies have had the same number of 51% group companies for many years.

Which of the three companies will NOT have to pay corporation tax by quarterly instalments for the current accounting period?

A   Asher Ltd
B   Barton Ltd only
C   Chelfry Ltd only
D   Barton Ltd and Chelfry Ltd

13 David received the following income for the tax year 2017–18:

Property income	£20,000
Interest from UK Government securities (gilts)	£2,400
Dividends	£2,400

What is David's total income tax liability for the tax year 2017–18?

Select... ▼
£1,980
£4,280
£2,080
£2,160

14 Gita died on 17 May 2017. At the date of her death she owned the following assets:

	£
House	390,000
Chattels and cash	70,000
Shares held in an individual savings account (ISA)	60,000

At the date of her death, Gita owed income tax of £25,000 in respect of the tax year 2016–17.

Gita left £100,000 of her estate to her husband, with the remainder of the estate left to her daughter.

What is Gita's chargeable estate for inheritance tax purposes?

A   £335,000
B   £395,000
C   £495,000
D   £420,000

15 Anika sold her entire holding of 3,000 £1 ordinary shares in Distribo Ltd, a trading company, to her son, Hemi, for £53,000 on 14 July 2017. The market value of the shares on that date was £98,000. Anika had purchased the 3,000 shares on 28 October 2006 for £41,500. She has never worked for Distribo Ltd.

Identify, by clicking on the relevant boxes in the table below, the amount of gift (holdover) relief (if any) that could be claimed in respect of the disposal of these shares, and Anika's chargeable gain for the tax year 2017–18 after taking account of any available relief.

	Amount			
Gift relief	£0	£11,500	£45,000	£56,500
Gain	£0	£11,500		

(30 marks)

Section B

This section of the exam contains **three OT cases**.
Each OT case contains a scenario which relates to **five OT questions**.
Each question is worth **2 marks** and is compulsory.

The following scenario relates to questions 16–20.

Zoyla's capital gains tax (CGT) liability for the tax year 2017–18 is calculated as follows:

	Gain £
Ordinary shares in Minor Ltd	98,400
Ordinary shares in Major plc	44,100
Annual exempt amount	(11,300)
	131,200
CGT: 10,600 at 10%	1,060
120,600 at 20%	24,120
	25,180

Minor Ltd is an unquoted trading company with an issued share capital of 200,000 £1 ordinary shares. Zoyla has been a director of this company since 1 April 2012. On 20 June 2017, Zoyla sold 20,000 of her holding of 45,000 ordinary shares in Minor Ltd. She had originally purchased 22,500 shares on 15 August 2016 for £117,000. On 12 December 2016, Minor Ltd made a 1 for 1 rights issue. Zoyla took up her allocation under the rights issue in full, paying £7.40 for each new share issued.

Major plc is a quoted trading company with an issued share capital of 2,000,000 £1 ordinary shares. Zoyla has been an employee of Major plc since 1 November 2016 when she acquired 16,000 ordinary shares in the company. On 6 March 2018, Zoyla sold her entire holding of shares in Major plc to her son for £152,000. On that date, shares in Major plc were quoted on the stock exchange at £9.62 – £9.74.

Zoyla will not make any other disposals in the foreseeable future, and her taxable income will remain unchanged.

16 Complete the following sentences to explain why neither of Zoyla's share disposals during the tax year 2017–18 qualified for entrepreneurs' relief.

The disposal of shares in Minor Ltd did not qualify for entrepreneurs' relied in the tax year 2017-18 due to:

The disposal of shares in Major plc did not qualify for entrepreneurs' relied in the tax year 2017-18 due to:

Minorv Ltd
Holding period
Size of shareholding

Major plc
Holding period
Size of shareholding

17 What cost figure will have been used in calculating the chargeable gain on Zoyla's disposal of 20,000 ordinary shares in Minor Ltd?

- A £126,000
- B £104,000
- C £148,000
- D £252,000

18 What proceeds figure will have been used in calculating the chargeable gain on Zoyla's disposal of 16,000 ordinary shares in Major plc?

- A £152,000
- B £154,400
- C £153,920
- D £154,880

19 If Zoyla had delayed the sale of her 16,000 ordinary shares in Major plc until 6 April 2018, by how long would the related CGT liability have been deferred?

Select... ▼
11 months
12 months
1 month
6 months

20 Assuming that the tax rates and allowances for the tax year 2017–18 continue to apply, how much CGT would Zoyla have saved if she had delayed the sale of her 16,000 ordinary shares in Major plc until the following tax year?

- A £1,060
- B £4,380
- C £3,320
- D £2,260

The following scenario relates to questions 21–25.

Roman died on 7 August 2017, and his wife Paris died on 18 February 2018.

The couple had attempted to mitigate their inheritance tax (IHT) liabilities when they both made substantial gifts during 2015. These gifts made full use of their respective nil rate bands of £325,000, but unfortunately neither Roman nor Paris then survived long enough for any of the gifts to benefit from taper relief. Neither Roman nor Paris had made any previous lifetime gifts, nor did either own any residential property.

Roman

On 4 March 2015, Roman made a cash gift of £210,000 to his daughter. On 26 August 2015, he made a cash gift of £190,000 to a trust. No lifetime IHT arose in respect of the gift to the trust.

Roman's estate for IHT purposes was valued at £560,000. Under the terms of his will, Roman left £300,000 to Paris (his wife) and the residue of his estate to his daughter.

Paris

On 12 December 2015, Paris made a gift of 75,000 £1 ordinary shares in Capital Ltd, an unquoted investment company, to her son. Before the transfer, Paris owned 100,000 of Capital Ltd's 250,000 ordinary shares. The market value of Capital Ltd's ordinary shares on 12 December 2015 was as follows:

Holding	Market value per share
10%	£5
30%	£6
40%	£8

Paris also made cash gifts of £80, £210, £195 and £460 to various friends during February 2016. The gifts of £80 and £195 were to the same friend.

Paris' estate for IHT purposes was valued at £840,000, including the inheritance from Roman (her husband). Under the terms of her will, Paris left a specific legacy of £20,000 to a friend and the residue of her estate to her grandchildren.

21   How much IHT will be payable in respect of the gift made to the trust by Roman as a result of his death?

         A   £26,400
         B   £30,000
         C   £27,600
         D   £13,200

22   Who will be responsible for paying the IHT arising from Roman's gift to the trust as a result of his death, and when will the tax be due?

         A   The personal representatives of Roman's estate on 30 April 2018
         B   The personal representatives of Roman's estate on 29 February 2018
         C   The trustees of the trust on 30 April 2018
         D   The trustees of the trust on 29 February 2018

23 For IHT purposes, what was the amount of the transfer of value as a result of Paris' gift of 75,000 ordinary shares in Capital Ltd?

    A £450,000
    B £600,000
    C £675,000
    D £425,000

24 What is the amount of the cash gifts made by Paris to her friends during February 2016 NOT covered by the small gifts exemption?

    A £735
    B £460
    C £670
    D £0

25 What is the amount of IHT payable in respect of Roman's and Paris' estates on death?

	Roman's estate	Paris' estate
A	£224,000	£336,000
B	£104,000	£336,000
C	£104,000	£328,000
D	£224,000	£328,000

The following scenario relates to questions 26–30.

Ardent Ltd was incorporated on 1 April 2017 and commenced trading on 1 January 2018. The company voluntarily registered for valued added tax (VAT) on 1 January 2018, preparing its first VAT return for the quarter ended 31 March 2018. Ardent Ltd's sales have been as follows:

		Standard rated £	Zero-rated £
2018	January	24,800	30,100
	February	42,600	28,700
	March	58,300	22,700
		125,700	81,500

Where applicable, the above figures are stated exclusive of VAT.

During the period 1 April to 31 December 2017, Ardent Ltd incurred input VAT of £120 each month in respect of payments made for advertising services. The company also incurred input VAT totalling £400 (£200 each) in respect of the purchase of two laptop computers on 10 July 2017. One of the laptop computers was scrapped on 30 November 2017 at a nil value, and the other laptop was not used until Ardent Ltd commenced trading on 1 January 2018.

During the quarter ended 31 March 2018, Ardent Ltd received standard rated invoices totalling £56,400 (inclusive of VAT) in respect of purchases and expenses. As at 31 March 2018, £11,400 (inclusive of VAT) of the purchases were unsold and therefore included in inventory.

Ardent Ltd was late in submitting its VAT return for the quarter ended 31 March 2018, and in paying the related VAT liability. The company currently does not use either the VAT cash accounting scheme or the annual accounting scheme.

26 From what date would Ardent Ltd have been required to be compulsorily registered for VAT?

Select... ▼
1 February 2018
1 March 2018
1 April 2018
1 May 2018

27 What amount of pre-registration input VAT was Ardent Ltd able to recover in respect of the inputs incurred prior to it registering for VAT on 1 January 2018?

  A £920
  B £1,120
  C £1,480
  D £1,280

28 Ignoring pre-registration input VAT, what amount of VAT should Ardent Ltd have paid to HM Revenue and Customs in respect of the quarter ended 31 March 2018?

  A £17,640
  B £32,040
  C £13,860
  D £15,740

29 How and by when should Ardent Ltd have filed its VAT return for the quarter ended 31 March 2018?

  A Either by paper or electronically by 30 April 2018
  B Electronically by 7 May 2018
  C Electronically by 30 April 2018
  D Either by paper or electronically by 7 May 2018

30 Drag and drop the correct period and VAT scheme from the options below to correctly identify for which period after 31 March 2018 Ardent Ltd will need to avoid further defaults in order to revert to a clean default surcharge record, and which VAT scheme may help in avoiding such further defaults.

Period
6 months
12 months
VAT scheme
Cash accounting scheme
Annual accounting scheme

Period after 31 March 2018	VAT scheme
Period	Scheme

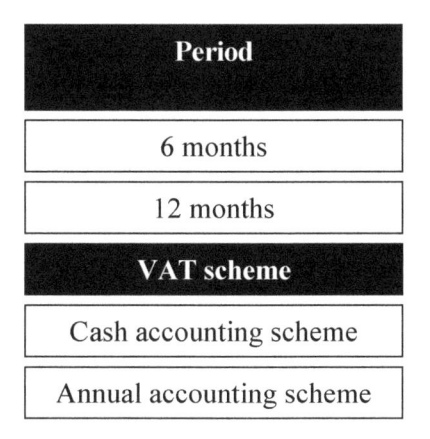

(30 marks)

TAXATION (TX-UK) (F6) – REVISION QUESTION BANK

Section C

This section of the exam contains **three constructed response** questions, each containing a scenario which relates to one or more requirement(s).
Each constructed response question is worth **10** or **15 marks**
All questions are compulsory.

31   You should assume that today's date is 15 March 2018 and that the tax rates and allowances for the tax year 2017–18 continue to apply.

Jack, aged 44, is a widower following the recent death of his wife. He has just cashed in a substantial share portfolio and is now considering what to do with the proceeds.

Gift to a trust

The value of Jack's estate is in excess of £1,000,000, and he is worried about the amount of inheritance tax which will be payable should he die. His wife's nil rate band was fully used when she died.

Jack is therefore planning to make an immediate lifetime cash gift of £300,000 to a trust with the funds then being held for the benefit of his two children aged 10 and 12. Jack has not made any previous lifetime gifts.

Personal pension contribution

The only pension contributions which Jack has made previously is the gross amount of £500 per month which he saves into a personal pension scheme. Jack has continued to make these contributions throughout the tax year 2017–18. Although Jack has been saving into this scheme for the previous 15 years, he is concerned that he is not saving enough for his retirement. Jack therefore wants to make the maximum possible amount of additional gross personal pension contribution for the tax year 2017–18, but only to the extent that the contribution will attract tax relief at the higher rate of income tax.

Jack is self-employed, and his trading profit for the tax year 2017–18 is £100,000. He does not have any other income and expects to make the same level of profit in future years.

Individual savings account (ISA)

Jack has never invested any amounts in ISAs. During the next 30 days he would like to invest the maximum possible amounts into stocks and shares ISAs.

Required:

(a)   **Explain, with supporting calculations where necessary, why it is good inheritance tax planning for Jack to make the immediate lifetime cash gift of £300,000 to a trust.**

        Note: You are not expected to consider taper relief.   (3 marks)

(b)   (i)   **Advise Jack of the amount of additional gross personal pension contribution he can make for the tax year 2017–18 which will benefit from tax relief at the higher rate of income tax, and explain why this is a tax efficient approach to pension saving.**   (4 marks)

(ii) Calculate the amount of unused pension annual allowances which Jack will be able to carry forward to the tax year 2018–19 if the contribution in (i) above is made. (1 mark)

(c) Advise Jack as to the maximum possible amount which he can invest into stocks and shares ISAs during the next 30 days. (2 marks)

(10 marks)

32 Array Ltd provides its employees with various benefits.

The benefits were all provided throughout the tax year 2017–18 unless otherwise stated.

Alice

Alice was provided with a petrol-powered motor car which has a list price of £24,600. The motor car has an official CO_2 emissions rate of 118 grams per kilometre. Alice made a capital contribution of £5,600 towards the cost of the motor car when it was first provided to her by Array Ltd.

Alice was also provided with fuel for her private journeys. The total cost to Array Ltd of fuel for the motor car during the tax year 2017–18 was £1,500.

During the tax year 2017–18, Alice drove a total of 12,000 miles, of which 8,000 were for business journeys.

Buma

Buma was provided with a loan of £48,000 on 1 October 2015, which she used to renovate her main residence. Buma repays £1,000 of the capital of the loan to Array Ltd each month, and by 6 April 2017 the amount of the loan outstanding had been reduced to £30,000. In addition, Buma paid loan interest of £240 to Array Ltd during the tax year 2017–18.

The taxable benefit in respect of this loan is calculated using the average method.

Claude

On 6 July 2017, Claude was provided with a mobile telephone. The telephone is a smartphone which is mainly used by Claude for personal internet access. It was purchased by Array Ltd on 6 July 2017 for £600.

On 6 January 2018, Claude was provided with a home entertainment system for his personal use. This was purchased by Array Ltd on 6 January 2018 for £3,200. The market value of the home entertainment system on 5 April 2018 was £2,400.

Denise

During May 2017, Array Ltd paid £10,400 towards the cost of Denise's removal expenses when she permanently moved to take up her new employment with Array Ltd, as she did not live within a reasonable commuting distance. The £10,400 covered both her removal expenses and the legal costs of acquiring a new main residence.

During February 2018, Array Ltd paid for £340 of Denise's medical costs. She had been away from work for three months due to an injury, and the medical treatment (as recommended by a doctor) was to assist her return to work.

Required:

(a) State how employers are required to report details of employees' taxable benefits to HM Revenue and Customs following the end of the tax year, and the deadline for submitting this information for the tax year 2017–18. (2 marks)

(b) Calculate the taxable benefits which Array Ltd will have to report to HM Revenue and Customs in respect of each of its employees for the tax year 2017–18.

Note: Your answer should include an explanation for any benefits which are exempt or partially exempt. (11 marks)

(c) Calculate the class 1A national insurance contributions which Array Ltd would have had to pay in respect of its employees' taxable benefits for the tax year 2017–18, and state when this would have been due if paid electronically. (2 marks)

(15 marks)

33 Wretched Ltd commenced trading on 1 August 2017, preparing its first accounts for the eight-month period ended 31 March 2018.

Wretched Ltd is incorporated in the United Kingdom, but its three directors are all non-resident in the United Kingdom. Board meetings are always held overseas.

The following information is available:

Trading loss

The trading loss based on the draft accounts for the eight-month period ended 31 March 2018 is £141,200. This figure is before making any adjustments required for:

(1) Advertising expenditure of £7,990 incurred during April 2017. This expenditure has not been deducted in arriving at the trading loss for the eight-month period ended 31 March 2018 of £141,200.

(2) The premium which was paid to acquire a leasehold office building on a 10-year lease.

(3) Capital allowances.

Premium paid to acquire a leasehold office building

On 1 August 2017, Wretched Ltd paid a premium to acquire a leasehold office building on a ten-year lease. The amount of premium assessed on the landlord as income was £34,440. The office building was used for business purposes by Wretched Ltd throughout the eight-month period ended 31 March 2018.

Plant and machinery

On 1 August 2017, Wretched Ltd purchased three laptop computers at a discounted cost of £400 per laptop. The original price of each laptop was £850, but they were sold at the discounted price because they were ex-display.

Wretched Ltd also purchased three second hand motor cars on 1 August 2017. Details are:

	Cost £	CO_2 emissions rate
Motor car [1]	8,300	64 grams per kilometre
Motor car [2]	12,300	110 grams per kilometre
Motor car [3]	14,100	145 grams per kilometre

Business property income

Wretched Ltd lets out a warehouse which is surplus to requirements. The warehouse was let out from 1 August to 31 October 2017 at a rent of £1,400 per month. The tenant left on 31 October 2017, and the warehouse was not re-let before 31 March 2018.

During the eight-month period ended 31 March 2018, Wretched Ltd spent £2,100 on advertising for tenants.

Due to a serious flood, Wretched Ltd spent £5,900 on repairs during January 2018. The damage was not covered by insurance.

Loss on the disposal of shares

On 20 March 2018, Wretched Ltd sold its entire 1% shareholding of £1 ordinary shares in Worthless plc for £21,400. Wretched Ltd had purchased these shares on 5 August 2017 for £26,200.

The indexation factor from August 2017 to March 2018 is 0.019 (notional).

Other information

Wretched Ltd does not have any 51% group companies.

Wretched Ltd will continue to trade for the foreseeable future.

Required:

(a) **State, giving reasons, whether Wretched Ltd is resident or not resident in the United Kingdom for corporation tax purposes.** (1 mark)

(b) **Assuming that Wretched Ltd is resident in the United Kingdom, calculate the company's trading loss, property business loss and capital loss for the eight-month period ended 31 March 2018.**

   Note: You should assume that the company claims the maximum available capital allowances. (11 marks)

(c) **Explain how Wretched Ltd will be able to relieve its trading loss, property business loss and capital loss for the eight-month period ended 31 March 2018.** (3 marks)

(15 marks)

TAXATION (TX-UK) (F6) – REVISION QUESTION BANK

MARCH/JUNE 2017 SAMPLE QUESTIONS

Section C

This section of the exam contains **three constructed response** questions, each containing a scenario which relates to one or more requirement(s).
Each constructed response question is worth **10** or **15 marks**
All questions are compulsory.

31 **You should assume that today's date is 15 December 2017.**

Zhi has been self-employed since 2001, preparing accounts to 31 December. On 1 December 2017, Zhi purchased a new freehold warehouse for £164,000 for use in his business, but this purchase has resulted in Zhi having cash flow problems. He has various tax payments becoming due over the next two months, and would like to reduce or postpone these payments as much as possible.

Income tax and national insurance contributions (NICs)

Zhi's income tax liabilities and class 4 NICs for the tax years 2015–16, 2016–17 and 2017–18 are, or are forecast to be:

	2015–16 £	2016–17 £	2017–18 £
Income tax liability	25,200	27,600	18,000
Class 4 NICs	4,084	4,204	3,724

Zhi has not made any claims to reduce his payments on account.

Capital gains tax (CGT)

Zhi has a CGT liability of £12,940 becoming due for payment on 31 January 2018. This is in respect of a freehold office building which was sold for £210,000 on 10 December 2016, resulting in a chargeable gain of £76,000. The office building had always been used for business purposes by Zhi.

Zhi is a higher rate taxpayer. No claim has been made for rollover relief.

Value added tax (VAT)

Zhi has forecast that he will have to pay VAT of £20,200 on 7 February 2018 to HM Revenue and Customs (HMRC) in respect of the VAT quarter ended 31 December 2017.

On 12 December 2017, Zhi despatched goods relating to an exceptionally large credit sale of standard rated goods of £45,600 (inclusive of VAT). He has not yet issued a sales invoice for this sale.

Because the customer is unlikely to pay until 28 February 2018, Zhi is considering not issuing a sales invoice until 1 February 2018.

PAYE and NICs

Zhi will have to pay PAYE and NICs of £5,724 electronically on 22 January 2018 to HMRC in respect of his two employees for the tax month running from 6 December 2017 to 5 January 2018.

This includes amounts for bonuses which Zhi was planning to pay to his two employees on 1 January 2018, but could delay payment until 10 January 2018. The bonuses are in respect of the year ended 31 December 2017, and they will be treated as being received on whichever is the date of payment.

The first employee has a gross annual salary of £20,000 and is to be paid a bonus of £1,500. The second employee has a gross annual salary of £55,000 and is to be paid a bonus of £5,000.

Required:

(a) Calculate the amount by which Zhi can claim to reduce his self-assessment income tax and NICs due for payment on 31 January 2018 without incurring interest or penalties. (2 marks)

(b) Calculate the amount by which Zhi's CGT liability due for payment on 31 January 2018 will be reduced if he makes a claim for rollover relief based on the warehouse purchased on 1 December 2017 for £164,000. (3 marks)

(c) Explain whether Zhi can reduce the amount of VAT payable on 7 February 2018 by not issuing a sales invoice for the credit sale of £45,600 until 1 February 2018, and, if so, by how much the payment will be reduced. (2 marks)

(d) Calculate the amount by which Zhi's PAYE and NICs due on 22 January 2018 will be reduced if he delays the payment of employee bonuses until 10 January 2018, and state when the postponed amount will be payable. (3 marks)

Note: Your calculations should be based on annual income tax and NIC thresholds.

(10 marks)

32 Petula has been employed as a sales manager by Downtown plc since 6 April 2010. The following information is available in respect of the tax year 2017–18:

(1) During the tax year 2017–18, Petula was paid a gross annual salary of £230,000.

(2) In addition to her salary, Petula has been paid the following bonuses by Downtown plc:

Amount £	Date of payment	Date of entitlement	In respect of the six-month period ended
21,200	30 April 2017	1 April 2017	31 December 2016
18,600	31 October 2017	1 October 2017	30 June 2017
22,400	30 April 2018	1 April 2018	31 December 2017

(3) During the tax year 2017–18, Petula used her private motor car for both private and business journeys. The total mileage driven by Petula throughout the tax year was 26,000 miles, with all of this mileage reimbursed by Downtown plc at the rate of 60p per mile. However, only 21,000 miles were in the performance of Petula's duties for Downtown plc.

(4) Petula pays an annual professional subscription of £630 which is relevant to her employment with Downtown plc. Petula also pays an annual subscription membership fee of £1,840 to a golf club which she uses to entertain Downtown plc's clients. Downtown plc does not reimburse Petula for either of these costs.

(5) During the tax year 2017–18, Petula paid interest of £140 on a personal loan taken out on 6 April 2017 to purchase a computer for sole use in her employment with Downtown plc.

(6) Each tax year since 6 April 2010 (including the tax year 2017–18), Downtown plc has contributed £20,000 into the company's HM Revenue and Customs' registered money purchase occupational pension scheme on Petula's behalf. Petula has never personally made any pension contributions.

(7) Petula owns a freehold house which was let out furnished throughout the tax year 2017–18. The total amount of rent received during the tax year was £12,000.

During August 2017, Petula purchased a new washer-dryer for the property at a cost of £730. This was a replacement for an old washing machine which was scrapped, with nil proceeds. The cost of a similar washing machine would have been £420.

During November 2017, Petula purchased a new dishwasher for the property at a cost of £580. The property did not previously have a dishwasher.

The other expenditure on the property for the tax year 2017–18 amounted to £1,640, and all of this is allowable.

(8) During the tax year 2017–18, Petula rented out one furnished room of her main residence. During the year, she received rent of £8,900 and incurred allowable expenditure of £2,890 in respect of the room. Petula always uses the most favourable basis as regards the tax treatment of the furnished room.

(9) On 1 July 2017, Petula purchased £250,000 (nominal value) of gilts paying interest at the rate of 3% for £300,000. Interest is paid half-yearly on 30 June and 31 December based on the nominal value. Petula sold the gilts on 31 October 2017 for £302,500 (including accrued interest).

Required:

(a) **Calculate Petula's taxable income for the tax year 2017–18.** (12 marks)

Note: Your computation should list all of the items referred to in notes (1) to (9), indicating with the use of zero (0) any items which are not taxable or deductible.

(b) **Advise Petula of the total amount of her unused pension annual allowances which are available to carry forward to the tax year 2018–19.** (3 marks)

Note: You should assume Petula's adjusted income for 2016–17 was £240,000.

(15 marks)

33 The following information is available in respect of Online Ltd for the year ended 31 March 2018:

Operating profit

Online Ltd's operating profit for the year ended 31 March 2018 is £896,700. Depreciation of £21,660 and amortisation of leasehold property of £9,000 (see the leasehold property note below) have been deducted in arriving at this figure.

Leasehold property

On 1 April 2017, Online Ltd acquired a leasehold office building, paying a premium of £90,000 for the grant of a ten-year lease. The office building was used for business purposes by Online Ltd throughout the year ended 31 March 2018.

Plant and machinery

On 1 April 2017, the tax written down values of plant and machinery were as follows:

	£
Main pool	56,700
Special rate pool	12,400

The following transactions took place during the year ended 31 March 2018:

		Costs/(proceeds) £
14 May 2017	Sold a motor car	(18,100)
18 July 2017	Sold all items included in the special rate pool	(9,300)
27 January 2018	Purchased a motor car	13,700

The motor car sold on 14 May 2017 for £18,100 was originally purchased during the year ended 31 March 2017 for £17,200. This expenditure was added to the main pool.

The motor car purchased on 27 January 2018 for £13,700 has a CO_2 emission rate of 90 grams per kilometre. The motor car is used as a pool car by the company's employees.

Qualifying charitable donations

During the year ended 31 March 2018, Online Ltd made qualifying charitable donations of £6,800. These were not included in arriving at the operating profit above.

Disposal of shareholding in Network plc

On 20 March 2018, Online Ltd sold its entire shareholding of £1 ordinary shares in Network plc for £90,600. Online Ltd had originally purchased 40,000 shares (less than a 1% shareholding) in Network plc on 24 June 2011 for £49,300. On 7 October 2014, Online Ltd sold 22,000 of the shares for £62,200.

Assume indexation factors are as follows:

June 2011 to October 2014	0·096
June 2011 to March 2018	0·190
October 2014 to March 2018	0·086

Brought forward losses

As at 1 April 2017, Online Ltd had the following brought forward amounts of unused losses:

	£
Capital loss	4,700
Property business loss	12,500

Planned acquisition

Online Ltd currently does not have any 51% group companies. However, Online Ltd is planning to acquire a 60% shareholding in Offline Ltd in the near future. Offline Ltd is profitable and will pay regular dividends to Online Ltd.

Required:

(a) **Calculate Online Ltd's taxable total profits for the year ended 31 March 2018.**
(13 marks)

(b) **Briefly explain how the acquisition of Offline Ltd will affect the calculation and payment of Online Ltd's corporation tax liability in future years.** (2 marks)

(15 marks)

Answer 1 GENERAL CONCEPTS AND PRINCIPLES

Item   Answer   Justification

1.1   D   VAT is an indirect tax on the sale of goods and services.

Tutorial note: *National insurance contributions are a form of direct taxation.*

1.2   B   HM Revenue and Customs is responsible for tax administration.

Tutorial note: *HMRC is the non-ministerial department set up by the Commissioners for Revenue and Customs Act 2005 (when it replaced the Inland Revenue and Customs and Excise). HM Treasury is a ministerial department (presided over by the Chancellor of the Exchequer).*

1.3

Failing to record cash sales	YES	
Claiming personal expenses through the business	YES	
Understating the value of closing inventory	YES	
Postponing a sale of shares from 5 April until 6 April		NO

Tutorial note: *The postponement of the sale is legitimate tax planning and so is tax avoidance rather than evasion.*

1.4   B   The automatic overseas tests, which result in the individual being treated as not UK resident, include working full-time overseas with no significant breaks and less than 91 days spent in the UK.

Tutorial note: *An individual **not** previously resident is automatically treated as non-resident if present in the UK for less than 46 days.*

1.5   A   Regardless of whether or not Anna was previously resident she will be not resident as she spent less than 16 days in the UK.

Tutorial note: *Barbara's stay should not have exceeded 45 days for her to remain non-resident. If Carol had not been UK resident in any of the previous three tax years she would have been non-resident as her days in the UK did not exceed 45. Danita is not automatically non-resident as her employment in Italy is not full-time.*

1.6   B   Tax avoidance is not illegal, so the other statements are all incorrect.

1.7   C   Using the table in the rates and allowances sheet, it can be seen that – as previously resident – if Samuel spends 60 days in the UK he will be UK resident with three ties or more. To achieve non-resident status he can therefore only have a maximum of two ties.

1.8

A Ltd, a company incorporated in the UK, with its central management and control exercised in the UK	RESIDENT	
B Ltd, a company incorporated overseas, with its central management and control exercised in the UK	RESIDENT	
C Ltd, a company incorporated in the UK, with its central management and control exercised overseas	RESIDENT	
D Ltd, a company incorporated overseas, with its central management and control exercised overseas		NOT RESIDENT

TAXATION (TX-UK) (F6) – REVISION QUESTION BANK

1.9

Classification	Tax
Capital	Inheritance
Revenue	National insurance contributions
Neither	Value added

Answer 2 INCOME TAX COMPUTATIONS

Item   Answer   Justification

2.1

☑ Interest received on a repayment of income tax

☑ Dividends received from an Individual Savings Account

2.2   D   As his net income exceeds £100,000 his personal allowance will be reduced at the rate of £1 for every £2 of excess. The effect of this progressive reduction is that net incomes between £100,000 and £123,000 actually suffer an effective marginal tax rate of 60%.

2.3   A

	£
Taxable income £(29,360 – 11,500)	17,860

	£
20% on £17,860	3,572
Less: PAYE	(3,517)
Income tax payable	55

2.4   D   The annual allowance for the tax years 2016–17 and 2017–18 is £40,000 pa. Allowance is first available on opening the scheme in the tax year 2015–16. There is no unused allowance from this year as contributions exceeded the limit. Unused allowance in the tax year 2016–17 available in the tax year 2017–18 is £23,000 (40,000 – 17,000). This plus the allowance for the tax year 2017–18 is available.

2.5   B   The annual allowance for the tax years 2015–16 to 2017–18 is £40,000 and for previous tax years £50,000.

	£
Unused allowance brought forward:	
2014–15, 2015–16 and 2016–17 ((40,000 – 33,000) × 3)	21,000
Annual allowance 2017–18	40,000
	61,000
Contributions	113,000
Excess subject to annual allowance tax charge	52,000

2.6

Directors	YES	
Employees	YES	
Self-employed persons	YES	

Tutorial note: *Relief for contributions paid into personal pension schemes is available to all individual tax payers.*

2.7   D   1,771 × 30% (W) = £531

WORKING

(53,000 − 50,000) ÷ 100 = 30%

2.8

☑ A contribution into an employer's HMRC registered occupational pension scheme

☑ A charitable donation made under the payroll deduction scheme

Answer 3 PROPERTY AND INVESTMENT INCOMES

Item   Answer   Justification

3.1   Rent for 8 months is £8,000 (£12,000 × $^8/_{12}$). Allowable expenses total £3,620 (5,120 − 1,500) so property income is **£4,380**.

Tutorial note: *Only expenditure on improvements to the property is not allowable.*

3.2

Property A		NO
Property B	YES	

Tutorial note: *Both properties are available to let for 8 months (i.e. > 210 days).*

*Property A does **not** qualify as the single letting of more than 31 consecutive days does not count. The longer letting was 42 days so actual holiday letting was less than 105 days (140 − 42 = 98 days). Property B satisfies all conditions.*

3.3   A   Losses from letting FHA can be relieved only against future profits from FHA lettings.

Tutorial note: *Remember that income from FHA is treated as earned income and losses cannot be offset against unearned income.*

3.4   C   Stocks and shares ISAs are most appropriate for higher (and additional) rate taxpayers who already have sufficient gains to make use of the annual exempt amount and nil rate bands. In addition to avoiding the higher rate income tax liability on dividend income, Caleb will also save capital gains tax at the higher rate of 20%.

3.5   D   £(20,000 − 6,000) = £14,000

3.6   82,000 − (82,000 × 2% × (15 − 1)) = **£59,040**

3.7 B

	£
Property business profits	86,500
Add back disallowed interest	
for which only basic rate relief available (24,000 × 25%)	6,000
	92,500
Personal allowance	(11,500)
	81,000
33,500 @ 20%	6,700
47,500 @ 40%	19,000
	25,700
Basic rate interest relief (6,000 × 20%)	(1,200)
	24,500

3.8

☑ It applies to finance costs including those incurred for property repairs

☑ The restriction is being phased in over four years

Answer 4 EMPLOYMENT INCOME

Item   Answer   Justification

4.1   C   The rate of approved mileage allowance for the first 10,000 business miles is 45p per mile, and 25p per mile thereafter. Sharon can therefore claim £5,900 ((10,000 × 0.45) + (5,600 × 0.25)).

4.2   A   The property was owned more than six years before first being available, so the additional benefit is based on the excess of open market value over £75,000 (i.e. £134,000 (209,000 – 75,000)).

Tutorial note: *The improvements were made before the valuation and so were taken account of in the valuation.*

4.3   C   Using the average method the average loan outstanding is ½ (15,400 +9,800) = £12,600 and the benefit, assessed at the official rate of interest is £12,600 × 2.5% = £315.

4.4   C

	£
Childcare vouchers £(45 – 28) × 52	884
Luncheon vouchers (£5 × 240)	1,200
	2,084

Tutorial note: *As a higher rate tax payer £28 per week is exempt. Luncheon vouchers are taxable in full.*

REVISION QUESTION BANK – TAXATION (TX-UK) (F6)

4.5 B   £20,000 × 34% (W) × $^9/_{12}$ = £5,100

WORKING

	%
95 grams	18
Additional amount ((160 – 95) ÷ 5)	13
Diesel supplement	3
Taxable %	34

Tutorial note: *The benefit is time apportioned as the car was available from 1 July 2017.*

4.6

☑ Legal fees of a successful appeal against a tax assessment

☑ Cost of taking out a new five-year lease on business premises

4.7 £ **1701**

	Car <130g/km £		Allowances £
Addition	21,000		
WDA 18% × $^9/_{12}$	(2,835)	× 60%	1,701

Answer 5 UNINCORPORATED TRADERS – ASSESSMENT AND PROFITS

Item   Answer   Justification

5.1 A   Where CO_2 emissions are more than 130 grams per kilometre, then 15% of a motor car's leasing costs are disallowed. Therefore, £3,100 is fully deductible.

Tutorial note: *15% of leasing costs of a car with CO_2 emissions > 130 grams per kilometre are added back to trading profit as disallowable expenditure considered "too remote from the performance of the trade".*

5.2 C   Trading profit assessed in tax year 2017–18: ($^{12}/_{14}$ × £49,700) = £42,600

Tutorial note: *Trade commences in tax year 2016–17. The basis of the assessment for the first tax year is actual (i.e. from 1 January to 5 April 2017). The second tax year is 2017–18. The accounting period ending in this tax year is more than 12 months so the 12 months ending on the first permanent accounting date is taxed.*

5.3 A   The basis period for the tax year 2016–17 (the first tax year) is 1 October 2016 to 5 April 2017. Taxable profits are £9,830 ($^6/_{12}$ × £19,660).

5.4 A   The basis period for the tax year 2016–17 is 1 October 2016 to 5 April 2017. The basis period for the tax year 2017–18 is the year to 30 September 2017. Therefore the overlap period is 1 October 2016 to 5 April 2017 and overlap profits are £9,830 ($^6/_{12}$ × £19,660).

5.5   The basis period for the tax year 2016–17 is the year to 31 December 2016. Therefore the basis period for tax year 2017–18 (the final tax year) is 1 January to 30 September 2017, with taxable profits of **£8,900** (10,500 – 1,600).

TAXATION (TX-UK) (F6) – REVISION QUESTION BANK

Answer 6 CAPITAL ALLOWANCES

Item	Answer	Justification
6.1	B	There is no private use adjustment where a motor car is used by an employee (because the employee is assessed on the private use benefit), so there is no need for separate treatment. A car with CO_2 emissions of more than 130 grams per kilometre will be included in the special rate (8%) pool.

Tutorial note: *The special rate pool only includes expenditures on high CO_2 emission cars, long life assets, thermal insulation and other integral features of buildings. The item-by-item basis applies only to cars other than very low CO_2 emission cars subject to private use by the proprietor and elected short life assets.*

6.2   D

	Main pool £	Special rate £	Allowances £
Brought forward	32,000	15,000	
Addition: equipment	7,000		
Annual investment allowance (AIA)	(7,000)		7,000
Disposal proceeds	(6,000)		
	26,000	15,000	
Writing down allowance	× 18%		4,680
Writing down allowance		× 8%	1,200
			12,880

6.3   £ **285000**

	Main pool £	Special rate £	Allowances £
Brought forward	300,000	0	
Additions			
Plant and equipment	150,000		
Factory cooling system		250,000	
Annual investment allowance (AIA)		(200,000)	200,000
	450,000	50,000	
Writing down allowance	× 18%		81,000
Writing down allowance		× 8%	4,000
			285,000

Tutorial note: *For maximum capital allowance AIA is used against the expenditure qualifying for 8% writing down allowance.*

6.4   D

CO_2 emissions	Rate	Allowance £
120 grams per kilometre (£24,000)	18%	4,320
75 grams per kilometre (£13,500)	100%	13,500
		17,820

Tutorial note: *The WDA on the car subject to private use is not restricted to reflect the private use; private use is taxed as a benefit on the managing director.*

6.5	B		£
		Invoice total including VAT	11,220
		Less: Insurance	(225)
			10,995

Tutorial note: *Input VAT on new cars with any amount of private use is irrecoverable and therefore included in the cost for capital allowance purposes.*

6.6 6,200 + 1,600 – 9,800 = **£2,000**

Answer 7 UNINCORPORATED TRADERS – RELIEF FOR TRADING LOSSES

Item Answer Justification

7.1 B Unrelieved loss £9,250 brought forward is deducted from the £11,150 profit for the year to 31 March 2018 to give trading income of £1,900.

	£
Loss	(17,500)
Relief 2016–17 (trading profit)	8,250
Unrelieved loss c/f to the tax year 2017–18	9,250

7.2 D It can be carried forward against first available future profits arising from the same trade only (*s.83* ITA07).

Tutorial note: *This must be agreed with HMRC within four years following the year of the tax loss.*

7.3 D For set off against total income (*s.64* ITA07) the loss must be claimed by 31 January following the first anniversary of the tax year of loss (i.e. 31 January 2020 for a loss in the tax year 2017–18).

7.4 A Before loss relief, the total income for the tax year 2016–17 is £18,800 (14,900 + 3,900). Therefore loss relief of £18,800 is given in this year, leaving total income for the year of £Nil.

Tutorial note: *There is actually no point in claiming loss relief against total income in the tax year 2016–17, since the income of £3,900 for that year can be covered by the personal allowance, however the question calls for maximum relief as soon as possible.*

7.5

Any remaining overlap profits arising from the commencement of trade is deducted from the loss for the last 12 months.		INCORRECT
This relief is given against trading profits of the tax year of permanent discontinuance and the three preceding tax years on a LIFO basis	CORRECT	

Tutorial note: *The first statement is incorrect as overlap profit relief is deducted from trading profit on cessation of a trade and therefore **added** in calculating a terminal loss.*

7.6 24,000 + 50,000 = £ **74000**

TAXATION (TX-UK) (F6) – REVISION QUESTION BANK

Answer 8 UNINCORPORATED TRADERS – OTHER MATTERS

Item	Answer	Justification

8.1   A   The admission of Phil has no effect on the basis periods for Vanessa (or Josh). She will continue to be taxed on the current year basis, so her basis period for tax year 2017–18 is the year to 30 June 2017.

8.2   A

	Xavier £	Yolanda £	Total £
Profit			42,300
Salary	6,700	4,400	(11,100)
4% interest (on £33,000/£27,000)	1,320	1,080	(2,400)
Balance to share 2:1	19,200	x	28,800
	27,220		

8.3   A

	Total £	Larimar £	Amber £
Interest on capital (5%)	3,000	1,800	1,200
Balance (35%:65%)	117,000	40,950	x
Tax adjusted profits	120,000	**42,750**	x

8.4   C

	Cate £	Dani £	Total £
Profit			33,000
Salary	5,000	4,000	(9,000)
6% interest (on £35,000/£20,000)	2,100	1,200	(3,300)
Balance to share 3:2	x	8,280	20,700
		13,480	

8.5

A partner who has a trading loss for a tax year can choose whichever form of loss relief best suits his individual circumstances.	TRUE	
Each partner is liable for any income tax due on their other partners' shares of the partnership profits.		FALSE

Tutorial note: *(1) is true – for an established partnership this usually means choosing between the more immediate relief against total income (s.64 ITA07) and later relief against future shares of trading profit (s.83 ITA07). (2) is false – partners are separate taxable persons for income tax (and capital gains tax). Each partner is liable only for his own share of partnership profits.*

8.6 B

	Old PSR 9 months	New PSR 3 months	Total
Profit	36,000	12,000	48,000
Laurel's share	½	⅓	
	18,000	4,000	22,000

Answer 9 CAPITAL GAINS TAX – BASIC PRINCIPLES

Item   Answer   Justification

9.1   C   £(95,000 + 2,600 + 6,700) = £104,300

Tutorial note: *The roof repairs are not enhancement expenditure.*

9.2   B

	£	Tax rate	£
Chargeable gain	33,600		
Less Annual exempt amount	11,300		
	22,300		
Unused basic rate band (33,500 – 27,985)	5,515	10%	551
Excess	16,785	20%	3,357
			3,908

9.3

The rate of CGT will be minimised		FALSE
The due date will be delayed as long as possible		FALSE
The benefit of the basic rate tax band will be maximised		FALSE
The benefit of the annual exempt amount will be maximised	TRUE	

9.4   B   (1) The racehorse is a wasting asset and the gain on the sale is therefore exempt. Correct treatment will therefore *decrease* taxable gains.

(2) Auctioneer's fees have been correctly deducted so there is no effect.

9.5   B

	£
Sales proceeds	1,250,100
Less: Estate agents' fees	(120,000)
Net sale proceeds	1,130,100
Less: Original cost	(642,000)
Chargeable gain	488,100
Less: Annual exempt amount	(11,300)
Taxable gain	476,800
CGT liability (476,800 × 20%)	95,360

Tutorial note: *As his taxable income exceeds the basic rate limit the taxable amount of the gain is assessed at the higher rate.*

TAXATION (TX-UK) (F6) – REVISION QUESTION BANK

9.6

Investment property	Two cars
Chargeable gain	Exempt

9.7   B

	£
Proceeds	321,000
Less: Cost	(156,000)
Fees	(4,500)
Extension	(32,000)
Unindexed gain	128,500

Tutorial note: *The repair is not enhancement expenditure.*

9.8   A   Indexation factor is: $(281.8 - 171.1) \div 171.1 = 0.647$.

Tutorial note: *Remember that this must be rounded to 3 decimal places.*

	£
Proceeds	315,000
Less: Cost	(154,000)
Unindexed gain	161,000
Less: Indexation allowance (0.647 × 154,000)	(99,638)
Gain	61,362

9.9   C   The set-off of the brought forward capital losses is restricted to £11,800 (23,100 – 11,300) so that chargeable gains are reduced to the amount of the annual exempt amount. Samantha therefore has unused capital losses of £13,900 (25,700 – 11,800) to carry forward to the tax year 2018–19

9.10 $6,100 - (23,700 - 10,400 - 11,300) = £$ **4100**

9.11   C $28,800 - (21,000 \times {}^{9}/_{15}) = £16,200$

9.12

An individual is subject to capital gains tax on the disposal of chargeable assets during any tax year in which they are resident in the UK	TRUE	
A company is subject to corporation tax on gains from the disposal of chargeable assets if it is resident in the UK	TRUE	
The disposal of a chargeable asset between civil partners is an exempt disposal		FALSE
The transfer of chargeable assets between companies in a chargeable gains group is automatically treated as an exempt disposal		FALSE

Tutorial note: *Inter-spouse and intra-group transfers are treated as nil gain/nil loss disposals.*

9.13 C Chargeable gains will be reduced to Nil by the current period losses and £6,000 of the b/fwd capital losses. Taxable total profits will therefore only consist of the £45,000 trading profits.

Capital losses of £4,000 (10,000 − (26,000 − 20,000)) will be carried forward.

9.14

When a limited company has a capital loss, it is first set off against any chargeable gains arising in the same accounting period	TRUE	
Any remaining capital loss may be set against other income of the accounting period		FALSE
Any capital loss unutilised in the accounting period is then carried forward and set off against the first available chargeable gains of future accounting periods	TRUE	
Any capital loss unutilised in the accounting period may be carried back and set off against the chargeable gains of the immediately preceding accounting period		FALSE

Answer 10 CAPITAL GAINS TAX – CHATTELS, LAND AND BUILDINGS

Item   Answer   Justification

10.1   B   The cost relating to the six acres of land sold is £40,000 (56,000 × 69,000 ÷ (69,000 + 27,600)).

10.2   The painting is a non-wasting asset. There is a disposal because compensation was received. None of the compensation was applied in restoring the asset so the "no gain/no loss" option that applies when at least 95% of the proceeds is applied to restoration is not available. This is therefore treated as a part disposal with A = £20,000 and B = £60,000. The "cost" is therefore £18,750 (75,000 × 20,000 ÷ (20,000 + 60,000)) so the chargeable **gain** is **£1,250** (20,000 − 18,750).

10.3   C   The chargeable gain is restricted to £10,167 ((12,100 − 6,000) × $^5/_3$) as this is less than the normal gain of £10,400 (12,100 − 1,700).

10.4   B   The gain (before PPR exemption) is £150,000.

The period of ownership (2 April 1991 to 31 March 2018) is 27 years. For 4½ years (54 months) it was not Anna's PPR. However, the last 18 months count as a period of occupation, so the proportion of the gain which is exempt is 24 years' worth.

The amount chargeable to CGT is therefore £16,667 ($^3/_{27}$ × 150,000).

10.5   D   Both statements are incorrect. A principal private residence is exempt from CGT (i.e. not a chargeable asset). However, if part of it is used exclusively for business purposes, that part is not exempt

10.6   73,000 − 37,200 + 41,700 = £ **77500**

TAXATION (TX-UK) (F6) – REVISION QUESTION BANK

Answer 11 CAPITAL GAINS TAX – SHARES

Item   Answer   Justification

11.1   A   Only a disposal of shares of the same class in the same quoted company is matched under the identification rules.

11.2   B   The order of matching is firstly against the shares acquired on the same day (i.e. 1,200 bought on 22 August 2016).

11.3   C   There is no purchase on the same day and no shares were acquired in the *next* 30 days. Therefore the cost will be 500 shares at the pool cost of £3 a share (£(1,250 + 4,400 + 4,850) ÷ (500 + 1,500 + 1,500)) = £10,500 ÷ 3,500).

11.4   B   The bonus issue increases the number of shares to 2,640 but has no effect on the cost of £6,600. Therefore the cost of the shares sold is £1,000 ($^{400}/_{2,640}$ × 6,600). Hence there is a loss of £100 (900 – 1,000).

Answer 12 CAPITAL GAINS TAX – BUSINESS ASSETS

Item   Answer   Justification

12.1   A   Chargeable gains less allowable loss is £148,200 (176,000 – 16,500 – 11,300 annual exempt amount). Entrepreneurs' relief (ER) means a preferential tax rate of 10% so the liability is £14,820.

   Tutorial note: *The fact that Christos is a higher rate taxpayer is irrelevant. ER up to the lifetime limit can be claimed by all personal taxpayers for significant disposals of business assets.*

12.2   B   The reinvestment must take place between 12 months before and three years after the date of disposal of the warehouse.

12.3   C

	£
Profit on the sale (620,000 – 155,000)	465,000
Chargeable gain = proceeds retained (620,000 – 420,000)	200,000
Rollover	265,000

12.4   C   The gain is £58,800 (82,500 – 23,700). This gain may be held-over in full since all of the company's chargeable assets are business assets.

12.5

☑ A warehouse

☑ Fixed plant and machinery

☑ Furnished holiday accommodation

Tutorial note: *Motor vehicles and moveable plant and machinery are not qualifying assets.*

12.6   (184,000 – 143,000) = 41,000 > £38,600

The base cost is the actual cost of £ **143000** . There is no rollover relief because the proceeds not reinvested are greater than the chargeable gain.

Answer 13 CORPORATION TAX – THE TAX COMPUTATION

Item Answer Justification

13.1 B The first corporation tax accounting period (chargeable accounting period) is 1 February 2016 to 31 January 2017.

Tutorial note: *A chargeable accounting period cannot exceed 12 months.*

13.2

- ☑ Employer's national insurance contributions
- ☑ Replacement of roof tiles on the company's head office building

13.3

- ☑ Interest payable on a loan to purchase an investment property
- ☑ Interest payable on a loan to purchase shares in Dim Ltd, another trading company

13.4

Net amount assessable	Deductible interest
£78,300	£27,200

Non-trading loan relationship = £97,000 – £5,300 – £13,400 = £78,300

Tutorial note: *The interest on the loans to acquire an investment property and shares in a subsidiary company are non-trade related and therefore included as non-trading loan relationships. Bank interest receivable is non-trade (unless the company's trade is financial). Allowable interest for trade profits in this question only includes the loan to purchase a factory.*

13.5 D (1) A qualifying donation to charity – decrease. (2) Recovery of previously written off trade debts – increase.

Answer 14 CORPORATION TAX – LOSS RELIEFS

Item Answer Justification

14.1 B Loss relief of £19,500 will be given against the trading profit only. The loss cannot be relieved against the bank interest receivable. This is therefore the total taxable profits for the year to 31 December 2017.

14.2 Loss relief available in the year to 31 March 2017 is £79,600 (90,000 – (8,100 + 2,300)).

	£
Adjusted trading profit	72,000
Property business profits	9,000
Chargeable gains	8,100
Total profits	89,100
Less: Loss relief	(79,600)
Less: Qualifying charitable donations	(1,800)
Total taxable profit	**7,700**

14.3   B   £6,600 of the trading loss is relieved against the chargeable gains of the year to 31 March 2018, leaving £18,200 to be relieved. Chargeable profits for 9 months to 31 March 2017 is £7,200 (21,900 + 3,500 – 18,200).

14.4   D   The year to 30 June 2016 began more than 12 months before the loss-making period. Therefore interest on any repayment of corporation tax for that year runs from the due date of payment for the loss-making period itself (i.e. 1 January 2019).

14.5   £ **52500**

Tutorial note: *£47,000 will be relieved first against the five-months to 31 December 2016. The relief is then restricted to the lower of unutilised loss (120,000 – 47,000 = 73,000) and time apportioned profits ($^{7}/_{12}$ × 90,000 = 52,500)*

Answer 15 CORPORATION TAX – GROUPS OF COMPANIES

Item   Answer   Justification

15.1   £ **145000**

Tutorial note: *Group relief is restricted to a maximum of £145,000, being the lower of £145,000 and £168,750 (225,000 × $^{9}/_{12}$).*

15.2   B   It is not possible to surrender capital losses as part of a group relief claim.

15.3

Banana Ltd		NO
Custard Ltd		NO
Dairy Ltd	YES	
Eden Ltd		NO

Tutorial note: *A is the parent of B, which is the parent of C, which is the parent of both D and E. Thus there is indirect ownership of subsidiaries C, D and E. Companies form a chargeable gains group if at each level in the group structure there is a 75% shareholding and the head of the group (A) owns at least 50% of each sub-subsidiary. A's indirect interest in E is <50% (85% × 75% × 75%). Hence E is not part of A's chargeable gains group.*

15.4   D   The election has to be made within two years of the end of the accounting period in which the asset is disposed of outside the group.

15.5   D   The holdings are insufficient to meet the criteria for either group relationship.

Answer 16 INHERITANCE TAX

Item   Answer   Justification

16.1   A   When making gifts (either during lifetime or on death) it can be beneficial to "skip a generation". This avoids a further charge to IHT when the daughter (in this case) dies. Gifts will then only be taxed once before being inherited by the grandchildren, rather than twice.

16.2 D   The measure of the transfer of value is the amount by which Katrina's estate has been reduced by the gift (the "diminution in value").

	£
Before (11,000 × £37)	407,000
After (8,000 × £24)	192,000
Diminution	215,000

16.3 B   Amanda is paying the IHT liability, so the amount of the gift (£550,000) is net and must be grossed up by £56,250 ((500,000 – 325,000) × $^{20}/_{80}$).

16.4 B   The PET on 12 July 2010 is IHT exempt as it was made more than seven years before Margaret died. The PET on 21 December 2012 utilises £75,000 of the nil rate band, so £350,000 (325,000 + 100,000 residence band – 75,000) is available against the estate. The IHT liability is therefore £40,000 (40% × (450,000 – 350,000)).

16.5 C   Ben's personal representatives can claim Bella's unused nil rate band of £211,250 (325,000 × 65%), so the amount of nil rate band available is therefore £536,250 (325,000 + 211,250).

16.6 C   The gift on 14 July 2016 utilises all Ray's annual exemption for the tax year 2016–17. Therefore, the value of the PET made on 17 October 2017 is £3,700 (6,700 less the annual exemption of 3,000 for the tax year 2017–18).

16.7 **31 May 2018.** The due date is the **later** of 30 April following the end of the tax year in which the gift is made and **six months from the end of the month** in which the gift is made.

16.8 **The trustees on 30 June 2018.** Tax is payable by transferee, due by 6 months from end of month of death.

16.9

Deducted	Not deducted
An outstanding repayment mortgage	A verbal promise to pay a friend's debt
Funeral expenses	Credit card debts
An outstanding interest-only mortgage	An outstanding endowment mortgage

16.10   890,000 – 260,000 – 120,000 – 276,000 = £ **234000**

16.11

Changing the terms of her will so that the residue of her estate goes to her grandchildren rather than her children		NOT EFFECTIVE
Making lifetime gifts to trusts up to the value of the nil rate band every seven years	EFFECTIVE	
Changing the terms of her will so that the residue of her estate goes to her husband rather than her children	EFFECTIVE	
Making lifetime gifts to her grandchildren early in life	EFFECTIVE	

Tutorial note: *Although changing the terms of her will so that the residue of her estate goes to her grandchildren rather than her children would not reduce IHT on her estate, it may be a valid tax planning strategy for reducing later tax on the transfer of wealth from children to grandchildren.*

TAXATION (TX-UK) (F6) – REVISION QUESTION BANK

Answer 17 NIC, PAYE AND SELF-ASSESSMENT

Item   Answer   Justification

17.1   A   31 January 2019. The balancing payment is due 31 January following the end of the year of assessment.

17.2   D   As an individual taxpayer Angela can amend her return at any time within the 12 months following the prescribed filing date (i.e. on or before 31 January 2020 for the return for the tax year 2017–18).

Tutorial note: *HMRC can amend the return at any time after submission. Companies can similarly correct returns within 12 months of the filing date, however, HMRC can correct obvious errors only within 9 months from the actual filing date.*

17.3   B   P11Ds must be completed by 6 July following the end of the tax year (i.e. 6 July 2018 for the tax year 2017–18).

Tutorial note: *31 May is the date for providing relevant employees with their P60 form. The 19th of each month is the due date for paying tax and NIC withheld to HMRC (22nd if paying electronically).*

17.4   C   Form P60 must be given to each employee to help him complete his annual tax return by 31 May after the end of the tax year (i.e. 31 May 2018 for the tax year 2017–18).

17.5

Bluish Ltd	Jasmine
31 March 2024	31 January 2024

Tutorial note: *A company must keep its records for six years from the end of the chargeable accounting period. An individual conducting a trade must keep all records (not just those relating to his business) for five years from 31 January following the tax year (i.e. 31 January 2024 for the tax year 2017–18).*

17.6   B

	£
Class 2: 52 × £2.85	148
Class 4: 9% (£25,000 – £8,164)	1,515
	1,663

17.7   C   Employers pay Class 1 and Class 1A NICs. Class 2 and Class 4 NICs relate to self-employed individuals.

17.8   **0**   Payments on account are not required because the relevant amount for 2016–17 (300 + 320 = £620) does not exceed £1,000.

17.9

Year ended 31 December 2016		INCORRECT
None of the years ended 31 December 2015, 2016 or 2017		INCORRECT
Year ended 31 December 2017	CORRECT	
Year ended 31 December 2015		INCORRECT

17.10

		£
Employed – Class 1 ((36,000 – 8,164) × 12%)		3,340
Self-employed – Class 4 ((36,000 – 8,164) × 9%)		(2,505)
– Class 2 (52 × 2·85)		(148)
		687

17.11

Paper tax return	Online tax return
31 October 2018	31 January 2019

Answer 18 TAX COMPLIANCE

Item   Answer   Justification

18.1

(1)	A taxpayer can appeal against a determination and apply for postponement of payment		INCORRECT
(2)	The taxpayer must first apply for an internal review before making an appeal to the First-tier Tribunal		INCORRECT
(3)	A taxpayer can appeal against and apply to postpone the tax due under an assessment raised as a result of an enquiry into a tax return	CORRECT	

(1) is incorrect – tax is payable on a determination without appeal.
(2) is also incorrect – an internal review is optional.

Tutorial note: *A "discovery assessment" is one that arises from an HMRC compliance check. A determination of tax payable is issued by HMRC when a tax return has not been filed.*

18.2   B

35% × (£18,000 × 40%) = £2,520

Tutorial note: *The maximum penalty for deliberate understatement is 70% of the tax lost to HMRC (calculated at the higher rate). Esther's prompted disclosure means that the penalty can be reduced to 35%.*

18.3   B

A taxpayer is required to notify HMRC of the need to complete a self-assessment return by 5 October following the tax year in which a new source of income is acquired. As Carmen commenced to trade in the tax year 2016–17 she is required to notify by 5 October 2017.

18.4   D

There are two components of the interest on late paid tax:

	£
(i) On 1 November 2017 payment of £90,000	
This is one month late: ($1/12$ × £90,000 × 2.75%)	206
(ii) 31 January 2018 payment of further £12,000	
Interest on this amount also runs from the due date	
1 October 2017: ($4/12$ × £12,000 × 2.75%)	110
	316

18.5   A

£12,000 × 2.75% × $2/12$ = £55

TAXATION (TX-UK) (F6) – REVISION QUESTION BANK

18.6 **10%.** Balancing payment is due 31 January 2018. A 5% penalty surcharge arises if this is unpaid for more than a month, and a further 5% if unpaid for 6 months (and a further 5% if outstanding for a year).

Tutorial note: *Interest will also be charged on the late payment.*

18.7 C Willard can make an amendment within 12 months of the prescribed filing date; HMRC can initiate a compliance check within 12 months of the actual filing date.

18.8 $166,250 \times 2.75\% \times {}^{4}/_{12} =$ **£1,524** (period 1 April to 31 July 2018)

Answer 19 VALUE ADDED TAX

Item Answer Justification

19.1

☑ He can register voluntarily if he makes only zero-rated supplies

☑ If he makes both zero-rated and standard-rated supplies he must register only if taxable supplies exceed the VAT registration limit

Tutorial note: *Sug can voluntarily register for VAT if he makes only zero-rated supplies. If he makes both zero-rated and standard-rated supplies he is required to register only if the level of taxable supplies exceeds the VAT registration limit.*

19.2 D 31 January 2018

Turnover	£
March-September (£7,500 × 7)	52,500
October-November (2 × £10,500)	21,000
December	12,000
	85,500

The VAT registration limit is therefore exceeded at the end of December.

19.3

Amount	£21.00
Payable by	**Dan**

Tutorial note: *Amount of VAT payable by Dan is £126 × ${}^{20}/_{120}$ = £21*

19.4 D 14 June

Since Gosia operates under the cash accounting scheme output VAT is accounted for when the payment is received from the customer.

Tutorial note: *The tax point is the date of supply; it is used to decide in which return period a transaction falls and the rate of VAT that applies.*

19.5

31 May	31 August
£375	£2,125

WORKINGS

Quarter to 31 May – £375 (2,250 × $^{20}/_{120}$)
Quarter to 31 August – £2,125 ((2,250 ÷ 15%) × $^{20}/_{120}$ – 375)

Tutorial note: *A normal (i.e. accruals based) accounting system should be assumed for unincorporated traders unless a special scheme is mentioned in the question.*

19.6   A   Output VAT = £19,650 × 20% = £3,275

19.7   D   Input VAT = £(600 + 1,338) = £1,938

19.8

Equipment	New car
Irrecoverable	Irrecoverable

Tutorial note: *In the absence of a VAT invoice the VAT on the equipment is irrecoverable. VAT on the car is also irrecoverable as there is an element of private use.*

19.9   A   0% of tax lost.

Tutorial note: *The error was a genuine mistake. The disclosure to HMRC was unprompted and therefore the penalty can be reduced to 0% of potential lost revenue.*

19.10

- ☑ Relief for impairment losses on trade debts is given automatically
- ☑ Output VAT is accounted for when cash is received from the customer

19.11

- ☑ The flat rate scheme may be used in conjunction with the annual accounting scheme
- ☑ A trader can join if VAT exclusive turnover for the next 12 months is not expected to exceed £150,000
- ☑ There is no recovery of input VAT

19.12

Output VAT	Input VAT
£68	£100

WORKINGS

Output VAT: (408 × $^{20}/_{120}$) = £68
Input VAT: (600 × $^{20}/_{120}$) = £100

19.13   (6 + 3) × 110 = £ **990**

19.14   D

	£
16.5% × (30,000 × 120%)	5,940
14% × (30,000 × 120%)	5,040
	900

Tutorial note: *Under the flat rate scheme, no separate relief is given for input costs. However, if Brian were to leave the flat rate scheme his liability for the quarter would be only £5,880 (i.e. (30,000 – 600) × 20%).*

Answer 20 ASPECTS OF A TAX SYSTEM

(a) **Objectives of taxation in a developed economy**

- To collect money to fund public sector expenditure (e.g. for health, defence, education, infrastructure, etc).

- As a tool for macroeconomic management of the domestic economy (e.g. to stimulate growth or improve international competitiveness).

- A mechanism for redistributing wealth between societal groups (e.g. from rich to poor, or as part of a regional policy).

- To influence behaviour (e.g. carbon, tobacco, alcohol duties).

(b) **Sources of tax law**

These include:

- Acts of Parliament – annual Finance Acts and periodic consolidated unifying acts such as the Income Tax Act 2007;

- Statutory Instruments;

- European Union regulations (directly applicable) and directives (requiring local adoption);

- Case Law, the accumulation of judgements and precedents from cases heard in the High Court, the Court of Appeal, the Supreme Court and the European Court of Justice; and

- HM Revenue and Customs Statements of Practice and Extra-Statutory Concessions.

(c) **Avoidance and evasion**

Tax *avoidance* is the minimisation of tax liabilities achieved through the organisation of a taxpayer's financial affairs within the limits of tax law. In large measure, tax avoidance is the utilisation of tax reliefs and exemptions and ensuring the lowest rate(s) of tax ultimately apply to taxable incomes, chargeable gains and taxable supplies for VAT purposes.

Tax avoidance schemes may be challenged under the General Anti-Abuse Rule (GAAR) whereby unreasonably abusive actions can be challenged by HM Revenue and Customs. In such cases just and reasonable adjustments may be made as necessary in order to counteract the tax advantage which would otherwise arise.

If a legal tax avoidance arrangement becomes too costly for the government or is deemed to run contrary to the intention of the law, the tax advantages of the arrangement can be removed by specific changes to the tax law (i.e. anti-avoidance legislation).

Tax *evasion* is the **illegal** avoidance of tax achieved by negligence or fraud (i.e. non-disclosure of income or gains or deliberate illegal actions).

Answer 21 SHIV AND SHANKER

(a) UK residency status

(i) Shiv

To establish residence, the statutory test first considers those criteria which would result in an automatic non-residence status. These are less than 16 days in UK, less than 46 days if not recently UK resident, or less than 91 days if working full-time overseas.

Shiv does not fall within any of the automatic non-resident tests, so the automatic UK tests are next considered. Again it appears that these do not conclusively determine residence – he is in the UK for less than 183 days and his work is not full time in the UK.

As Shiv is previously resident in the UK, and is present in the UK between 121 and 182 days in the year, he will be UK resident if he has at least one UK "tie". In fact he has at least three ties – accommodation, work, and country tie – and so Shiv will be treated as UK resident.

(ii) Shanker

The same procedures apply in determining Shanker's UK residence. Again he is not treated as automatically non-resident, nor can we conclude that he is automatically resident.

As he is in the UK for only 86 days, he will be treated as UK resident if he has three or more UK ties. Shanker has a close family tie, an accommodation tie, and a country tie (more time spent in UK than any other country), so will therefore be UK resident. He may additionally have a 90 day tie and also a work tie, but we do not need to know as the criterion is already met.

(b) Poppy's bookshop

(i) Real time information

An employer is required to submit a full payment submission (FPS) to HM Revenue and Customs every time a payroll payment is made. The electronic submission should be made on or before the time of the payroll payment. Poppy could be liable to a £100 penalty for each late submission (up to £400 if she had a greater number of employees).

Penalties would also apply for errors in the FPS, and also for any late payment. Payments made electronically in respect of monthly payroll should generally be received by the 22nd of the following month.

The final FPS will include year-end accumulations for employees, but the following forms and returns are also required:

- P60 – to employees by 31 May;
- P11D – to relevant employees by 6 July;
- P11D(b) – to HM Revenue and Customs also by 6 July, showing Class 1A National Insurance liability which should be paid by 22 July.

Penalties apply if these are submitted late (£100 per month) or incorrectly and interest is charged on any late payment.

Tutorial note: *Although benefits are not specifically referred to in the scenario relevant returns are included for completeness.*

(ii) *iXBRL*

iXBRL stands for inline extensible business reporting language, and refers to the standardised way accounts and computations may be electronically tagged. It is a mandatory presentation for submissions accompanying the online filing of form CT600 by companies (and also certain charities, clubs and friendly societies).

It is not a requirement for unincorporated businesses so no action is required by Poppy in this respect.

Answer 22 BAYLE DEFENDER

(a) **NIC if Fyle Guardian is an employee**

Fyle

Fyle's annual salary is £39,600 (£3,300 × 12), so below the £45,000 threshold for employee's contributions reducing to 2%.

Fyle will pay employee Class 1 NIC for 2017–18 of £1,257 ((39,600 – 8,164) × $^4/_{12}$ × 12%).

Bayle

Bayle will pay employer's Class 1 NIC for 2017–18 of £Nil as the employment allowance fully covers the liability of £1,446 ((39,600 – 8,164) × $^4/_{12}$ × 13.8%).

(b) **Fyle Guardian becomes a partner**

(i) *Trading income assessment for 2017–18*

	£
Basis period: 1 December 2017 to 5 April 2018 (216,000 × $^4/_{12}$)	72,000
Profit share (72,000 × 20%)	14,400

Trading income assessment for 2018–19

	£
Basis period: 1 December 2017 to 30 November 2018	
216,000 × $^{10}/_{12}$	180,000
240,000 × $^2/_{12}$	40,000
	220,000
Profit share (220,000 × 20%)	44,000

Tutorial notes:

(1) *The commencement rules apply to Fyle for 2017–18 since he will join as a partner on 1 December 2017.*

(2) *The assessment for 2018–19 is for the 12 months from when Fyle joins the partnership.*

(ii) *NIC*

Fyle will pay Class 2 NIC for 2017–18 of £51 (18 × £2.85).
He will pay Class 4 NIC for 2017–18 of £561 (14,400 – 8,164 = 6,236 at 9%).

There are no NIC implications for Bayle.

Answer 23 JOSIE JONES

Income tax computation 2017–18

	£	£
Trading profit (W1)		64,000
Employment income		
Salary (15,100 × 8)		120,800
Removal expenses (11,600 – 8,000)		3,600
Beneficial loan (33,000 × 2.5% × 7/12)		481
Staff canteen		0
Property business profit		
Property two (7,200 – 2,100)	5,100	
Property one	0	
		5,100
Building society interest		11,200
Dividends		7,200
Premium bond prize		0
		212,381
Personal allowance		0
Taxable income		212,381

£		
39,000 (W3) × 20%		7,800
116,500 (155,500 – 39,000) × 40%		46,600
49,681 (212,381 – 7,200 – 155,500) × 45%		22,356
5,000 × 0%		0
2,200 (7,200 – 5,000) × 38.1%		838
212,381		
Income tax liability		77,594

Tutorial notes:

(1) Only £8,000 of the relocation costs is exempt.

(2) The provision of meals in a staff canteen does not give rise to a taxable benefit.

(3) The furnished holiday letting loss from property one can only be carried forward against future furnished holiday letting profits.

(4) Premium bond prizes are exempt from income tax.

(5) No personal allowance is available as Josie's adjusted net income of £206,881 (212,381 – 5,500) exceeds £123,000.

(6) No savings income nil rate band is available as Josie is an additional rate taxpayer.

(7) The £5,000 dividend nil rate band is available to all taxpayers. Dividends are treated as the top slice of income so the balance of Josie's dividends are taxed at the additional rate of 38.1%.

WORKINGS

(1) Trading profit

	£	£
Year ended 30 April 2017	56,500	
Capital allowances (W2)	(2,376)	
		54,124
Period ended 30 June 2017	16,600	
Balancing allowance (W2)	(6,724)	
		9,876
		64,000

(2) Capital allowances

	Main pool £	Allowances £
Year ended 30 April 2017		
WDV brought forward	13,200	
WDA – 18%	(2,376)	2,376
WDV carried forward	10,824	
Period ended 30 June 2017		
Addition	3,600	
Proceeds	(7,700)	
Balancing allowance	(6,724)	6,724

(3) Tax bands

- Josie's basic and higher rate tax bands are extended by £5,500 (4,400 × $^{100}/_{80}$) to £39,000 (33,500 + 5,500) and £155,500 (150,000 + 5,500) in respect of the gift aid donations.

Answer 24 SOPHIA WONG

(a) Profits withdrawn as director's remuneration

- Employer's class 1 NIC will be £8,711 (80,000 – 71,289).

- Sophia's income tax liability for the tax year 2017–18 will be:

	£
Director's remuneration	71,289
Personal allowance	(11,500)
Taxable income	59,789

Income tax

	£
33,500 × 20%	6,700
26,289 × 40%	10,516
59,789	
Income tax liability	17,216

- Sophia's employee class 1 NIC for the tax year 2017–18 will be £4,946 ((45,000 – 8,164 = 36,836 × 12%) + (71,289 – 45,000 = 26,289 × 2%)).

- There is no corporation tax liability for the new company as the profits are entirely withdrawn as director's remuneration.

- The total tax and NIC cost if all of the new company's profits are withdrawn as director's remuneration is £30,873 (8,711 + 17,216 + 4,946), which is £6,010 (30,873 – 24,863) more than the cost on a self-employed basis.

(b) Profits withdrawn as dividends

- There will be no class 1 NIC.

- The corporation tax liability of the new company for the year ended 5 April 2018 will be £15,200 (80,000 × 19%) and dividends paid to Sophia will be £64,800 (80,000 – 15,200).

- Income tax payable by Sophia for the tax year 2017–18:

	£
Dividends	64,800
Personal allowance	(11,500)
Taxable income	53,300

Income tax

£	
5,000 × 0%	0
28,500 (33,500 – 5,000) × 7·5%	2,137
19,800 (53,300 – 33,500) × 32·5%	6,435
53,300	
Income tax liability	8,572

- The total tax and NIC cost if all of the new company's profits are withdrawn as dividends is £23,772 (15,200 + 8,572), which is £1,091 (24,863 – 23,772) less than the cost on a self-employed basis.

Answer 25 JOHN BEACH

(a) Income tax computation 2017–18

	£	£
Employment income		
Director's remuneration		184,000
Mileage allowance (W1)		1,425
		185,425
Occupational pension contributions		(28,000)
		157,425
Car benefit (W2)	4,112	
Fuel benefit (22,600 × 35% × 5/12)	3,296	
Beneficial loan (W3)	710	
		8,118
Property business profit		6,730
		172,273
Personal allowance		0
Taxable income		172,273
33,500 × 20%		6,700
116,500 (150,000 – 33,500) × 40%		46,600
22,273 × 45%		10,023
172,273		
Annual allowance charge (W4)		
30,000 × 45%		13,500
Income tax liability		76,823

WORKINGS

(1) Mileage allowance

- The mileage allowance received by John was £3,576 (5,960 × £0.60).

- Ordinary commuting does not qualify for relief, so the tax free amount is £2,151 ((4,270 + 510) × £0.45).

- The taxable benefit is therefore £1,425 (3,576 – 2,151).

(2) Car benefit

- The relevant percentage for the car benefit is 35% ((18% + 17% (180 – 95) ÷5)).
- The motor car was available during the period 1 November 2017 to 5 April 2018, so the benefit for the tax year 2017–18 is £4,112 (28,200 × 35% × 5/12).

TAXATION (TX-UK) (F6) – REVISION QUESTION BANK

(3) Beneficial loan

- John repaid £24,000 (12,000 + 12,000) of the loan during the tax year 2017–18, so the outstanding balance at 5 April 2018 is £60,000 (84,000 – 24,000).

- Benefit calculated using the average method is £710:

	£
½ (84,000 + 60,000) × 2.5%	1,800
Interest paid	(1,090)
	710

(4) Effect of tapered annual allowance

- John's adjusted income for calculating his annual allowance will be in excess of £210,000 (172,273 + 28,000 + 12,000 = 212,273), the annual allowance will be tapered down to the minimum of £10,000.

- The excess pension input of £30,000 (28,000 + 12,000 – 10,000) is subject to annual allowance charge at John's marginal rate of 45%

Tutorial note: No personal allowance is available as John's adjusted net income of £172,273 exceeds £123,000.

(b) National insurance contributions

- Employee class 1 NIC for the tax year 2017–18 is £7,229 (((45,000 – 8,164) × 12%) + ((185,425 – 45,000) × 2%)).

Answer 26 PHIL JONES

(a) Income tax computation 2017–18

	£	£
Property business income		
Rent receivable		22,000
Repairs	2,800	
Insurance	2,300	
		(5,100)
		16,900
Personal allowance		(11,500)
Taxable income		5,400
Income tax (5,400 × 20%)		1,080
Income tax liability		1,080

Capital gains tax computation 2017–18

	£	£
House		
Disposal proceeds		504,000
Cost	420,000	
Enhancement expenditure	5,300	
Incidental costs of disposal	8,600	
		(433,900)
Chargeable gain		70,100
Annual exempt amount		(11,300)
		58,800
Capital gains tax (using residential property rates)		
28,100 (33,500 – 5,400) × 18%		5,058
30,700 × 28%		8,596
58,800		
Capital gains tax liability		13,654

Tutorial note: *The cost of replacing the property's chimney is revenue expenditure as the chimney is a subsidiary part of the house. The cost of the new boundary wall is capital expenditure as the wall is a separate, distinct, entity.*

(b)   FHL as trade

- Furniture and equipment purchased for use in the furnished holiday letting will qualify for capital allowances instead of only replacement furniture relief.

- The profit from the furnished holiday letting will qualify as relevant earnings for pension tax relief purposes.

- Capital gains tax entrepreneurs' relief, rollover relief and holdover relief will potentially be available when the furnished holiday letting is disposed of.

Answer 27 RICHARD FEAST

(a)   Trading profit for the year ended 5 April 2018

	£
Net profit	32,200
Motor expenses – Richard (4,710 × 70%)	3,297
Motor expenses – Chef	0
Parking fines	280
Property expenses (16,200 × 1/5)	3,240
Decorating – Restaurant	0
– Apartment	1,320
Other expenses – Legal fees	2,590
Capital allowances (W1)	(3,780)
Trading profit	39,147

WORKING

(1) Capital allowances

	Pool £	Motor car £	Allowances £
Additions			
Motor car [1]		14,000	
Motor car [2]	16,800		
WDA – 18%		(2,520) ×30%	756
WDA – 18%	(3,024)		3,024
WDV carried forward	13,776	11,480	3,780

Tutorial note: *Both motor cars have CO_2 emissions between 76 and 130 grams per kilometre, and therefore qualify for writing down allowances at 18%. The private use of a motor car by an employee is irrelevant, since such usage will be assessed on the employee as a benefit.*

(b) National insurance contributions (NIC) as employer

Chef

- Employer's class 1 NIC for the tax year 2017–18 is £5,221 (37,836 (46,000 – 8,164) × 13·8%).

- The relevant percentage for the car benefit is 20% (18% + 2% ((105 – 95) ÷ 5)).

- The motor car was available throughout 2017–18, so the benefit for the tax year 2017–18 is £3,360 (16,800 × 20%).

- Employer's class 1A NIC for the tax year 2017–18 is therefore £464 (3,360 × 13·8%).

Waitress

- No NICs were payable as the waitress earned less than the £8,164 earnings threshold.

Assistant chef

- The monthly earnings threshold is £680 ($^1/_{12}$ × 8,164).
- Employer's Class 1 NIC for the tax year 2017–18 is therefore £1,678 ((2,200 – 680) × 13·8% × 8).

Tutorial note: *The alternative approach using the annual earnings threshold and then taking $^8/_{12}$ × an annual NIC figure is acceptable.*

Total

Employer's class 1 NIC for the tax year 2017–18 is £5,221 (chef), £1,678 (assistant chef), less £3,000 (employment allowance), i.e. £3,899.

Employer's class 1A NIC total is £464 (re chef's car benefit only).

Answer 28 FANG AND HONG

(a)   Fang

(i)   Assessments

	£
2015–16 (1 August 2015 to 5 April 2016) (45,960 × $^{8}/_{12}$)	30,640
2016–17 (Year ended 31 July 2016)	45,960
2017–18 (Year ended 31 July 2017)	39,360

■ In the tax year 2016–17 there are overlap profits of £30,640 (i.e. the eight-month period 1 August 2015 to 5 April 2016).

(ii)   Pre-trading expenditure

■ The trading expenditure will be treated as incurred on 1 August 2015 provided it was incurred within the previous seven years and would have been allowable if the trade had already commenced.

■ The computer equipment which Fang already owned will be an addition for capital allowances purposes based on its market value at 1 August 2015.

(b)   Hong

Taxable income 2016–17

	£
Trading profit	29,700
Loss relief brought forward *(s.83 ITA 2007)*	(2,600)
	27,100
Property business profit	3,900
	31,000
Loss relief *(s.64 ITA 2007)*	(31,000)
	0
Personal allowance	0
Taxable income	0

Taxable gain tax year 2016–17

	£
Chargeable gain	17,800
Loss relief *(s.261B TCGA 1992)* (W)	(11,600)
	6,200
Capital losses b/fwd	(6,200)
Taxable gain	0

WORKING

Loss relief

- The loss relief claim against the chargeable gain is restricted to £11,600 (chargeable gain of 17,800 less the capital loss brought forward of 6,200), which is lower than the available trading loss of £14,800 (45,800 – 31,000).

- Therefore, the trading loss carried forward is £3,200 (14,800 – 11,600).

Answer 29 KLM AND RICHARD MORRIS

(a) Kang, Ling and Ming

Allocation of profits

	Kang £	Ling £	Ming £
Year ended 30 June 2016			
148,800 × $\frac{1}{3}$	49,600	49,600	49,600
Year ended 30 June 2017			
1 July to 31 October 2016			
136,800 × $\frac{4}{12}$ × $\frac{1}{3}$	15,200	15,200	15,200
1 November 2016 to 30 June 2017			
136,800 × $\frac{8}{12}$ × $\frac{1}{2}$	45,600	45,600	0
	60,800	60,800	15,200

Trading income assessments

	Kang £	Ling £	Ming £
2016–17			
Year ended 30 June 2016	49,600	49,600	49,600
Period ended 31 October 2016			15,200
			64,800
Relief for overlap profits			(29,400)
			35,400
2017–18			
Year ended 30 June 2017	60,800	60,800	

Tutorial note: *The cessation rules apply to Ming for the tax year 2016–17 since she ceased to be a partner on 31 October 2016.*

(b) Richard Morris

(i) Child benefit income tax charge

- Richard's adjusted net income of £90,000 exceeds £60,000, so the child benefit income tax charge will be £1,752 (the amount of child benefit received).

- The tax charge will be collected through the self-assessment system along with any remaining income tax payable.

(ii)   Personal pension scheme contribution

- Richard was not a member of a pension scheme prior to the tax year 2017–18, so the annual allowances for the tax years 2014–15, 2015–16 and 2016–17 are not available.

- Although net relevant earnings are £80,000 (65,000 + 15,000), the maximum amount of tax relievable personal pension contribution is effectively restricted to the annual allowance of £40,000 for the tax year 2017–18.

- Personal pension contributions are made net of basic rate tax, so Richard would have paid £32,000 (40,000 less 20%) to the pension company.

- Higher rate tax relief would have been given by extending Richard's basic rate tax band for the tax year 2017–18 by £40,000 (gross amount of the pension contribution).

Answer 30 CHI NEEDLE

(a)   Trading profit of £52,400

(i)   Income tax liability 2017–18

	£
Trading profit	52,400
Personal allowance	(11,500)
Taxable income	40,900

£	
33,500 × 20%	6,700
7,400 × 40%	2,960
40,900	
Income tax liability	9,660

(ii)   National insurance contributions

- Class 2 national insurance contributions for the tax year 2017–18 will be £148 (52 × 2·85).

- Class 4 national insurance contributions for the tax year 2017–18 will be £3,463 ((45,000 – 8,164 = 36,836 × 9%) + (52,400 – 45,000 = 7,400 × 2%)).

(iii)   Tax payments

- Chi's balancing payment for the tax year 2017–18 will be £13,123 (9,660 + 3,463).

- In addition, she will have to make the first payment on account for the tax year 2018–19 of £6,561 (13,123 × 50%).

- The total amount payable on 31 January 2019 will therefore be £19,832 (13,123 + 6,561 + 148).

(b)   Tax return deadlines

- Unless the return is issued late, the latest date that Chi can file a paper self-assessment tax return for the tax year 2017–18 is 31 October 2018.

- Should Chi wish to make an amendment to this return, then the deadline for doing so will be 31 January 2020 (12 months from the latest (electronic) filing date for the return of 31 January 2019).

Answer 31 QI PIN

(a) Trading profit for the year ended 5 April 2018 using the cash basis

	£	£
Revenue (71,900 – 1,600)		70,300
Expenses		
Motor expenses (W)	5,300	
Other expenses (8,200 – 900)	7,300	
Office equipment	4,020	
Capital allowances	0	
		(16,620)
Trading profit		53,680

WORKING

	£
10,000 miles × 45p	4,500
3,200 miles × 25p	800
	5,300

Tutorial note: *Capital allowances are not relevant, since purchases of equipment are deducted as an expense. The running and capital costs of owning a motor car are replaced by the deduction based on approved mileage allowances.*

(b) Mobias

(i) Maximum gross personal allowance and contributions for relief

- There is no maximum limit to the amount of additional personal pension contribution which Mobias could make for the tax year 2017–18.

- The maximum contribution which will qualify for tax relief is £68,000 (relevant earnings of £78,000 less the £10,000 of contributions already made).

- However, tax relief will effectively be restricted to the available annual allowances of £44,000 (£14,000 (40,000 – 26,000) from the tax year 2016–17 and £30,000 (40,000 – 10,000) from the tax year 2017–18).

Tutorial note: *No allowance is available for the tax year 2015–16 as Mobius was not a member of a personal pension scheme for that year.*

(ii) Use of ISA limits

- Since Mobias has already invested £2,400 into a cash ISA, he can invest a maximum of £17,600 (20,000 – 2,400) into a stocks and shares ISA in the tax year 2017–18.

- Alternatively, he could invest up to a further £17,600 into the existing cash ISA, with any balance being invested into a stocks and shares ISA (with either the same or a new account manager).

Tutorial note: *Mobias could also invest the maximum limit of £20,000 into a stocks and shares ISA by transferring his existing cash ISA. However, ISA transfers are outside the scope of the F6(UK) syllabus.*

REVISION QUESTION BANK – TAXATION (TX-UK) (F6)

(c) **Road Ltd**

(i) *VAT returns and payments*

- VAT registered businesses have to file their VAT returns online and pay the VAT which is due electronically.

- The deadline for doing this is one month and seven days after the end of each quarter. For example, for the quarter ended 31 March 2018 a business will have until 7 May 2018 to file its VAT return and pay any VAT which is due.

(ii) *PAYE real time reporting*

- Real time PAYE information must be filed electronically, so Road Ltd will have to either run payroll software or use the services of a payroll provider.

- Road Ltd will have to send real time PAYE information to HM Revenue and Customs electronically by the end of each calendar month (the time when employees are paid).

- Form P60 must be provided to employees following the end of the tax year.

- Form P11D/P9D detailing the benefits provided to the employees must be submitted to HM Revenue and Customs following the end of the tax year, with a copy provided to the employees. In addition, Form P11D(b) should be submitted detailing Class 1A national insurance contributions.

Answer 32 ALFRED KING

(a) **Income tax computation 2017–18**

	£
Trading profit (W1)	72,750
Dividends (6,060 – 720)	5,340
	78,090
Personal allowance	(11,500)
Taxable income	66,590

	£
35,900 (W3) × 20%	7,180
25,350 (66,590 – 5,340 – 35,900) × 40%	10,140
5,000 × 0%	0
340 × 32·5%	110
66,590	
Income tax liability	17,430
Class 4 national insurance contributions (W4)	3,870
	21,300
Payments on account	(20,200)
Balancing payment	1,100

WORKINGS

(1) Trading profit

		£
Trading profit		228,000
Capital allowances (W2)		(34,000)
		194,000

Profit share
6 April to 31 December 2017	194,000 × 9/12 × ⅓	48,500
1 January to 5 April 2018	194,000 × 3/12 × ½	24,250
		72,750

(2) Capital allowances

	£	Main pool £	Allowances £
WDV brought forward		10,000	
Additions qualifying for AIA			
False ceiling	0		
Display units	15,100		
Tiled flooring	0		
Movable partitions	17,100		
	32,200		
AIA – 100%	(32,200)	0	32,200
WDA – 18%		(1,800)	1,800
WDV carried forward		8,200	
Total allowances			34,000

Tutorial note: Expenditure forming part of a building, such as the false ceiling and tiled flooring, does not qualify as plant. The display units and the movable partition walls are not treated as forming part of the shop building, and therefore do qualify as plant.

(3) Tax band

- Alfred's basic rate tax band is extended by £2,400 (1,920 × 100/80) to £35,900 (33,500 + 2,400) as a result of making the gift aid donations.

(4) Class 4 national insurance contributions

- Class 4 NIC for the tax year 2017–18 is £3,870 ((45,000 – 8,164 = 36,836 × 9%) + (72,750 – 45,000 = 27,750 × 2%)).

(b) Self-assessment

(i) Latest date

Unless the return is issued late, the latest date when Alfred can file his self-assessment tax return online for the tax year 2017–18 is 31 January 2019.

(ii) Records retention

As Alfred was in business during the tax year 2017–18, all of his tax records (both business and non-business) must be retained until five years after 31 January following the tax year, which is 31 January 2024.

Answer 33 EDWARD KING

Item   Answer   Justification

1   Mileage allowance received (12,000 × 35p)   4,200
    Less: 10,000 miles × 45p   4,500
            2,000 miles × 25p   500
                                                       ─────
                                                                            (5,000)
                                                                            ─────
                                                                            (800)

2   Edward will have been taxed on benefits totalling £3,120 (5,200 × 20% × 3) for the tax years 2014–15, 2015–16 and 2016–17.

    The benefit for the acquisition of the home entertainment system in the tax year 2017–18 is the market value at the date of gift of **£2,200**, as this is greater than £2,080 (5,200 – 3,120).

3   • £9,560

    Pension contributions (179,000 × 4%)   7,160
    Charitable payroll deductions (12 × 200)   2,400
                                                                           ─────
                                                                            9,560

4   £
    33,500 × 20%   6,700
    116,500 × 40%   46,600
    21,670 × 45%   9,751
    ─────
    171,670
    ─────

    Income tax liability   63,051
    Tax suffered at source – PAYE   (62,600)
                                                                          ──────
    Balancing payment   **451**

5

If Edward completes a paper tax return by 31 October 2018, then HM Revenue and Customs will prepare a self-assessment tax computation on his behalf	CORRECT	
Edward's tax records must be retained until 31 January 2022		INCORRECT

Answer 34 SOPHIE SHAPE

(a) Schedule of tax payments

Due date	Tax year	Payment	£
31 July 2018	2017–18	Second payment on account	3,240
(5,240 + 1,240) × 50%			
31 January 2019	2017–18	Balancing payment	6,128
12,608 (6,100 + 1,480 + 4,880 + 148) – (3,240 × 2)			
31 January 2019	2018–19	First payment on account	3,790
(6,100 + 1,480) × 50%			

Tutorial notes:

(1) The second payment on account for 2017–18 is based on Sophie's income tax and class 4 NIC liability for 2016–17.

(2) The balancing payment for 2017–18 includes the capital gains tax liability for that year and the class 2 NIC liability for that year.

(3) The first payment on account for 2018–19 is based on Sophie's income tax and class 4 NIC liability for 2017–18.

(b) Implications of reducing payments to nil without justification

- If Sophie's payments on account for 2017–18 were reduced to nil, then she would be charged interest on the payments due of £3,240 from the relevant due date to the date of payment.

- A penalty based on the amount of underpaid tax will be charged as the claim to reduce the payments on account to nil would appear to be made fraudulently or negligently.

(c) Latest date for filing self-assessment return

- Unless the return is issued late, the latest date when Sophie can file a paper self-assessment tax return for 2017–18 is 31 October 2018.

(d) Compliance check

Notification

- If HM Revenue and Customs (HMRC) intend to carry out a compliance check into Sophie's 2017–18 tax return they will have to notify her within 12 months of the date when they receive the return.

Possible reasons

- HMRC has the right to carry out a compliance check as regards the completeness and accuracy of any return, and such a check may be made on a completely random basis.

- However, compliance checks are generally carried out because of a suspicion that income has been undeclared or because deductions have been incorrectly claimed. For example, where accounting ratios are out of line with industry norms.

Answer 35 FERGUS

(1) Income tax liability 2017–18

	£	
Director's remuneration	18,000	½
Dividends	40,000	½
	58,000	
Personal allowance	(11,500)	½
Taxable income	46,500	

Income tax

£		
6,500 (18,000 – 11,500) × 20%	1,300	½
5,000 × 0%	0	½
22,000 (33,500 – 6,500 – 5,000) × 7.5%	1,650	1
13,000 (40,000 – 22,000 – 5,000) × 32.5%	4,225	1
46,500		
Income tax liability	7,175	

(2) National insurance contributions (NIC) 2017–18

	£	
Employee class 1 ((18,000 – 8,164) × 12%)	1,180	1
Employer's class 1 ((18,000 – 8,164) × 13·8%)	1,357	1
Employment allowance – not available	(0)	1
	1,357	

(3) Corporation tax liability of incorporated business for the year ended 5 April 2018

	£	
Trading profit	100,000	½
Director's remuneration	(18,000)	½
Taxable total profits	82,000	
Corporation tax (82,000 × 19%)	15,580	½

(4) The total tax and NIC cost if Fergus incorporates his business is £25,292 (7,175 + 1,180 + 1,357 + 15,580). ½

(5) Therefore, if Fergus incorporated his business there would be an overall saving of tax and NIC for the year of £7,971 (33,263 – 25,292) compared to continuing on a self-employed basis. ½

Answer 36 WAI

(a) Taxable income 2017–18

Employment income	£	
Salary (10,200 × 12)	122,400	½
Bonus	8,100	1
Mileage allowance (W1)	2,763	W1
Car benefit (W2)	1,326	W2
Incidental expenses	0	½
Mobile telephone (400 × 20%)	80	1
Living accommodation – Annual value	4,600	½
– Additional benefit (W3)	2,470	W3
	141,739	
Personal allowance	0	1
Taxable income	141,739	

Tutorial notes:

(1) The bonus of £4,600 will have been treated as being received during 2016–17 as Wai became entitled to it during that tax year. Similarly, the bonus of £2,900 will be treated as received during 2018–19.

(2) The exemption for mobile telephones does not apply to the second telephone.

(3) No personal allowance is available as Wai's adjusted net income of £141,739 exceeds £123,000.

WORKINGS

(1) Mileage allowance

	Miles	£	
Reimbursement (13,860 × 55p)		7,623	½
Business mileage			
Ordinary commuting	0		½
Travel to clients' premises	8,580		½
Temporary workplace	2,860		½
	11,440		
Tax free amount			
10,000 miles × 45p		(4,500)	½
1,440 miles × 25p		(360)	½
Taxable benefit		2,763	

Tutorial note: Travel to the temporary workplace qualifies as business mileage because the 24-month limit was not exceeded.

(2) Car benefit

- The relevant percentage for the car benefit is 17% because the motor car has CO_2 emissions between 76 and 94 grams per kilometre. ½

- The motor car was available during the period 1 September 2017 to 5 April 2018, so the benefit for 2017–18 is £1,326 (13,370 × 17% × $^7/_{12}$). 1

(3) Living accommodation additional benefit

- The benefit is based on the cost of the property plus subsequent improvements incurred before the start of the tax year.

	£
Cost	149,600
Improvements (14,400 + 9,800)	24,200
	173,800
Limit	(75,000)
	98,800

- The additional benefit is therefore £2,470 (98,800 × 2.5%).

(b) Form P60

- Form P60 will show Wai's taxable earnings, income tax deducted, final tax code, national insurance contributions (NIC), and Qaz plc's name and address.
- This form should have been provided to Wai by 31 May 2018.

Form P11D

- Form P11D will detail the expenses and benefits provided to Wai.
- This form should have been provided to Wai by 6 July 2018.

Answer 37 DANIEL, FRANCINE AND GREGOR

(a) Daniel – Trading income assessment 2017–18

	£
1 May to 31 October 2017 (96,000 × ¼ × 6/12)	12,000
1 November 2017 to 5 April 2018 (180,000 × ¼ × 5/12)	18,750
	30,750

Tutorial note: *Daniel joined as a partner on 1 May 2017, so the commencement rules apply to him for 2017–18. The basis period is the 11-months from 1 May 2017 to 5 April 2018.*

(b) Francine – Beneficial loan 2017–18

	£	£
½ (96,000 + (96,000 + 14,000)) × 2·5% × 8/12		1,717
Interest paid – 96,000 × 1·5% × 2/12	240	
– 110,000 × 1·5% × 6/12	825	
		(1,065)
Taxable benefit		652

(c) **Gregor – Trading loss carried forward**

		£	
Trading loss		68,800	
2016–17	– Claim against total income (14,700 + 4,600 + 1,300)	(20,600)	1
2017–18	– Claim against total income	(900)	1
	– Claim against chargeable gain (W)	(14,500)	W ½
Loss carried forward		32,800	½

WORKING

Claim against chargeable gain

The loss relief claim against the chargeable gain is restricted to £14,500 (chargeable gain of 17,400 less the capital loss brought forward of 2,900).   1

                                                                                                    4

Tutorial note: *Gregor can claim loss relief against his total income (under s.64 ITA 2007) and chargeable gains (under s.261B TCGA 1992) for 2016–17 and 2017–18.*   **10**

Answer 38 SAMSON & DELILAH

(a) **Samson – Income tax computation 2017–18**

	£	
Employment income – Salary	112,000	½
Building society interest (½ × 9,600)	4,800	½
	116,800	
Personal allowance (W1)	(3,100)	W1
Taxable income	113,700	

£		
33,500 × 20%	6,700	½
75,400 (113,700 – 4,800 – 33,500) × 40%	30,160	½
500 (savings nil rate band) × 0%	0	½
4,300 (4,800 – 500) × 40%	1,720	1
113,700		
Income tax liability	38,580	

WORKING

(1) Personal allowance

Samson's adjusted net income exceeds £100,000, so his personal allowance of £11,500 is reduced to £3,100 (11,500 – ½ (116,800 – 100,000)).   1

Delilah – Income tax computation 2017–18

	£	
Employment income		
Salary	184,000	½
Charitable payroll deductions (250 × 12)	(3,000)	½
	181,000	
Car benefit (W1)	24,192	W1
Chauffeur	9,400	½
	214,592	
Professional subscription	(450)	½
Golf club membership	0	½
	214,142	
Trading profit ((93,600 – 8,000) × 40%)	34,240	1
Building society interest (½ × 9,600)	4,800	½
	253,182	
Interest paid	(6,200)	½
	246,982	
Personal allowance	0	½
Taxable income	246,982	

£		
39,500 (W2) × 20%	7,900	½
116,500 × 40%	46,600	½
90,982 × 45%	40,942	½
246,982		
Income tax liability	95,442	

Tutorial notes:

(1) The car benefit does not cover the cost of a chauffeur, so this is an additional benefit.

(2) The golf club membership is not an allowable deduction despite being used to entertain customers.

(3) The loan interest paid of £6,200 is deductible because the loan was used by Delilah for a qualifying purpose.

(4) No personal allowance is available as Delilah's adjusted net income of £240,982 (246,982 – 6,000) exceeds £123,000.

(5) No savings income nil rate band is available as Delilah is an additional rate taxpayer.

WORKINGS

(1) Car benefit

- The relevant percentage is 36% (18% + ((185 – 95) ÷ 5 × 1%)). — 1

- The motor car was available throughout 2017–18 (even though Delilah was unable to use it for a period due to her accident), so the benefit is £24,192 (67,200 × 36%). — ½

TAXATION (TX-UK) (F6) – REVISION QUESTION BANK

    (2)   **Tax bands**

Delilah's basic and higher rate tax bands are extended by £6,000 to £39,500 (33,500 + 6,000) and £156,000 (150,000 + 6,000) in respect of the charitable gift aid donations.   ½

                                                                                                              13

(b)   **Building society interest**

Transferring the building society deposit account into Delilah's sole name would have saved Samson income tax of £2,680 ((4,800 × 60%) – (500 × 40%)).   2

                                                                                                              15

Tutorial note: *Because of the loss of the personal allowance, Samson's effective marginal rate of income tax is 60%, but this is offset by the loss of the nil rate band saving at 40%.*

Answer 39   GEORGE

(a)   **Indicators of employee status**

- The contract is for a relatively long period of time.   ½ each
- George is required to do the work personally.   max 2
- Xpee plc exercises control over George via the weekly meetings and instructions.
- George will not incur any significant expenses in respect of the contract.
- George will only be working for Xpee plc.
- George is not taking any significant financial risk.

(b)   **Income tax liability 2017–18**

	£	
Income	40,000	½
Capital allowances (3,600 × 100%)	(3,600)	1
Trading profit	36,400	
Personal allowance	(11,500)	½
Taxable income	24,900	
Income tax liability at 20%	4,980	½

National insurance contributions 2017–18

- Class 2 national insurance contributions will be £148 (52 × 2·85).   ½
- Class 4 national insurance contributions will be £2,541 ((36,400 – 8,164) × 9%).   1

                                                                                                               4

(c)   **Treatment as employee**

(i)   *Why income tax liability will be payable earlier*

- If George is treated as employed in respect of his contract with Xpee plc, then the company will be required to deduct tax under PAYE every time that George is paid during 2017–18.   1

- If treated as self-employed, George's income tax liability for 2017–18 would not be payable until 31 January 2019.   1

                                                                                                                2

(ii) Additional NIC suffered

- If George is treated as employed in respect of his contract with Xpee plc, then his Class 1 national insurance contributions for 2017–18 will be £3,820 ((40,000 – 8,164) × 12%).   1½

- The additional amount of national insurance contributions which he will suffer for 2017–18 is therefore £1,131 (3,820 – 148 – 2,541).   ½

             2
             10

Tutorial note: *For income tax purposes, capital allowances will reduce employment income in the same way that they are deducted in calculating the trading profit. However, there is no deduction for capital allowances when it comes to calculating Class 1 national insurance contributions.*

Answer 40 PATIENCE

Income tax computation 2017–18

	£	
Employment income		
Salary (3,750 × 9)	33,750	1
Pension contributions – Patience (33,750 × 6%)	(2,025)	½
– Employer	0	½
	31,725	
School place	540	1
Long-service award	0	½
Beneficial loan	0	½
Trading profit (W1)	16,100	W1
Pensions (2,025 + 6,000 + 2,725)	10,750	1
Property business profit (W3)	3,500	W3
	62,615	
Personal allowance	(11,500)	½
Taxable income	51,115	

£		
38,000 (W4) × 20%	7,600	W4 ½
13,115 × 40%	5,246	½
51,115		
Income tax liability	12,846	

Tutorial notes:

(1) A non-cash long-service award is not a taxable benefit if it is for a period of service of at least 20 years, and the cost of the award does not exceed £50 per year of service.

(2) There is no taxable benefit if beneficial loans do not exceed £10,000 during the tax year.

WORKINGS

(1) Trading profit

	£	£
Year ended 31 July 2017		14,800
Period ended 31 December 2017	6,900	
Balancing allowance (W2)	(1,900)	
		5,000
		19,800
Relief for overlap profits		(3,700)
		16,100

(2) Capital allowances

	Main pool £	Allowances £
WDV brought forward	2,200	
Addition – Laptop computer	1,700	
Proceeds (1,200 + 800)	(2,000)	
Balancing allowance	(1,900)	1,900

(3) Property business profit

	£
Rent received (3,600 + 7,200)	10,800
Expenditure (4,700 + 2,600)	(7,300)
Property business profit	3,500

(4) Tax band

Patience's basic rate tax band is extended by £4,500 to £38,000 (33,500 + (3,600 × $^{100}/_{80}$)) in respect of the personal pension contributions.

Capital gains tax computation 2017–18

		£	£
Property one	– Disposal proceeds	122,000	
	– Cost	(81,400)	
			40,600
Property two	– Disposal proceeds	98,000	
	– Cost	(103,700)	
			(5,700)
			34,900
Annual exempt amount			(11,300)
			23,600
Capital gains tax (23,600 × 28%, residential property higher rate)			6,608

Answer 41 STEVIE DEE

Net income under continued employment

	£
Salary	40,000
Assessable benefit re van	0
	40,000
Personal allowance	(11,500)
Taxable income	28,500
Income tax @ 20%	5,700
Class 1 NIC (40,000 – 8,164) @ 12%	3,820
	9,520
Net income (40,000 – 9,520)	30,480

Net income under self-employment

	£	£
Income		45,000
Use of home (£18 × 12)	216	
Motor expenses (flat rate mileage 45p × 500 × 12)	2,700	
Other expenses	3,000	
		(5,916)
		39,084
Personal allowance		(11,500)
Taxable income		27,584
Income tax @ 20%		5,517
Class 2 NIC (£2.85 × 52)		148
Class 4 NIC (39,084 – 8,164) @ 9%		2,783
		8,448
Net income (45,000 – 8,448 – 1,800 – 3,000)		31,752

Conclusion

Stevie's net income would be £1,272 higher (31,752 – 30,480) as a self-employed engineer.

TAXATION (TX-UK) (F6) – REVISION QUESTION BANK

Answer 42 BASIL AND YOKO

(a) Overall tax saving

Original tax position			Basil		Yoko	
		£	£	£	£	
Salary			96,000			
Property income						18,000
Interest			4,000			4,000
Dividends			5,000			2,000
			105,000			24,000
Personal allowance (restricted for Basil)			(9,000)			(11,500)
Taxable income			96,000			12,500
Other income	20%	33,500	6,700	6,500	1,300	
	40%	53,500	21,400			
Interest	0%	500	0	1,000	0	
	20%			3,000	600	
	40%	3,500	1,400			
Dividends	0%	5,000	0	2,000	0	
Income tax liability		96,000	29,500	12,500	1,900	

Chargeable gains (after £11,300 annual exempt amount)
10%   20,700   2,070

Total tax payable (29,500 + 1,900 + 2,070)   **£33,470**

Revised tax position			Basil		Yoko	
		£	£	£	£	
Salary			96,000			
Property income						18,000
Interest			0			8,000
Dividends			5,000			2,000
			101,000			28,000
Personal allowance (restricted for Basil)			(11,000)			(11,500)
Taxable Income			90,000			16,500
Other income	20%	33,500	6,700	6,500	1,300	
	40%	51,500	20,600			
Interest	0%	0	0	1,000	0	
	20%			7,000	1,400	
Dividends	0%	5,000	0	2,000	0	
Income tax liability		90,500	27,300	16,500	2,700	

Chargeable gains will be nil as fully covered by Basil's b/fwd losses and the annual exempt amount.

Total tax payable (27,300 + 2,700)	**£30,000**
Overall tax saving (33,470 – 30,000)	**£3,470**

(b) **Questions raised**

(i) Brought forward capital losses are only utilised to the extent that chargeable gains are not covered by the annual exempt amount. Basil will therefore have capital losses to carry forward of £9,300 (30,000 – (32,000 – 11,300)).

(ii) Even though Basil's dividend income is fully covered by the dividend allowance so taxable at a nil rate, it would still be worthwhile transferring some of the shareholdings to Yoko. If the holdings were rearranged such that £1,000 of dividend income went to Yoko instead of Basil, then his personal allowance would not be restricted, resulting in a further tax saving of £200 (£500 × 40%).

Answer 43 WINSTON KING

Item   Answer   Justification

1 *CGT liability 2017–18 (No sale of business)*

		£
Chargeable gain on painting		45,960
Annual exempt amount		(11,300)
		34,660
CGT liability:	11,810 × 10%	1,181
	22,850 × 20%	4,570
		5,751

2 Freehold shop (140,000 – 80,000)   **60000**

3

	£
Painting	45,960
Capital loss on freehold warehouse (102,000 – 88,000)	(14,000)
	31,960
Annual exempt amount	(11,300)
	20,660

Tutorial note: *The capital loss on the sale of the freehold warehouse and the annual exempt amount are set against the chargeable gain from the sale of the painting as this saves CGT at the higher rate of 20%.*

4 No effect. Winston has £11,810 (33,500 – 21,690) of his basic rate tax band unused.

The unused basic rate tax band of £11,810 is set against the gain qualifying for entrepreneurs' relief of £60,000 even though this has no effect on the 10% tax rate. If Winston's income was £10,000 higher there would still be no effect.

5	Chattels may be defined as tangible moveable property, so include items such as paintings and securities		INCORRECT
	Chattels are exempt from CGT if they are wasting assets	CORRECT	
	Chargeable disposals of chattels cannot give rise to a CGT loss		INCORRECT
	Marginal relief can apply to the gain on disposal of a chattel if the sale proceeds are less than £6,000	CORRECT	

Tutorial note: *Securities are not tangible property so are not generally regarded as chattels. Disposals of non-exempt chattels can give rise to a loss for CGT purposes.*

Answer 44 AOM AND LEROY

Item	Answer	Justification		
1	C	Disposal proceeds		213,000
		Cost		(184,000)
				29,000
		Rollover relief		(0)
				29,000

No rollover relief is available as the amount not reinvested of £45,000 (213,000 – 168,000) exceeds the chargeable gain.

2	B	Disposal proceeds		180,000
		Cost		(113,000)
				67,000
		Rollover relief (67,000 – 12,000)		(55,000)
				12,000

The sale proceeds are not fully reinvested, and so £12,000 (180,000 – 168,000) of the chargeable gain cannot be rolled over.

3	D	The gift gives rise to a chargeable disposal, for which the mid-price is used as market value, and the cost is established by reference to the share pool (neither FIFO nor LIFO).

REVISION QUESTION BANK – TAXATION (TX-UK) (F6)

4	D	Disposal proceeds		83,400
		Cost (W)		(20,400)
				63,000

WORKING   Share pool

	Number	Cost £
Purchase 1 March 2009	20,000	19,800
Purchase 20 July 2013	8,000	27,800
	28,000	47,600
Disposal 23 October 2017 (47,600 × 4,000 ÷ 28,000)	(4,000)	(6,800)
	24,000	40,800
Disposal 2 April 2018 (40,800 × 12,000 ÷ 24,000)	(12,000)	(20,400)
Balance carried forward	12,000	20,400

5   C   Delaying the sale of the 12,000 shares in Jerk-Chic plc until 6 April 2018 would have deferred the due date for the related capital gains tax liability from 31 January 2019 to 31 January 2020.

Answer 45 MICK STONE

Item Answer   Justification

1   £ **165000**

	£	£
Disposal proceeds		522,000
Cost	258,000	
Enhancement expenditure – Extension	99,000	
– Floor	0	
		(357,000)
Chargeable gain		165,000

Tutorial note: *The cost of replacing the warehouse's floor is revenue expenditure as the floor is a subsidiary part of the property.*

2

☑ Whether it was purchased before or after 19 May 2016

☑ Whether it cost more or less than £522,000

Tutorial note: *The acquisition date of the replacement warehouse is required, since relief will only be available if this is after 19 May 2016 (one year before the date of disposal), and the cost of the replacement warehouse is required, since relief will be restricted if the sale proceeds of £522,000 have not been fully reinvested.*

3			£
	Disposal proceeds		81,700
	Cost: 167,400 × (81,700 ÷ (81,700 + 268,000))		(39,109)
	Chargeable gain		**42,591**

4   £ **3137400**

	£
Disposal proceeds	3,675,000
Cost (Working)	(537,600)
Chargeable gain	3,137,400

WORKING – Share pool

	Number	Cost £
Purchase June 2009	500,000	960,000
Bonus issue December 2014 500,000 × 3/2	750,000	0
	1,250,000	960,000
Disposal September 2017 960,000 × 700,000 ÷ 1,250,000	(700,000)	(537,600)
Balance carried forward	550,000	422,400

5   A

	£
Deemed proceeds (24,000 × ½ (6.98 + 7.10))	168,960
Cost	(76,800)
Chargeable gain	92,160

Answer 46 PATRICK AND EMILY GRANT

Item Answer Justification

1   B   The UK ties are having a house in the UK which is made use of, and being in the UK for more than 90 days during the previous two tax years.

Tutorial note: *For the tax year 2017–18, Patrick and Emily have spent too long in the UK to be automatically treated as non-resident, and will not automatically be treated as resident because they do not meet the only home test.*

2   B

	£
Disposal proceeds (8,000 at £11·50)	92,000
Cost (8,000 at £1·00)	(8,000)
Chargeable gain	84,000
Annual exempt amount	0
Taxable gain	84,000

The disposal proceeds are based on £11·50 per share, as given the need for a quick sale there is no reason to believe that this is not a bargain at arm's length.

3	C	Capital gains tax (70,000 × 10%)	7,000
		Net of tax proceeds (70,000 + 8,000 – 7,000)	71,000

The disposal will qualify for entrepreneurs' relief as Emily is a director of Shore Ltd, Shore Ltd is a trading company, and her shareholding of 8% (8,000 ÷ 100,000 × 100) is more than the minimum required holding of 5%.

The £8,000 original cost is not a current cash flow in establishing the net of tax proceeds.

			£
4	A	Disposal proceeds (32,000 at £2·88)	92,160
		Cost (75,600 × 32,000 ÷ 54,000)	(44,800)
			47,360
		Patrick – 50%	23,680
		Annual exempt amount	(11,300)
			12,380
		Capital gains tax (12,380 × 10%)	1,238

5   D   Although Patrick and Emily will have the same chargeable gain as each other, the taxable amount will differ as Emily has already utilised her annual exempt amount. Emily has income of £46,400 so will suffer capital gains tax at 20% whereas Patrick's liability will only be calculated at 10%.

Answer 47 RUBY

(a)   Capital gains tax liability 2017–18

		£	
Chargeable gain on investment property		45,800	
Annual exempt amount		(11,300)	½
		34,500	
Capital gains tax:	15,900 (33,500 – 17,600) × 10%	1,590	1
	18,600 (34,500 – 15,900) × 20%	3,720	½
		5,310	2

(b) Disposal of shareholding in Pola Ltd

Ordinary shares in Pola Ltd	£	
Disposal proceeds	61,000	½
Cost	(23,700)	½
Chargeable gain qualifying for entrepreneurs' relief	37,300	
Other chargeable gain		
Investment property	45,800	½
Annual exempt amount	(11,300)	1
	34,500	
Capital gains tax: (37,300 × 10%)	3,730	1
(34,500 × 20%)	6,900	1
	10,630	

Tutorial note: *The chargeable gain of £37,300 qualifying for entrepreneurs' relief reduces Ruby's available basic rate tax band. Therefore, the chargeable gain on the investment property is taxed at 20%.*

Disposal of shareholding in Aplo plc

Ordinary shares in Aplo plc	£	
Disposal proceeds	59,000	½
Cost (40,000 × £2·18 (i.e. mid-price £2·24 – £2·12))	(87,200)	1½
Capital loss	(28,200)	
Investment property	45,800	½
Annual exempt amount	(11,300)	½
	6,300	
Capital gains tax (6,300 × 10%)	630	½

8

Answer 48 JEROME

Chargeable gains 2017–18

House

The gift of the house does not give rise to any gain or loss because it is a transfer between spouses. ½

Reward Ltd

	£	
Deemed proceeds	98,400	½
Cost	(39,000)	½
	59,400	
Gift relief (W1)	(50,600)	W1
Chargeable gain	8,800	

WORKING

(1) Gift relief

Gift relief is restricted to £50,600 (59,400 × 460,000 ÷ 540,000), being the proportion of chargeable business assets to chargeable assets. 1½

Antique bracelet

	£	
Disposal proceeds	12,200	½
Cost	(2,100)	½
Chargeable gain	10,100	

This is lower than the maximum gain of £10,333 ($^5/_3$ × (12,200 – 6,000)). 1

Land

	£	
Disposal proceeds	78,400	½
Cost	(26,460)	W1
Chargeable gain	51,940	

WORKING

(1) Cost

The cost relating to the nine acres of land gifted is £26,460 (37,800 × 78,400 ÷ (78,400 + 33,600)). 1½

7

(b) Base cost for CGT purposes

- The house has a base cost of £112,800. 1
- The 12,000 £1 ordinary shares in Reward Ltd have a base cost of £47,800 (98,400 – 50,600). 1
- The bracelet has a base cost of £12,200. ½
- The nine acres of land have a base cost of £78,400. ½

3

10

Answer 49 SAM SHIRE

Item   Answer   Justification

1

Since Sam has already invested £4,000 into a cash ISA, he can invest a maximum of £16,000 (20,000 – 4,000) into a stocks and shares ISA for the tax year 2017–18	CORRECT	
Dividend income received within a stocks and shares ISA is exempt from income tax, only chargeable gains are taxable		INCORRECT

TAXATION (TX-UK) (F6) – REVISION QUESTION BANK

2

		£
Value transferred		450,000
Annual exemption 2017–18		(3,000)
Gross chargeable transfer		447,000
IHT liability	325,000 × 0%	0
	122,000 × 20%	**24400**

3
- £30,500

		£
Net chargeable transfer		447,000
IHT liability	325,000 × 0%	0
	122,000 × ²⁰⁄₈₀	30,500
Gross chargeable transfer		477,500

4   The potentially exempt transfer made on 20 December 2016 will utilise **£194,000** (200,000 less annual exemptions for the tax years 2015–16 and 2016–17) of the nil rate band of £325,000.

5
- ☑ Inheritance tax will be payable at a rate of 40% on transfers above the nil rate band
- ☑ The inheritance tax liability can be reduced by 40% taper relief

Answer 50 PERE JONES

Item   Answer   Justification

1   D

		£
Value transferred		320,000
Marriage exemption	5,000	
Annual exemptions 2005–06	3,000	
2004–05	3,000	
		(11,000)
Potentially exempt transfer		309,000

2   B

		£
IHT liability	325,000 × 0%	0
	(380,000 – 325,000) × 40%	22,000
Taper relief reduction – 60%		(13,200)
		8,800

Tutorial note: *The gift is a potentially exempt transfer that becomes chargeable as a result of Pere dying within seven years of making it.*

REVISION QUESTION BANK – TAXATION (TX-UK) (F6)

			£
3	C	Value of estate	880,000
		Spouse exemption (½ × 880,000)	(440,000)
		Chargeable estate	440,000
		IHT liability	
		440,000 × 40%	176,000

Tutorial note: *The IHT liability for the death estate is all at 40% as the nil rate band was fully utilised by the lifetime transfer now chargeable.*

4   D   Gifts from grandparents are exempt only up to £2,500. Gifts from siblings (and other non-ancestral relatives or unrelated parties) are exempt only up to £1,000.

5   B   The due date is 30 September 2018, being six months after the end of the month in which the donor died.

However, if the personal representative files the estate returns earlier, then the IHT will also be payable at this earlier date.

Answer 51 AFIYA

Item	Answer	Justification

1   D   Gift to husband is exempt as a transfer to spouse.
Two of the gifts to her nieces are exempt as small gifts under £250.

			£
2	C	Value of shares held before the transfer (8,000 × £8)	64,000
		Value of shares held after the transfer (1,500 × £3)	(4,500)
		Value transferred	59,500

				£
3	B	Net chargeable transfer		400,000
		Inheritance tax (IHT) liability	325,000 × 0%	0
			75,000 × $^{20}/_{80}$	18,750
		Gross chargeable transfer		418,750

			£
4	A	Value of estate	620,000
		Spouse exemption	(150,000)
		Chargeable estate	470,000
		IHT liability (470,000 × 40%)	188,000

Tutorial note: *The IHT liability is all at 40% as the nil rate band was fully utilised by the lifetime gifts.*

TAXATION (TX-UK) (F6) – REVISION QUESTION BANK

5   C   The due date for the IHT liability arising on the chargeable lifetime transfer payable by Afiya (per the question) was 31 July 2017, being six months from the end of the month in which the gift was made. The due date for the additional liability arising on death is 31 May 2018, being six months after the end of the month in which the donor died, payable by the trustee(s).

Answer 52 KENDRA OLDER

Item   *Answer*   *Justification*

1   C

	£
Potentially exempt transfer	247,000
Inheritance tax liability	
185,000 (325,000 – 140,000) × 0%	0
62,000 (247,000 – 185,000) × 40%	24,800
	24,800

2   £ 1624000

	£
Property	970,000
Building society deposits	387,000
Individual savings accounts	39,000
Savings certificates	17,000
Proceeds of life assurance policy	225,000
	1,638,000
Funeral expenses	(14,000)
Chargeable estate	1,624,000

3   B   The chargeable lifetime transfer made on 20 June 2010 is not relevant when calculating the inheritance tax on the death estate as it was made more than seven years before the date of Kendra's assumed death.

Therefore, only the potentially exempt transfer made on 5 October 2016 is taken into account, and this utilises £247,000 of the nil rate band for the tax year 2017–18.

4

The potential benefit of the residence nil rate band would be lost	YES	
Capital gains tax of £48,720 would be payable	YES	
Capital gains tax of £31,320 would be payable		NO
No capital gains would be payable as a transfer on death is an exempt disposal		NO

The residence nil rate band is only available for transfers on death of qualifying property.

Tutorial note: *As the property is not expected to increase in value in the near future, there is no inheritance tax benefit in making a lifetime gift. Kendra would need to live for three more years for taper relief to be available.*

A lifetime gift would result in a capital gains tax liability of £48,720 (174,000 × 28%) for 2017–18.

A transfer on death would be an exempt disposal, but this would not apply if Kendra made the transfer as a lifetime gift.

5

The IHT on her estate would be reduced		FALSE
The IHT on her estate would be unchanged	TRUE	
There may be an IHT benefit by avoiding a further charge when the children die	TRUE	
This would only be beneficial if Kendra's children were to die within seven years of Kendra's death		FALSE

Tutorial note: *It can be beneficial to skip a generation so that gifts are made to grandchildren rather than children, particularly if the children already have significant assets. This avoids a further charge to inheritance tax when the children die. Gifts will then only be taxed once before being inherited by the grandchildren, rather than twice.*

Answer 53 TOBIAS

Item   Answer   Justification

1

	£	£
Property		660,000
Interest-only mortgage		(14,300)
		645,700
Portfolio of ordinary shares		92,600
Motor car		21,900
		760,200
Credit card debts	9,400	
Medical costs	0	
Funeral expenses	5,800	
		(15,200)
Chargeable estate		**745,000**

Tutorial note: *The promise to pay the friend's medical costs is not deductible as it is not legally enforceable.*

2   £ **138000**

Inheritance tax liability	£
(325,000 + (325,000 × 40%)) × 0%	0
(800,000 – 455,000) × 40%	138,000
	138,000

Tutorial note: *The residence nil rate band is not available as Tobias is not a direct descendent.*

3   A   The gift will be a potentially exempt transfer of £89,000 (£100,000 less the marriage exemption of £5,000 and annual exemptions of £3,000 for the tax years 2017–18 and 2016–17).

4   Tax relief will effectively be restricted to the available annual allowances of **£44,000** (£14,000 (40,000 – 26,000) from 2016–17 and £30,000 (40,000 – 10,000) from 2017–18).

Tutorial note: There is no annual allowance available for 2015–16 as Tobias was not a member of a scheme in that year. Had he been a member, the annual allowance would be £40,000, but total effective relief would be capped at his total earnings for 2017–18 (£78,000, less £10,000 contributions already made).

5

Tobias must make the gifts as part of his normal expenditure out of income	YES	
The standard of living of Tobias must not be affected by the gifts	YES	
The pattern of making the gifts should be habitual	YES	
Each gift must be less than £1,000		NO

Tutorial note: There is no financial limit on the size of gifts out of income; if the other conditions met they can be regarded as exempt for IHT purposes.

Answer 54 ZOE

(a)   Importance of differentiating potentially exempt and chargeable lifetime transfers

- A potentially exempt transfer only becomes chargeable to inheritance tax (IHT) if the donor dies within seven years of making the gift.

- In contrast, a chargeable lifetime transfer is immediately charged to IHT. An additional IHT liability may then arise if the donor dies within seven years of making the gift.

(b)   Additional IHT liability arising on the chargeable transfer on death

	£	
Gross chargeable transfer (W1)	690,000	W1
IHT liability 131,000 (W2) × 0%	0	W2
559,000 × 40%	223,600	½
Taper relief reduction – 40%	(89,440)	1
	134,160	
IHT already paid (W1)	(73,000)	W1 ½
Additional liability	61,160	

WORKINGS

(1) Chargeable lifetime transfer

	£	
Value transferred	620,000	
Annual exemption 2013–14	(3,000)	½
Net chargeable transfer	617,000	
IHT liability 325,000 × 0%	0	½
292,000 × $^{20}/_{80}$	73,000	1
Gross chargeable transfer	690,000	

Tutorial note: *The potentially exempt transfer made on 7 March 2013 utilises the annual exemption for 2012–13.*

(2) Available nil rate band

	£	£	
Nil rate band – Zoe		325,000	½
– Husband (325,000 × 20%)		65,000	1
		390,000	
Potentially exempt transfer			
Value transferred	270,000		½
Marriage exemption	(5,000)		1
Annual exemptions 2012–13	(3,000)		½
2011–12	(3,000)		½
		(259,000)	
		131,000	8
			10

Tutorial note: *The gift made on 7 March 2013 is a potentially exempt transfer which becomes chargeable as a result of Zoe dying within seven years of making it.*

Answer 55 MARCUS

(a) IHT Legislation

(i) Chargeable persons

- Married couples (and registered civil partnerships) are not chargeable persons for inheritance tax (IHT) purposes, because each spouse (or civil partner) is taxed separately.   1

(ii) Married couples

- Gifts to spouses (and registered civil partners) are exempt from IHT. This exemption applies both to lifetime gifts and transfers on death.   1

- Any proportion of the nil rate band unused on a person's death can be transferred to their surviving spouse (or registered civil partner).   1

  2

(b) Additional IHT liability arising on death

14 January 2009

No additional IHT is due because the chargeable lifetime transfer (CLT) was made more than seven years before 10 March 2018.

3 February 2015

		£
Gross chargeable transfer (420,000 + 96,250)		516,250
IHT liability	(325,000 – 290,000) × 0%	0
	481,250 × 40%	192,500
Taper relief reduction (3–4 years) – 20%		(38,500)
		154,000
IHT already paid		(96,250)
Additional liability		57,750

17 March 2015

	£
Value of shares held before the transfer (100,000 × £12)	1,200,000
Value of shares held after the transfer (70,000 × £9)	(630,000)
Potentially exempt transfer	570,000
IHT liability (570,000 × 40%)	228,000

Tutorial notes:

(1) Although the CLT on 14 January 2009 was made more than seven years prior to Marcus's death, it reduces the nil rate band available against the CLT on 3 February 2015 as it was made within seven years of that transfer.

(2) Although no details are given, there would be no IHT liability in respect of Marcus's estate because this is left entirely to his spouse.

Answer 56 JAMES

(a) Inheritance tax arising on death

Lifetime transfers within seven years of death

14 May 2016

		£
Value transferred		420,000
Annual exemptions	2016–17	(3,000)
	2015–16	(3,000)
Potentially exempt transfer		414,000
Inheritance tax liability	296,000 (W1) × 0%	0
	118,000 × 40%	47,200
		47,200

James' daughter will be responsible for paying the inheritance tax of £47,200.

2 August 2016

	£
Chargeable lifetime transfer	260,000
Inheritance tax liability (260,000 × 40%)	104,000

The trust will be responsible for paying the inheritance tax of £104,000.

Death estate

	£
Chargeable estate	870,000
Residence nil rate band (2 × 100,000)	(200,000)
	670,000
Inheritance tax liability 670,000 × 40%	268,000

The personal representatives of James' estate will be responsible for paying the inheritance tax of £268,000.

WORKING

(1) **Available nil rate band**

	£	£
Nil rate band		325,000
Chargeable lifetime transfer 9 October 2010		
Value transferred	35,000	
Annual exemptions 2010–11	(3,000)	
2009–10	(3,000)	
Chargeable transfer		(29,000)
		296,000

(b) **Portion of estate to grandchildren rather than children**

Skipping a generation avoids a further charge to inheritance tax when the children die. Gifts will then only be taxed once before being inherited by the grandchildren, rather than twice.

(c) **Lifetime gifts within seven years of death**

- Even if the donor does not survive for seven years, taper relief will reduce the amount of IHT payable after three years.

- The value of potentially exempt transfers and chargeable lifetime transfers are fixed at the time they are made.

- James therefore saved inheritance tax of £20,000 ((310,000 – 260,000) × 40%) by making the lifetime gift of property.

Answer 57 BLACK LTD

(a) Group relief

- The group relief claim by Black is calculated after deducting brought forward trading losses and qualifying charitable donations.

- The maximum potential claim by Black is therefore £355,600 (396,800 − 57,900 + 21,100 − 4,400).

- White's qualifying charitable donations of £5,600 cannot be surrendered as they can be fully relieved against the company's property business profit of £26,700.

- It is not possible to surrender capital losses as part of a group relief claim.

- Only current year trading losses can be group relieved, so the maximum potential surrender by White is £351,300.

- The maximum group relief claim is therefore £351,300.

(b) Softapp Ltd

(i) Joint election with Byte-size Ltd

- A joint election should be made so that Byte-Size Ltd is treated as having made Softapp Ltd's chargeable gain.

- This will mean that Byte-Size Ltd's otherwise unused capital loss of £48,200 can be set against Softapp Ltd's chargeable gain of £61,300.

(ii) Corporation tax returns

(1) Softapp's self-assessment corporation tax return for the year ended 31 March 2018 must be submitted by 31 March 2019.

(2) It will be possible for Softapp to amend its return at any time within 12 months after the filing deadline.

(3) Errors found after the period of possible amendment should be notified to HMRC immediately. If an overpayment arising from an incorrect return is discovered, then Softapp can make a claim for relief before 31 March 2022, being four years from the end of the accounting period.

(c) Accounting period

- An accounting period will normally start immediately after the end of the preceding accounting period.

- An accounting period will also start when a company commences to trade, or otherwise becomes liable to corporation tax.

- An accounting period will normally finish 12 months after the beginning of the accounting period or at the end of a company's period of account.

- An accounting period will also finish when a company ceases to trade, when it otherwise ceases being liable to corporation tax, or on the commencement of winding up procedures.

Answer 58 HEAVY LTD

Corporation tax computation for the year ended 31 December 2017

	£
Operating profit	140,000
Depreciation	12,880
Amortisation	9,000
Deduction for lease premium (W1)	(7,380)
Capital allowances (W2)	(34,500)
Trading profit	120,000
Chargeable gain	0
Taxable total profits	120,000
Corporation tax	
FY2016 120,000 × 3/12 × 20%	6,000
FY2017 120,000 × 9/12 × 19%	17,100
	23,100

Tutorial note: *The sale of the office building does not give rise to a chargeable gain as Soft is a 75% group company.*

WORKINGS

(1) Deduction for lease premium

	£
Premium received	90,000
Less: 90,000 × 2% × (10 – 1)	(16,200)
Amount assessed on the landlord	73,800

This is deductible over the life of the lease, so the deduction for the year ended 31 December 2017 is £7,380 (73,800 ÷ 10).

Tutorial note: *As the office building has been used for business purposes the proportion of the premium assessed as income on the landlord can be deducted, spread over the life of the lease.*

(2) Capital allowances

	Main pool £	Special rate pool £	Short life assets £	Allowances £
WDV brought forward		900	37,100	21,700
Addition qualifying for AIA				
Office equipment	22,400			
AIA – 100%	(22,400)			22,400
Proceeds		(14,600)	(12,300)	
Balancing allowance			9,400	9,400
		22,500		
WDA – 100%	(900)			900
WDA – 8%		(1,800)		1,800
WDV carried forward	0	20,700		
Total allowances				34,500

Tutorial notes:

(1) *The balance on the main pool is less than £1,000 so a writing down allowance equal to the unrelieved expenditure can be claimed.*

(2) *The motor cars are all high CO_2 emission and therefore qualify for 8% writing down allowance in the special rate pool. The private use of motor car [2] is irrelevant, since such usage will be assessed on the managing director as a benefit.*

Answer 59 SOFT LTD

(a) Relief for capital losses

- When a limited company has a capital loss, it is first set off against any chargeable gains arising in the same accounting period.

- Any remaining capital loss is then carried forward and set off against the first available chargeable gains of future accounting periods.

(b) Corporation tax liabilities for the 16-month period ended 31 December 2017

	Year ended 31 August 2017 £	Period ended 31 December 2017 £
Trading profit	90,150	30,050
Capital allowances	(4,320)	(947)
	85,830	29,103
Chargeable gain	16,650	0
Taxable total profits	102,480	29,103
Corporation tax at 20% ($^7/_{12}$ × 102,480)	11,956	-
Corporation tax at 19% ($^5/_{12}$ × 102,480)	8,113	5,530
	20,069	5,530

- Trading profits are allocated on a time basis: £90,150 (120,200 × $^{12}/_{16}$) to the year ended 31 August 2017 and £30,050 (120,200 × $^4/_{16}$) to the period ended 31 December 2017.

- Separate capital allowance computations are prepared for each accounting period as follows:

	Pool £	Allowances £
Year ended 31 August 2017		
WDV brought forward	24,000	
WDA – 18%	(4,320)	4,320
WDV carried forward	19,680	
Period ended 31 December 2017		
Proceeds	(3,900)	
	15,780	
WDA – 18% × $^4/_{12}$	(947)	947
WDV carried forward	14,833	

- The capital loss of £2,900 for the period ended 31 December 2017 is carried forward.

(c) **Corporation tax computation for the year ended 31 March 2018**

The maximum amount of group relief that can be claimed is Can Ltd's trading loss of £64,700.

Tutorial note: *Greenstew Ltd cannot claim group relief from Are Ltd as this company is not a 75% subsidiary.*

	£
Trading profit	277,700
Group relief	(64,700)
Taxable total profits	213,000
Corporation tax (213,000 × 19%)	40,470

Answer 60 GREENZONE LTD

(a) **Trading profit for the period ended 31 March 2017**

	£
Operating profit	239,700
Depreciation	28,859
Repainting office building	0
New reception area	19,800
Entertaining UK customers	3,600
Entertaining overseas customers	1,840
Political donations	740
Non-qualifying charitable donations	0
Gifts to customers – Pens	660
– Clocks	910
	296,109
Capital allowances (W1)	(18,409)
Trading profit	277,700

Tutorial notes:

(1) *The extension of the office building is not deductible, being capital in nature. The building has been improved rather than repaired.*

(2) *Gifts to customers are only an allowable deduction if they cost less than £50 per recipient per year, are not of food, drink, tobacco or vouchers exchangeable for goods and carry a conspicuous advertisement for the company making the gift.*

TAXATION (TX-UK) (F6) – REVISION QUESTION BANK

WORKING

(1) Plant and machinery

	Main pool £	Special rate pool £	Allowances £
WDV brought forward	48,150	9,200	
Addition – Motor car [2]	20,400		
	68,550		
Proceeds – Motor car [3]	(8,500)		
– Motor car [4]		(12,400)	
Balancing charge		3,200	(3,200)
	60,050		
WDA – 18%	(10,809)		10,809
Addition qualifying for FYA £			
Motor car [1] 10,800			
FYA – 100% (10,800)			10,800
		0	
WDV carried forward	49,241		
Total allowances			18,409

Tutorial notes:

(1) Motor car [1] has CO_2 emissions up to 75 grams per kilometre and therefore qualifies for the 100% first year allowance.

(2) Motor car [2] has CO_2 emissions between 76 and 130 grams per kilometre and therefore qualifies for writing down allowances at 18%.

(3) The proceeds for motor car [3] are restricted to the original cost figure of £8,500.

Answer 61 OPAL LTD

(a) Self-assessment

(i) Filing date

- Cuemore's self-assessment tax return for the year ended 31 March 2018 must be submitted by 31 March 2019.

(ii) iXBRL

- If Cuemore has straightforward accounts, it could use the software provided by HM Revenue and Customs. This automatically produces accounts and tax computations in the iXBRL format.

- Alternatively, other software that automatically produces iXBRL accounts and computations could be used.

- A tagging service could be used to apply the appropriate tags to the accounts and tax computations, or Cuemore could use software to tag documents itself.

(b)   Taxable total profits for the 14-month period of account ended 31 May 2018

	Year ended 31 March 2018 £	Period ended 31 May 2018 £
Trading profit	744,000	124,000
Capital allowances (W1)	(22,320)	(38,083)
Taxable total profits	721,680	85,917

Trading profits are allocated on a time basis: £744,000 (868,000 × $^{12}/_{14}$) to the year ended 31 March 2018 and £124,000 (868,000 × $^{2}/_{14}$) to the period ended 31 May 2018.

WORKING

(1)   Capital allowances

	£	Pool £	Allowances £
Year ended 31 March 2018			
WDV brought forward		124,000	
WDA – 18%		(22,320)	22,320
WDV carried forward		101,680	
Period ended 31 May 2018			
Addition qualifying for AIA			
Machinery	90,000		
AIA – 100% × 200,000 × $^{2}/_{12}$	(33,333)		33,333
		56,667	
		158,347	
WDA – 18% × $^{2}/_{12}$		(4,750)	4,750
WDV carried forward		153,597	
Total allowances			38,083

Answer 62 SOFTAPP LTD

Corporation tax computation for the year ended 31 March 2018

	£
Operating profit	519,300
Depreciation	10,170
Amortisation	2,500
Deduction for lease premium (W1)	(2,050)
Debenture interest payable	(67,200)
Capital allowances (W2)	(48,000)
Trading profit	414,720
Property business profit (W3)	21,800
Interest income (5,600 + 2,500)	8,100
Chargeable gain	61,300
Taxable total profits	505,920
Corporation tax (505,920 × 19%)	96,125

Tutorial note: *Interest paid in respect of a loan used for trading purposes is deductible in calculating the trading profit.*

WORKINGS

(1) Deduction for lease premium

- The amount assessed on the landlord is £82,000 calculated as follows:

	£
Premium received	100,000
Less: 100,000 × 2% × (10 – 1)	(18,000)
	82,000

- This is deductible over the life of the lease, so the deduction for the year ended 31 March 2018 is £2,050 ((82,000 ÷ 10) × $^{3}/_{12}$).

Tutorial note: *The office building has been used for business purposes, and so the proportion of the lease premium assessed on the landlord can be deducted, spread over the life of the lease.*

(2) Plant and machinery

	£	Main pool £	Special rate pool £	Allowances £
WDV brought forward		50,000		
Additions qualifying for AIA				
Building costs	0			
Heating system	3,600			
Ventilation system	4,600			
	8,200			
AIA – 100%	(8,200)		0	8,200
Furniture and furnishings	29,400			
Refrigerator and cooker	1,400			
	30,800			
AIA – 100%	(30,800)			30,800
		0		
WDA – 18%		(9,000)		9,000
WDV carried forward		41,000		
Total allowances				48,000

Tutorial notes:

(1) The expenditure which is integral to the building is included in the special rate pool.

(2) It is beneficial to claim the annual investment allowance initially against this expenditure, as it would otherwise only qualify for writing down allowance at 8%. (Although in this case all additions are covered by the AIA.)

(3) Property business profit

	£
Rent receivable ((15,600 + 15,600) × 5/6)	26,000
Security deposit	0
Advertising	(600)
Insurance (1,200 × 5/12)	(500)
Repairs (12,800 – 9,700)	(3,100)
Property business profit	21,800

Tutorial note: *A security deposit, less the cost of making good any damage, is returned to the tenant on the cessation of a letting. It is therefore initially not treated as income.*

Answer 63 LONG LTD

Item   Answer   Justification

1   £ **47690**

	£	Main pool £	Allowances £
WDV brought forward		44,800	
Addition qualifying for AIA			
Lorry	36,800		
AIA – 100%	(36,800)	0	36,800
Addition – Motor car		15,700	
		60,500	
WDA – 18%		(10,890)	10,890
WDV carried forward		49,610	
Total allowances			47,690

Tutorial note: *The motor car has CO_2 emissions between 76 and 130 grams per kilometre, and therefore qualifies for writing down allowances at 18%. The private use of the motor car is irrelevant, since such usage will be assessed on the managing director as a benefit.*

TAXATION (TX-UK) (F6) – REVISION QUESTION BANK

2 In respect of the leased vehicle, £540 should be added to Long Ltd's operating profit.

Tutorial note: The leased motor car has CO_2 emissions of more than 130 grams per kilometre, so 15% of the leasing costs are disallowed. £3,600 × 15% = £540

3

	£
Operating profit	62,900
Capital allowances (900 × 100%)	(900)
Amortisation	5,000
Deduction for lease premium (68,200 ÷ 20)	(3,410)
Taxable total profits	**63,590**

Tutorial note: The balance on the main pool is less than £1,000, so a writing down allowance equal to the unrelieved expenditure can be claimed.

4 £ –34900

	£
Operating loss	(26,100)
Donations	2,800
Capital allowances	(11,600)
Trading loss (available for surrender as group relief)	(34,900)

Tutorial notes: The motor car purchased on 3 October 2017 is pre-trading and is treated as incurred on 1 January 2018. The motor car has CO_2 emissions up to 75 grams per kilometre and therefore qualifies for the 100% first year allowance.

5 B

	£
Interest income	4,300
Qualifying charitable donations	(2,400)
Taxable total profits	1,900
Corporation tax (1,900 × 19%)	361

Answer 64 E-COMMERCE PLC

(i) **Revised computation for the year ended 31 March 2018**

	£	£
Operating profit		2,102,300*
Legal fees – Issue of preference shares	80,200	
– Issue of loan notes	0	
– Renewal of long lease	14,900	
– Breach of contract	0	
– Registration of trade marks	0	
		95,100
		2,197,400
Deduction for lease premium (14,400 × $^{12}/_{15}$)		(11,520)
Capital allowances	209,200*	
Motor car [1]	0	
Motor car [2]	0	
Motor car [3] (62,100 × 10% (18% – 8%))	(6,210)	
Motor car [4] (19,800 × 82% (100% – 18%))	16,236	
Short-life asset (1,512 × $^{82}/_{18}$)	6,888	
		(226,114)
Trading profit		1,959,766
Property business profit	156,700*	
Repairs (capital in nature)	95,300	
Rent accrual – March 2018 (16,200 × $^{1}/_{3}$)	5,400	
		257,400
Loan interest receivable	42,400*	
Accrual (4,800 – 3,500)	(1,300)	
		41,100
Taxable total profits		2,258,266
Corporation tax (2,258,266 × 19%*)		429,071

*Figures provided in question

Tutorial notes:

(1) Motor cars [1] and [2] have CO_2 emissions between 76 and 130 grams per kilometre, and qualify for writing down allowances at 18%. No adjustment is therefore required.

(2) Motor car [3] has CO_2 emissions over 130 grams per kilometre, and therefore only qualifies for writing down allowances at 8%.

(3) Motor car [4] has CO_2 emissions up to 75 grams per kilometre, and therefore qualifies for the 100% first year allowance.

(4) The scrapping of the computer equipment is a disposal for capital allowances purposes. The company should therefore have received a 100% balancing allowance rather than a writing down allowance at 18%. The $^{82}/_{18}$ adjustment represents the additional 82% (100% – 18%) of the brought forward WDV which can be deducted.

(b) Why quarterly instalments were not required

- Large companies have to make quarterly instalment payments in respect of their corporation tax liability. A large company is one with annual profits in excess of £1.5 million (reduced proportionately for the number of related group companies).

- However, a company is not required to make quarterly instalment payments in the first year that it is large. Therefore, E-Commerce plc will not have been required to make instalment payments for the year ended 31 March 2018 as it was not a large company in the year ended 31 March 2017. This is because the profits of £1,360,000 were less than £1,500,000.

- For the year ended 31 March 2019, this exception will not apply. Therefore, E-Commerce plc will have to make quarterly instalment payments.

Answer 65 CAIRO LTD AND KIGALI LTD

Item Answer Justification

1

	£
Dakar Ltd loss (54,600 × 8/12)	36,400
Cairo Ltd profit (87,000 × 8/12)	58,000

Group relief is restricted to the lower figure of £ **36400** .

2

Dakar Ltd	– Trading loss	£ 27,900
	– Capital loss	0
	– Qualifying charitable donations	600
		28,500
Cairo Ltd profit (87,000 × 4/12)		29,000

Group relief is restricted to the lower figure of **£28,500**.

3

It results in earlier relief, since Dakar will not make a trading profit until at least the year ended 31 March 2019	CORRECT	
It may allow taxation at a lower effective rate		INCORRECT
It allows some utilisation of the capital loss which might not otherwise be relieved		INCORRECT
It avoids wasting all of Dakar's qualifying charitable donations for the period ended 31 March 2017	CORRECT	

Tutorial note: *Unrelieved qualifying charitable donations can be group relieved, but it is not possible to surrender capital losses in a group loss relief claim.*

4 • £57,442

	£	£
Disposal proceeds		310,000
Cost	120,000	
Enhancement expenditure	42,000	
		(162,000)
		148,000
Indexation (162,000 × 0·559)		(90,558)
Chargeable gain		57,442

5

Kigali's chargeable gain may be subject to a rollover claim in respect of a qualifying acquisition by Maputo	CORRECT	
Kigali's chargeable gain may be subject to a rollover claim in respect of a qualifying acquisition by Niamey		INCORRECT
An acquisition qualifying for rollover would need to be made during the period one year before the date of disposal to three years after the date of disposal	CORRECT	
An acquisition qualifying for rollover would need to be made during the period three years before the date of disposal to one year after the date of disposal		INCORRECT

Answer 66 RETRO LTD

(a)   Trading loss for the year ended 31 March 2018

	£	
Loss before taxation	(120,000)	
Depreciation	27,240	½
Gifts to employees	0	½
Gifts to customers	0	½
Political donations	420	½
Qualifying charitable donations	680	½
Impairment loss	0	½
Lease of motor car (4,400 × 15%)	660	1
Health and safety fine	5,100	½
Legal fees – Internet domain name	0	½
Interest payable	0	½
Capital allowances (W)	(50,420)	W
Trading loss	(136,320)	

Tutorial notes:

(1) *Gifts to customers are an allowable deduction if they cost less than £50 per recipient per year, are not of food, drink, tobacco or vouchers for exchangeable goods and carry a conspicuous advertisement for the company making the gift. Gifts to employees are an allowable deduction because the gifts will potentially be assessed on the employees as benefits.*

(2) *Interest on a loan used for trading purposes is deductible on an accruals basis.*

WORKING

Capital allowances

	£	Main pool £	Allowances £	
WDV brought forward		39,300		½
Additions qualifying for AIA				
Delivery van	28,300			½
AIA – 100%	(28,300)		28,300	½
		0		
Addition – Motor car [1]		14,700		½
		54,000		
WDA – 18%		(9,720)	9,720	½
Addition qualifying for FYA				
Motor car [2]	12,400			½
FYA – 100%	(12,400)		12,400	½
		0		
WDV carried forward		44,280		
Total allowances			50,420	

9

Tutorial notes:

(1) *Motor car [1] has CO_2 emissions between 76 and 130 grams per kilometre, and therefore qualifies for writing down allowances at 18%.*

(2) *Motor car [2] has CO_2 emissions up to 75 grams per kilometre, and therefore qualifies for the 100% first year allowance.*

(b) Taxable total profits

	Year ended 31 August 2016 £	Period ended 31 March 2017 £	
Trading profit	56,600	47,900	½
Bank interest	1,300	0	½
	57,900	47,900	
Trading loss (s.37 CTA 2010) (W)	(24,125)	(47,900)	W1
	33,775	0	
Qualifying charitable donations	(540)		1
Taxable total profits	33,235	0	

REVISION QUESTION BANK – TAXATION (TX-UK) (F6)

WORKING

Trading loss

For the year ended 31 August 2016, loss relief is restricted to £24,125 (57,900 × $^5/_{12}$).   1

    4

(c) **Unrelieved trading loss**

- The amount of unrelieved trading loss at 31 March 2018 is £64,295 (136,320 – 47,900 – 24,125).   1

- The unrelieved trading loss can be carried forward and will be relieved against the first available trading profits of the same trade.   1

    2

    15

Answer 67 LUCKY LTD

(a) **Accounting periods**

- An accounting period will normally start immediately after the end of the preceding accounting period.   1

- An accounting period will also start when a company commences to trade, or otherwise becomes liable to corporation tax.   1

    2

(b) **Corporation tax computation for the four-month period ended 31 March 2018**

	£	
Operating profit	432,600	
Advertising	0	½
Depreciation	14,700	½
Amortisation	9,000	½
Deduction for lease premium (46,800 ÷ 12 × $^4/_{12}$)	(1,300)	1½
Capital allowances (W1)	(80,291)	W1
Trading profit	374,709	
Interest income	700	½
Taxable total profits	375,409	
Corporation tax (375,409 × 19%)	71,328	½

Tutorial note: *The advertising expenditure incurred during September 2017 is pre-trading, and is treated as incurred on 1 December 2017. It is therefore deductible and no adjustment is required.*

WORKINGS

(1) Capital allowances

	Main pool £	Special rate pool £	Allowances £	
Additions qualifying for AIA				
Integral feature		41,200		½
AIA – 100%		(41,200)	41,200	½
		0		
Computer	6,300			½
Office equipment	32,900			½
	39,200			
AIA (W2) – 100%	(25,467)		25,467	W2
	13,733			
WDA – 18% × 4/12	(824)		824	1
Addition qualifying for FYA				
Motor car	12,800			½
FYA 100%	(12,800)		12,800	½
	0			
WDV carried forward	12,909			
Total allowances			80,291	

WORKING

(2) Annual investment allowance

The annual investment allowance is reduced to £66,667 (200,000 × 4/12) because Lucky Ltd's accounting period is four months long.

1

—
9
—

Tutorial notes:

(1) The expenditure which is integral to the building is included in the special rate pool.

(2) It is beneficial to claim the annual investment allowance of £66,667 initially against this integral features expenditure, as it would otherwise only qualify for writing down allowance at 8%.

(3) The computer purchased on 19 August 2017 is pre-trading and is treated as incurred on 1 December 2017.

(4) The motor car has CO_2 emissions up to 75 grams per kilometre, and therefore qualifies for the 100% first year allowance.

(c) **Record retention**

- Lucky Ltd must retain the records used in preparing its self-assessment corporation tax return until six years after the end of the accounting period, which is 31 March 2024.   1

- A failure to retain records could result in a penalty of up to £3,000 per accounting period. However, the maximum penalty will only be charged in serious cases.   1

                                                                                                                                                                        2

                                                                                                                                                                        13

Answer 68 JUMP LTD

(a) **Trading loss for the three-month period ended 31 March 2018**

	£	
Operating loss	(144,700)	
Depreciation	8,100	½
Employee training courses	0	½
Employee pension contributions	0	½
Staff party	0	½
Lease of motor car (1,200 × 15%)	180	1
Accountancy	0	½
Legal fees – Issue of share capital	3,800	½
– Renewal of short lease	0	½
Entertaining UK customers	1,700	½
Entertaining overseas customers	790	½
Political donations	800	½
Balancing charge (W)	3,330	3½
Trading loss	(126,000)	½
		10

WORKING

(1) **Capital allowances**

	Main pool £	Special rate pool £	Allowances £	
WDV brought forward	12,100	5,700		½
Proceeds – Motor car [1]		(9,300)		1
– Motor car [2]	(6,100)			½
Balancing charge		3,600	(3,600)	½
	6,000			
WDA – 18% × 3/12	(270)		270	1
WDV carried forward	5,730			
Overall balancing charge			(3,330)	3

Tutorial note: *The proceeds for motor car [1] are restricted to the original cost figure of £9,300.*

(b) Trading loss

(i) Choice of loss relief

The main factor which will influence Jump Ltd's choice of loss relief or group relief claims is the timing of the relief obtained, with an earlier claim generally being preferable.

Tutorial note: *Another possible factor is the extent to which relief for qualifying charitable donations will be lost. However Jump Ltd has not made any charitable donations.*

(ii) Maximum amount which can be relieved against total profits

- The maximum loss relief claim for the seven-month period to 31 December 2017 is £42,400, being the total profits for this period.

- The loss relief claim for the year ended 31 May 2017 is restricted to £33,250 $((78,600 + 1,200) \times {}^5/_{12})$.

(iii) Maximum amount for group relief

- The maximum amount of trading loss which can be surrendered to Hop Ltd is £23,625, being the lower of £23,625 $(63,000 \times {}^3/_8)$ and £126,000.

- Skip Ltd is not a 75% subsidiary of Jump Ltd, so no group relief claim is possible.

Answer 69 WIKI LTD

Item	Answer	Justification		
1	B		£	£
		Disposal proceeds		308,600
		Cost	171,000	
		Incidental costs of acquisition	2,200	
				(173,200)
				135,400
		Indexation allowance (173,200 × 0.330 (W))		(57,156)
		Chargeable gain		78,244

WORKING

Indexation factor is 0.330 ((278.9 − 209.7) ÷ 209.7).

2 A No rollover relief is available as the amount not reinvested of £142,600 (308,600 − 166,000) exceeds the chargeable gain.

The base cost of the factory will be £166,000.

3 B The net sale proceeds are not fully reinvested, and so £12,600 (308,600 − 296,000) of the chargeable gain cannot be rolled over.

Tutorial note: *The base cost of the office building will be £230,356 (296,000 − (78,244 − 12,600)).*

4	D	Indexation allowance is based on retail price index; it cannot be used to create or enhance a loss.
5	C	A claim must be made within four years after the end of the accounting period (or tax year for individuals) in which the gain arises

Answer 70 ACEBOOK LTD

Item	Answer	Justification			
1	B	Share pool	Number	Cost	Indexed cost
				£	£
		Purchase June 2008	24,000	25,200	25,200
		Indexation to February 2013			
		25,200 × 0.142			3,578
		Rights issue February 2013			
		24,000 × 1/5 = 4,800 at £4·30	4,800	20,640	20,640
			28,800	45,840	49,418
2		Purchase June 2008	50,000	25,000	25,000
		Indexation to March 2017			
		25,000 × 0·242			6,050
					31,050
		Disposal March 2017	(50,000)	(25,000)	(31,050)

	£
Disposal proceeds (50,000 × 1·30)	65,000
Indexed cost	(31,050)
Chargeable gain	**33,950**

3   £ **15360**

	£
Disposal proceeds	192,000
Indexed cost	(153,600)
Enhancement expenditure	(23,040)
	15,360

The cost relating to the three acres of land sold is £153,600 (196,000 × 192,000 ÷ (192,000 + 53,000)).

The cost of clearing and levelling the land is enhancement expenditure. The cost relating to the three acres of land sold is £23,040 (29,400 × 192,000 ÷ 245,000).

TAXATION (TX-UK) (F6) – REVISION QUESTION BANK

4   B   The insurance proceeds not reinvested of £16,600 (189,000 – 172,400) are an immediate chargeable gain for the year ended 31 December 2017.

Tutorial note: *The balance of the gain of £34,000 (189,000 – 138,400 – 16,600) is deferred by deducting it from the cost of the replacement property.*

5

If no insurance proceeds or other compensation is received there is no disposal for tax purposes	TRUE	
If compensation is received, a chargeable disposal arises on the date the damage occurred		FALSE
If compensation is received, a chargeable disposal arises on the date of receipt	TRUE	
If at least 90% of proceeds are applied to restoration of the damaged asset, then a no gain/no loss disposal arises		FALSE

Tutorial note: *The relevant date for disposal is the receipt of proceeds (so statements 1 and 3 are correct and 2 is incorrect). A nil gain/nil loss disposal is applicable if at least 95% of the proceeds are applied to restoration.*

Answer 71 LUNA LTD

(a)   How indexation allowance can be used

Where a company makes a capital loss

- No indexation allowance is available because it cannot be used to increase a loss.   1

Where the indexation allowance is greater than a company's unindexed gain

- The gain is simply reduced to nil because the allowance cannot be used to create a loss.   1
                                                                                                                                                                                              ─
                                                                                                                                                                                              2

(b)   Chargeable gains for the year ended 31 March 2018

(1)   *Pluto plc*

	£	
Disposal proceeds	53,400	½
Indexed cost (W1)	(16,188)	(W1) 4
Chargeable gain	37,212	

(2)   *Asteroid plc*

	£	
Disposal proceeds (cash received)	65,000	1
Indexed cost (W2)	(19,500)	(W2) 2½
Chargeable gain	45,500	8
		──
		10

Tutorial note: *No chargeable gain arises in respect of the £1 ordinary shares in Asteroid plc because this is a paper-for-paper disposal.*

WORKINGS

(1) Share pool

	Number	Indexed cost £	
Purchase June 2011	16,000	36,800	½
Indexation to May 2013			
36,800 × ((250.0 – 235.2) ÷ 235.2)		2,316	1
		39,116	
Disposal May 2013			
39,116 × (10,000 ÷ 16,000)	(10,000)	(24,448)	1
	6,000	14,668	
Indexation to October 2017			
14,668 × ((275.9 – 250.0) ÷ 250.0)		1,520	1
		16,188	
Disposal October 2017	(6,000)	(16,188)	½

4

(2) Indexed cost

■ On the takeover, Luna Ltd received cash of £65,000 (10,000 × £6·50) and new ordinary shares valued at £45,000 (10,000 × £4·50).   1

■ The indexed cost attributable to the cash element is £19,500 (33,000 × 65,000 ÷ (65,000 + 45,000)).   1½

2½

Answer 72 FLICK PICK

Item	Answer	Justification
1	C	Using the flat rate scheme to calculate its VAT liability the partnership will have paid VAT of £7,164 (59,700 × 12%) for the quarter ended 31 March 2018.
2	B	If the partnership had used the normal basis it would have paid VAT of £5,400 ((59,700 – 27,300) × 20/120).
3	A	The partnership's sales are all to members of the general public, who cannot recover the input VAT.

It may not therefore be possible to pass the output VAT on to customers in the prices charged. To the extent this is not possible the partnership would have had to absorb all or some of this amount itself as a cost.

It was therefore not beneficial for the partnership to have voluntarily registered for VAT from 1 January 2018. For the quarter ended 31 March 2018 voluntary registration reduced the partnership's profits by a maximum of £7,164 (£5,400 if the normal basis had been used).

TAXATION (TX-UK) (F6) – REVISION QUESTION BANK

4   B   Output VAT must be accounted for according to the VAT period in which the supply is treated as being made. This is determined by the tax point.

                   The basic tax point is the date when the service is completed, which will be the date that a film is screened.

                   Where payment is received before the basic tax point, then this date becomes the actual tax point. The tax point for each 25% deposit is therefore the date that it is received.

                   Invoices are issued on the same day as the basic tax point, so this is the tax point for the balance of 75%.

5   D   The annual accounting scheme still requires regular payments on account during the course of the year. The cash accounting scheme, if used, applies to both sales and purchases.

Answer 73 CLUELESS LTD

Item   Answer   Justification

1   B   Clueless can use both schemes because its expected taxable turnover for the next 12 months does not exceed £1,350,000 exclusive of VAT.

                   A company needs to be up to date with its VAT payments, and with its VAT returns, however there is not a retrospective test. Companies may also join these schemes immediately on registration.

2   B   With the cash accounting scheme, output VAT will be accounted for two months later than at present since the scheme will result in the tax point becoming the date that payment is received from customers. The recovery of input VAT on expenses will not be affected as these are paid in cash.

                   With the annual accounting scheme, the reduced administration in only having to file one VAT return each year should save on overtime costs.

                   Both schemes may be used together.

3   A   Clueless will have to pay VAT of £4,400 (22,000 × 20%) to HM Revenue and Customs at the time of importation.

                   This will then be reclaimed as input VAT on the VAT return for the period during which the machinery is imported.

                   As the supplier is based outside of the EU and not VAT registered, no VAT information would appear on the invoice.

4   D   VAT will have to be accounted for according to the date of acquisition. This will be the earlier of the date that a VAT invoice is issued or the 15th day of the month following the month in which the machinery comes into the UK.

                   The VAT charged of £4,400 will be declared on Clueless's VAT return as output VAT, but will then be reclaimed as input VAT on the same VAT return. This is known as the reverse charge procedure.

5   C   It is referred to as an acquisition rather than an import. The terms export and despatch would refer to international sales by Clueless.

Answer 74 RICHARD FAMINE

Item   Answer   Justification

1 Richard would have been liable to compulsory VAT registration when his taxable supplies during any 12-month period exceeded £85,000.

This happened on 31 October 2017 when taxable supplies amounted to £86,000 (11,000 + 11,000 + 11,000 + 11,000 + 14,000 + 14,000 + 14,000).

Registration is required from the end of the month following the month in which the limit is exceeded, so Richard should have been registered from **1 December 2017**.

2 B   Both statements are correct.

3

Ceasing to act for Richard	YES	
Reporting under the money laundering regulations	YES	
Notifying HM Revenue and Customs that Inspire Co no longer acts for Richard and the reason for this		NO
Disclosing the matter fully to Richard's successor advisors when replying to their professional clearance letter		NO

Tutorial note: *The matter is one of professional judgement, and a firm of Chartered Certified Accountants would be expected to act honestly and with integrity. If Richard refuses to register for VAT, Inspire Co would be obliged to report under the money laundering regulations (as tax evasion is a money laundering offence).*

*Inspire Co should also cease to act for Richard and notify HMRC that the firm no longer acts for Richard. However, there is **no** requirement to provide any reason for this. (Therefore to disclose the reason, without Richard's permission, would be a breach of confidentiality.)*

*The matter would need to be carefully considered when replying to a professional clearance letter from a subsequent adviser, but full disclosure is likely to breach Inspire Co's duty of confidentially to Richard and so is **not** required.*

4 D   Retailers need only issue a VAT invoice if the customer requests one.

A simplified (or less detailed) VAT invoice can be issued by a supplier where the VAT inclusive total of the invoice is less than £250.

5

- ☑ A description of the goods or services supplied
- ☑ The supplier's name, address and VAT registration number

Tutorial note: *Neither the VAT exclusive amount nor the total amount of VAT need be shown. A simplified VAT invoice must show the following information:*

- *The supplier's name and address;*
- *The supplier's VAT registration number;*
- *The date of supply (the tax point);*
- *A description of the goods or services supplied;*
- *The VAT inclusive total;*
- *The rate of VAT.*

Answer 75 WRONG LTD

Item Answer Justification

1   Output VAT: Charge to director (140 × 40%)   £56
             Input VAT: Fuel   £140

   Tutorial note: *No adjustment is required in respect of the repairs to the motor car as such input VAT can be reclaimed provided there is some business use; and the question refers only to fuel anyway.*

2   £ 53780
                                                                        £
             Sales (52,640 – 1,760)   50,880
             Group sales (1,940 + 960)   2,900
                                                                     ──────
                                                                     53,780

   Tutorial note: *The tax point for the deposit is the date of payment, so this will have been included in output VAT for the quarter ended 31 December 2017.*

3   D   Hire of photocopier (18 × 51)   918

   Tutorial note: *Refunds of VAT are subject to a four-year time limit, so in addition to the input VAT for the hire of the photocopier incurred during the quarter ended 31 March 2018, Wrong Ltd can also claim for the input VAT incurred during the period 1 January 2014 to 31 December 2017.*

4   Output VAT   £0
             Input VAT   £0
                                                                      ────
             VAT payable/recoverable   £0

   Tutorial note: *Wind Ltd's sales are exempt from VAT, so the company cannot be registered for VAT.*

5   C   £   £
             Output VAT   0
             Input VAT
             Expenses   3,120
             Advertising   380
                                                          ─────
                                                                    (3,500)
                                                                    ───────
             VAT recoverable   (3,500)

   Tutorial note: *Input VAT on services incurred prior to registration is subject to a six-month time limit, so the input VAT of £640 in respect of the advertising expenditure incurred during April 2017 cannot be recovered.*

Answer 76 DEE-COMMERCE PLC

Item   Answer   Justification

1

☑ The further default will result in a surcharge of 10% of the amount of VAT outstanding

☑ The default surcharge period will be extended to the 12-month anniversary of the VAT quarter to which the default relates

2

• Submit four consecutive VAT returns on time and pay the related VAT on time

3

DEE-Commerce plc should account for VAT on the earlier of the date when the service is completed and the date the service is paid for	CORRECT	
DEE-Commerce plc should account for VAT according to the date on the suppliers invoice showing the VAT charged		INCORRECT
Input VAT will be claimed on the same VAT return as the output VAT	CORRECT	
No input VAT can be claimed as the supplier will not have charged VAT		INCORRECT

Tutorial note: *The UK customer of an imported service will not be charged VAT by the foreign supplier (i.e. he will receive an invoice without any VAT being added).*

4   B

■ DEE-Commerce plc will be permitted to disclose the underpayment of VAT of £8,200 by entering this amount on its next VAT return as the net error is less than the limit of £10,000.

■ Default interest is not charged where voluntary disclosure can be made by entering the underpayment on the next VAT return.

5

☑ It would be 30% of the VAT underpaid

☑ It could be reduced to nil as a result of unprompted disclosure at HMRC's discretion

Answer 77 ZIM

(a) Value added tax (VAT) for the year ended 31 March 2018

		£	£	
Output VAT				
Sales	– Standard rated (115,200 × 20/120)		19,200	½
	– Zero rated		0	½
Input VAT				
Impairment losses ((780 + 660) × 20/120)		240		1
Purchases	– Standard rate (43,200 × 20/120)	7,200		½
	– Zero rated	0		½
Rent ((1,200 × 13) 20/120)		2,600		1
Telephone (2,600 × (100% – 40%) × 20/120)		260		1
Entertaining	– UK customers	0		½
	– Overseas customers (240 × 20/120)	40		½
			(10,340)	
VAT payable			8,860	

Total: 6

Tutorial notes:

(1) *Relief for impairment losses is given once six months have expired from the time when payment was due, so relief can be claimed in respect of both impairment losses.*

(2) *Rent is a continuous supply, so the tax point for the April 2018 rental invoice is the date of payment. Therefore, input VAT is recoverable in respect of all 13 rental payments.*

(3) *An apportionment is made where a service such as the use of a telephone is partly for business purposes and partly for private purposes.*

(4) *Input VAT on business entertainment is not recoverable unless it relates to the cost of entertaining overseas customers.*

(b) Flat rate scheme

Permission to use

- Zim can join the flat rate scheme from 1 April 2018 because his taxable turnover (excluding VAT) for the next 12 months is not expected to exceed £150,000. 1

Leaving

- He can continue to use the scheme until his total turnover (including VAT, but excluding sales of capital assets) for the previous year exceeds £230,000. 1

Total: 2

Tutorial note: *It is also necessary to leave the flat scheme if total turnover is expected to exceed £230,000 during the following 30 days. Although candidates are not expected to be aware of this point, equivalent marks were awarded if this was given instead of the previous year limit.*

(c) Whether flat rate scheme would have been beneficial

- Using the flat rate scheme to calculate his VAT liability, Zim would have paid VAT of £15,120 (126,000 × 12%) for the year ended 31 March 2018. — 1

- It would therefore not have been beneficial to use the flat rate scheme as the additional cost of £6,260 (15,120 – 8,860) for the year would appear to outweigh the advantage of simplified VAT administration. — 1

2

10

Answer 78 SMART LTD

(a) Registration

- Smart Ltd was liable to register for VAT from 1 November 2017 because this is the date when it signed the contract valued at £86,000. — 1

- The company would therefore have known that its taxable supplies for the following 30-day period would have exceeded £85,000. Registration is required from the start of the 30-day period. — 1

- Smart Ltd would have had to notify HM Revenue and Customs by 30 November 2017, being the end of the 30-day period. — 1

3

(b) Returns and payments

- Smart Ltd will have to file its VAT returns online and pay the VAT which is due electronically. — 1

- The deadline for filing the VAT return and paying any VAT which is due is one month and seven days after the end of each quarter (for example, on or before 7 March 2017 for the quarter ended 31 January 2017). — 1

2

(c) Tax point

- Smart Ltd will have to account for output VAT at the time that payment is received if a customer pays before the basic tax point and before an invoice is issued (for example, if a deposit is paid). — 1

- The basic tax point for services is the date when they are completed. — 1

2

(d) Cash accounting scheme

- Output VAT will be accounted for 60 days later than at present, because the scheme will result in the tax point becoming the date when payment is received from customers. — 1

- The recovery of input VAT on purchase invoices will not be affected because Smart Ltd pays these immediately after they are received. — 1

- The scheme will provide automatic relief for an impairment loss should a customer default on the payment of a debt. — 1

3

10

TAXATION (TX-UK) (F6) – REVISION QUESTION BANK

Answer 79 GARFIELD

(a) **Value added tax (VAT) return for the quarter ended 31 March 2018**

	£	
Output VAT		
Sales	22,500*	
Discounted sale (4,300 × 90% × 20%)	774	1
Equipment (12,400 × 20%)	2,480	1
Fuel scale charge	60*	
Input VAT		
Purchases	(11,200)*	
Motor car	0*	
Equipment	(2,480)	½
Impairment losses (1,400 × 20%)	(280)	1
Entertaining – UK customers	0*	
– Overseas customers (960 × $^{20}/_{120}$)	(160)	1
Motor expenses ((1,008 + 660) × $^{20}/_{120}$)	(278)	1½
VAT payable	11,416	

*Figures provided in question.   1

                                                    ───
                                                     7

Tutorial notes:

(1) *Relief for an impairment loss is only available if the claim is made more than six months from the time when payment was due. Therefore, relief can only be claimed in respect of the invoice due for payment on 29 August 2017.*

(2) *Input VAT on business entertainment is recoverable if it relates to the cost of entertaining overseas customers.*

(b) **VAT schemes**

- Given Garfield's current annual turnover of £450,000, he can use the cash accounting scheme and the annual accounting scheme, but not the flat rate scheme.   1

- The cash accounting scheme would appear to be the most beneficial scheme for Garfield to use.   ½

- The scheme will provide automatic VAT relief for the impairment losses which he is incurring.   ½

- Where credit is given to customers, output VAT could be accounted for later than at present.   ½

- The recovery of input VAT on most purchases and expenses will not be affected as Garfield pays for these on a cash basis.   ½

                                                    ───
                                                     3
                                                    ───
                                                    10

Tutorial notes:

(1) *The annual turnover limit for both the annual accounting scheme and the cash accounting scheme is £1,350,000, but for the flat rate scheme it is £150,000.*

(2) *Although the annual accounting scheme would mean only having to submit one VAT return each year (reducing the risk of late return penalties), payments on account are based on the VAT payable for the previous year. From a cash flow viewpoint, this is not beneficial where turnover is decreasing.*

SPECIMEN EXAM

Section A

Item	Answer	Justification

1   C $((45,000 - 8,164) \times 9\%) + ((82,700 - 45,000) \times 2\%) = £4,069$

2
- ☑ Reporting under the money laundering regulations
- ☑ Advising the client to make disclosure

3

	£
Personal allowance	11,500
Restriction (½ × (109,400 – 800 – 100,000)	(4,300)
Restricted personal allowance	**7200**

4   D   Lower of:
$£135,000 (180,000 \times {}^9/_{12})$
$£168,000 (224,000 \times {}^9/_{12})$

5   B $¼ \times (£970,000 \times 19\%) = £46,075$

6 $60,000 \times 2.75\% \times {}^6/_{12} = £825$ (period 1 October 2018 to 31 March 2019)

7   A ${}^5/_3 \times (8,700 - 6,000) = £4,500$
This is less than £4,900 (8,700 – 3,800).

8   C $(800,000 - 325,000) \times {}^{20}/_{80} = £118,750$

9   Only the cash gift of **£175 to Winifred** is exempt.

Tutorial note: *The exemption is £250 or less per donee per tax year.*

10   D $49,750 \times {}^{120}/_{100} \times 12\% = £7,164$

11
- ☑ A motor car suitable for private use
- ☑ A UK Government security (gilt)

12   B $20,000 - 8,000 = £12,000$

13   As Ming is in business, she must keep **both** her business and non-business records until **31 January 2024**.

14   D $105,000 - 43,000 = £62,000$

15   A

TAXATION (TX-UK) (F6) – REVISION QUESTION BANK

Section B

16 A $(240{,}000 - 25{,}000) \times 20\% = £43{,}000$

17
- ☑ Entrepreneurs' relief would have been available
- ☑ The cash gift would not have been a chargeable disposal

18 C $^1/_3 \times (497{,}000 - 152{,}600) = £114{,}800$

19 B $(11{,}300 \times 28\%) + (33{,}500 \times (28\% - 18\%)) = £6{,}514$

20 The CGT liability would have been paid later.

21 C $374{,}000 + 442{,}000 - 160{,}000 = £656{,}000$

22 Personal loan £22,400 and funeral cost £5,200

23 B $(950{,}000 - (325{,}000 - 220{,}000)) \times 40\% = £338{,}000$

24 $220{,}000 \times 40\% = £88{,}000$

25
- ☑ The gifts must be habitual
- ☑ Opal must have enough remaining income to maintain her normal standard of living

26 $((44{,}600 - 35{,}200) \times 20\%) + 1{,}600 = £3{,}480$

27 D Output VAT $415 \times {}^{20}/_{120} = £\,\boxed{69}$

Input VAT $720 \times {}^{20}/_{120} = £\,\boxed{120}$

28 A Second default during surcharge period.

29 D

30 Glacier Ltd will be required to issue a VAT invoice when **a standard rated supply** is made to **a VAT registered customer**.

Section C

31 SARAH

(1) Income tax payable 2017–18

	£	
Director's remuneration	30,000	½
Dividends	10,000	½
	40,000	
Personal allowance	(11,500)	½
Taxable income	28,500	

Income tax
£
18,500 × 20%	3,700	½
5,000 × 0%	0	½
5,000 × 7.5%	375	½
28,500		
Income tax liability	4,075	3

(2) National insurance contributions (NIC) 2017–18

	£	
Employee class 1 ((30,000 – 8,164) × 12%)	2,620	1
Employer's class 1 ((30,000 – 8,164) × 13·8%)	3,013	1
		2

Tutorial note: *Employment allowance is not available as there are no other employees liable to NIC.*

(3) Corporation tax liability of the new limited company for the year ended 5 April 2018

	£	
Trading profit	50,000	½
Director's remuneration	(30,000)	½
Employer's class 1 NIC	(3,013)	½
Taxable total profits	16,987	
Corporation tax (16,987 × 19%)	3,228	½

(4) The total tax and NIC cost if Sarah incorporates her business is £12,936 (4,075 + 2,620 + 3,013 + 3,228). ½

(5) Therefore, if Sarah incorporated her business there would be an overall extra tax and NIC cost of £673 (12,936 – 12,263) compared to continuing on a self-employed basis. ½

8

(b) Advice to Sarah

- The relatively high tax cost of Sarah incorporating her business arises because of her salary attracting both employee and employer NICs. 1

- Restricting the salary to around £8,000, and taking a correspondingly higher amount of dividends, would significantly reduce her overall tax cost. 1

  —

  2

32 SIMON

(a) Taxable income 2017–18

	£	
Employment income		
Salary	23,700	½
Living accommodation – Annual value	4,600	½
– Additional benefit (W1)	1,700	W1
– Furniture (9,400 × 20%)	1,880	1
Beneficial loan (84,000 × 4/12 × 2.5%)	700	1
	32,580	
Trading profit (W2)	8,220	W2
Property income (W4)	4,040	W4
	44,840	
Personal allowance	(11,500)	½
Taxable income	33,340	

WORKINGS

(1) Living accommodation additional benefit

(1) The benefit is based on the market value when first provided.

	£	
Market value	143,000	1
Limit	(75,000)	½
	68,000	

(2) The additional benefit is therefore £1,700 (68,000 × 2.5%). ½

Tutorial note: *The property was purchased more than six years before first being provided, so the benefit is based on the market value when first provided.*

(2) Trading profit

(1) Simon's share of the partnership's trading profit for the period ended 30 April 2018 is £10,960 calculated as follows:

	£	
Trading profit	29,700	½
Capital allowances (W3)	(300)	W3
	29,400	
Salary paid to Art (6,000 × 4/12)	(2,000)	1
	27,400	
Profit share (27,400 × 40%)	10,960	½

(2) Simon's trading income assessment for 2017–18 is £8,220 (10,960 × 3/4).   1

Tutorial note: *Simon's assessment for 2017–18 is for the period 1 January to 5 April 2018.*

(3) Capital allowances

	Motor car £	Allowances	
Addition	18,750		½
WDA – 8% × 4/12	(500) × 60%	300	1½
WDV carried forward	18,250		

Tutorial note: *The partnership's motor car has CO_2 emissions over 130 grams per kilometre and therefore qualifies for writing down allowances at 8%.*

(4) Property income

	£	£	
Rent receivable (660 × 12)		7,920	1
Council tax	1,320		½
Furniture	2,560		
		(3,880)	1
Property income		4,040	

Tutorial note: *The cost of purchasing replacement furniture (but not initial acquisition or improvements) is allowable (following the withdrawal of wear and tear allowance). Capital allowances are not given in respect of plant and machinery used in a private dwelling.*

13

(b) Advantages of choosing accounting date

- The interval between earning profits and paying the related tax liability will be 11 months longer. This can be particularly beneficial where profits are rising.   1

- It will be possible to calculate taxable profits well in advance of the end of the tax year, making it much easier to implement tax planning and make pension contributions.   1

2

15

33 NAIVE LTD

(a) Corporation tax computation for the year ended 31 March 2018

	£	
Trading profit (W1)	248,340	W1
Loan interest	32,800	1
	281,140	
Qualifying charitable donations	(900)	½
Taxable total profits	280,240	
Corporation tax (280,240 × 19%)	53,246	½

WORKINGS

(1) Trading profit for the year ended 31 March 2018

	£	£	
Profit before taxation	274,530		
Depreciation	15,740		½
Donations to political parties	400		½
Qualifying charitable donations	900		½
Accountancy	0		½
Legal fees	0		½
Entertaining suppliers	3,600		½
Entertaining employees	0		½
Gifts to customers – pens	0		½
Gifts to customers – food hampers	1,650		½
Capital allowances (W2)		48,480	W2 ½
	296,820	48,480	
	(48,480)		
Trading profit	248,340		

Tutorial notes:

(1) The only exception to the non-deductibility of entertainment expenditure is when it is in respect of employees.

(2) Gifts to customers are an allowable deduction if they cost less than £50 per recipient per year, are not of food, drink, tobacco or vouchers for exchangeable goods, and carry a conspicuous advertisement for the company making the gift.

(2) Capital allowances

		Main pool £	Special rate pool £	Allowances £	
WDV brought forward		12,400	13,600		1
Additions qualifying for AIA					
Machinery	42,300				
AIA – 100%	(42,300)	0		42,300	1
Other additions					
Motor car [1]		13,800			½
Motor car [2]			14,000		½
Proceeds			(9,300)		½
		26,200	18,300		
WDA – 18%		(4,716)		4,716	½
WDA – 8%			(1,464)	1,464	1
WDV carried forward		21,484	16,836		
Total allowances				48,480	12

Tutorial notes:

(1) Motor car [1] has CO_2 emissions between 76 and 130 grams per kilometre and therefore qualifies for writing down allowances at 18%.

(2) Motor car [2] has CO_2 emissions over 130 grams per kilometre and therefore qualifies for writing down allowances at 8%. The private use of the motor car is irrelevant, since such usage will be assessed on the employee as a benefit.

(b) Options for use of iXBRL

- If Naive Ltd has straightforward accounts, it could use the software provided by HM Revenue and Customs. This automatically produces accounts and tax computations in the iXBRL format.   1

- Alternatively, other software which automatically produces iXBRL accounts and computations could be used.   1

- A tagging service could be used to apply the appropriate tags to the accounts and tax computations, or Naive Ltd could use software to tag documents itself.   1

                                                               3

                                                               15

TAXATION (TX-UK) (F6) – REVISION QUESTION BANK

SEPTEMBER 2016 EXAM

Section A

Item	Answer	Justification

1   A   £50,000 minus the balance of the 2017–18 annual exemption (AE) of £1,000 (3,000 – 2,000 PET) minus the balance of the 2016–17 AE of £500 (3,000 – 2,500) = £48,500.

2   C   168 – (72 – 18) = 114 months.

3   C   £40,000 (2017–18) + 2014–15 £0 (contribution exceeds £40,000) + 2015–16 £3,000 (40,000 – 37,000) + 2016–17 £12,000 (40,000 – 28,000) = £55,000.

4   Nine monthly payments of 47,700 × 90% ÷ 9 = £4,770

5   £ 14000

Lili Ltd can deduct the research into competitors incurred on 6 June 2012 (£12,000) and the donation to the local school on 15 December 2016 (£2,000).

Tutorial note: *It cannot deduct the initial market research as it was incurred more than seven years before the commencement of trade, nor the costs of entertaining customers and suppliers as this is disallowable expenditure under the normal rules.*

6   D   ((45,000 – 8,164) × 9%) + ((48,000 – 45,000) × 2%) = £3,375

7   True statement: National insurance is a direct tax suffered by employees, employers and the self-employed on earnings.

Tutorial note: *Corporation tax is a tax on the profits of companies, not the turnover. Inheritance tax is a tax on the transfer of assets not income. VAT is an indirect tax not a direct tax.*

8   C   If a taxpayer submits a paper return on time, they can ask HMRC to calculate the tax due. Tax returns submitted electronically automatically calculate the tax due.

9

Eric	SATISFIES	
Fran		DOES NOT SATISFY

Tutorial note: *Eric – less than 46 days and not previously resident. Fran – resident during the previous three years, so to be automatically not resident she must be in the UK for less than 16 days.*

10   The taxable benefit is **£1,600**. The market value when first made available less the taxable benefit in respect of the private use in 2016–17 (2,000 – (2,000 × 20%) = £1,600), as this is higher than the market value at the date of transfer (£1,400).

11   C   190,000 ((500,000 – (325,000 – 300,000)) × 40%) less 40% (4 – 5 years) = £114,000

12	D	A penalty will be imposed since the payment is more than 30 days late: 1,200 × 5% = **£60** Interest will be charged from 1 February to 30 June 2019: 1,200 × 2.75% × $^5/_{12}$ = **£14**
13	A	102,800 – 10,100 – 79,400 – 6,800 = £6,500. **Tutorial note:** *A corporate trading loss may be relieved against total profits of (a) the same period and (b) the preceding 12 months. The claim may be limited to (a) only, but **not** (b) only.*
14		Deferring the CGT due date. **Tutorial note:** *The CGT due date will be the same whether the asset is split between spouses (or civil partners) or not.*
15		½ × 4,840 = £ **2420**

Section B

16		325,000 + (325,000 × 80%) = **£585,000**
17		220,000 + 43,700 = £ **263700**
18		It is the **personal representatives** of someone's estate who will be responsible for paying any IHT on the death estate and this must be done by six months after the **end of the month** of death
19	C	£0. Neither gift would have made any difference to the amount payable.
20	B	(650,000 × 40%) – 52,250 = £207,750
21	C	(138,600 + 23,400) × 0.406 (W) = £65,772 WORKING (271.7 – 193.3) ÷ 193.3 = 0.406
22	A	272,000 – (120,700 – (364,000 – 272,000)) = £243,300
23	D	The gain will crystallise at the latest of the date the replacement is disposed of, the date the replacement ceases to be used for trade purposes and 10 years from the date of the replacement's acquisition. This is therefore 10 years from the date of the replacement's acquisition on 30 September 2018.
24	B	(90,000 + (90,000 × $^2/_3$ × 6.40)) × 20,000 ÷ (90,000 + (90,000 × $^2/_3$)) = £63,200
25	D	((27,900 – 11,300) × 20%) + (142,200 × 10%) = £17,540
26	B	((8,000 + 10,000) × 4) + 13,500 = £85,500. The historic test is met by 30 September 2017. Alisa should therefore have notified HMRC by 30 October 2017, with registration effective from **1 November 2017.**
27	D	((240 × $^{20}/_{120}$) + (180 × 20%)) × 6 = £456
28	C	(456 + 624) × $^{20}/_{120}$ = £180

TAXATION (TX-UK) (F6) – REVISION QUESTION BANK

29 All businesses must make their VAT payments **electronically** and this must be done no later than **one month and seven days after the end of the quarter** (i.e. 7 May 2018).

30 **The customer's VAT registration number** is NOT required to be included on a valid VAT invoice.

Section C

Answer 31 JOE

Profits withdrawn entirely as director's remuneration

(1) *Income tax liability 2017–18*

	£	
Director's remuneration	58,108	
Personal allowance	(11,500)	½
Taxable income	46,608	

Income tax
£
33,500 × 20%	6,700	½
13,108 × 40%	5,243	½
46,608		
Income tax liability	11,943	

(2) Joe's employee Class 1 NIC for 2017–18 are £4,682 (((45,000 – 8,164) × 12%) + (58,108 – 45,000) × 2%)).   1½

(3) There is no corporation tax liability for OK-Joe Ltd as the profits are entirely withdrawn as director's remuneration.   ½

Total tax and NIC is £23,517 (11,943 + 6,892 + 4,682).   ½

Profits withdrawn as a mix of director's remuneration and dividends

(1) *Income tax liability 2017–18*

	£	
Director's remuneration	8,000	
Dividends	46,170	½
	54,170	
Personal allowance	(11,500)	½
Taxable income	42,670	

Income tax
£
5,000 × 0%	0	½
28,500 × 7.5%	2,137	½
9,170 × 32.5%	2,980	½
42,670		
Income tax liability	5,117	

(2) There will be no class 1 NIC for either Joe or OK-Joe Ltd as the earnings of £8,000 are below the NIC lower thresholds.   1

(3) *OK-Joe Ltd corporation tax liability for the year ended 5 April 2018*

	£	
Trading profit	65,000	½
Director's remuneration	(8,000)	½
Taxable total profits	57,000	
Corporation tax (57,000 × 19%)	10,830	½

(4) Total tax and NIC is £15,947 (5,117 + 10,830). The overall tax and NIC saving if Joe extracts profits using a mix of director's remuneration and dividends is **£7,570** (15,947 – 23,517).

½
½

10

Answer 32 ASHURA

(a) Advantages of 5 April accounting date

- The application of the basis period rules is more straightforward.
- There will be no overlap profits.
- The basis period in the year of cessation will be a maximum of 12 months in length, rather than the potential 23 months which could arise with a 30 April year end.

1 mark per point – max 2

(b) Trading loss for the nine-month period ended 5 April 2018

	£	
Trading loss	(3,300)	
Advertising expenditure	(800)	1
Use of office (4,350 × $^1/_5$)	(870)	1
Capital allowances (W)	(2,960)	W ½
Revised trading loss	(7,930)	

WORKING – Capital allowances

	Main pool £	Motor car £	Allowances £	
Additions				
Laptop computer	2,600			½
Motor car		19,200		½
AIA – 100%	(2,600)		2,600	1
WDA – 8% × $^9/_{12}$		(1,152) × 2,500 ÷ 8,000	360	1½
WDV carried forward	0	18,048	2,960	

6

Tutorial notes:

(1) The advertising expenditure incurred during January 2017 is pre-trading, and is treated as incurred on 1 July 2017. An adjustment is therefore required.

(2) Ashura's motor car has CO_2 emissions over 130 grams per kilometre, and therefore only qualifies for writing down allowances at 8%.

(3) The laptop computer purchased on 10 June 2017 is pre-trading capital expenditure, and is therefore treated as incurred on 1 July 2017.

(c) Commencement of trade loss relief (s72 ITA 07)

- The loss of £7,930 would be relieved against total income for 2014–15 to 2016–17, earliest year first.   1

- Ashura's total income for 2014–15 of £10,400 is already covered by her personal allowance of £11,500, so a loss relief claim against this year would not result in any tax saving.   1

2

(d) Taxable income 2017–18

	£	
Employment income		
Salary	56,200	½
Mileage allowance (3,400 × 10p (55p – 45p))	340	1
Pension contributions – Occupational	(2,800)	½
– Personal pension	0	½
Subscriptions – Professional	(320)	½
– Health club	0	½
	53,420	
Loss relief	(7,930)	1
	45,490	
Personal allowance	(11,500)	½
Taxable income	33,990	

Tutorial notes:

(1) The personal pension scheme contribution does not affect the calculation of taxable income, but will instead extend Ashura's basic rate tax band by £3,400.

(2) The health club subscription is not an allowable deduction because membership is not necessary for Ashura to carry on her employment.

(3) The loss relief cap does not apply because Ashura's trading loss is less than the greater of £50,000 and 25% of her total income.

5

15

Answer 33 TENTH LTD

(a) Tenth Ltd – Taxable total profits for the four-month period ended 31 July 2017

	£	
Trading profit	52,400	½
Balancing charge (W1)	15,300	W1 ½
Revised trading profit	67,700	
Property business income (W2)	1,500	W2
Chargeable gain (180,300 – 164,500)	15,800	1
	85,000	
Qualifying charitable donations	(800)	½
Taxable total profits	84,200	

WORKINGS

(1) Balancing charge

	Main pool £	Charge £	
WDV brought forward	12,400		½
Addition	1,800		1
Proceeds (28,200 + 1,300)	(29,500)		1
	(15,300)		
Balancing charge	15,300	(15,300)	½

(2) Property business income

	£	
Rent receivable (1,200 × 4)	4,800	½
Impairment loss	(1,200)	½
Running costs (6,300 × 1/3)	(2,100)	½
Property business income	1,500	
		7

(b) Eleventh Ltd – Tax adjusted trading profit for the six-month period ended 31 March 2018

	£	
Operating profit	122,900	½
Depreciation	2,580	½
Amortisation	2,000	½
Deduction for lease premium (W1)	(1,440)	W1 ½
Interest payable (100,000 × 5% × 6/12)	(2,500)	1
Capital allowances (W2)	(14,334)	W2
Trading profit	109,206	

WORKINGS

(1) Deduction for lease premium

	£	
Premium paid	60,000	
Less: 60,000 × 2% × (15 – 1)	(16,800)	
Amount assessed on the landlord as income	43,200	1
Deduction (43,200 ÷ 15 years × 6/12)	1,440	1

(2) Capital allowances

	£	Main pool £	Allowances £	
Addition – Motor car [1]		12,600		½
WDA – 18% × 6/12		(1,134)	1,134	1
Addition qualifying for FYA				
Motor car [2]	13,200			½
FYA – 100%	(13,200)		13,200	1
	0			
WDV carried forward		11,466		
Total allowances			14,334	
				8
				15

Tutorial notes:

(1) The first motor car has CO_2 emissions between 76 and 130 grams per kilometre, and therefore qualifies for writing down allowances at 18%.

(2) The second motor car has CO_2 emissions up to 75 grams per kilometre, and therefore qualifies for the 100% first year allowance. The private use of the motor car is irrelevant because there are no private use adjustments in respect of a company.

REVISION QUESTION BANK – TAXATION (TX-UK) (F6)

DECEMBER 2016 EXAM

Section A

Item   Answer   Justification

1   320 + 1,250 = £ **1,570**

2   C   Acasta Ltd has 75% interest in Barge Ltd and greater than 50% effective interest in Dhow Ltd.

3   B
		£
Nil rate band (NRB) at Nadia's death		255,000
Band utilised on Nadia's death (£275,400 × 50%)		(137,700)
Unused NRB on Nadia's death		117,300
Percentage of NRB unused $\frac{£117,300}{£255,000}$		46%
Tareq's NRB in 2017–18		325,000
Transfer of Nadia's unused NRB (£325,000 × 46%)		149,500
Total NRB available		474,500

4   D
	£
Proceeds	27,900
Cost (£31,320 × $^{14}/_{30}$)	(14,616)
Chargeable gain	13,284

5   A   Concessions are a relaxation or mitigation of the strict statutory position.

6   Five years (i.e. 60 months) from filing due date (i.e. 31 January following the end of the tax year).

7   C   2017–18 is the second year of trading, so assessment is based on the first 12 months.
                 Trading profit = 8,800 + ($^{6}/_{12}$ × 24,400) = £21,000
                 Class 4 NICs will be (21,000 – 8,164) × 9% = £1,155

8   A   (3,000 × 12) – (200 × 12) = £33,600

9   D   A, B and C are automatic UK residency tests. D is a combination of two of the sufficient ties tests, but is not an automatic UK-residency test.

10   **30 April 2018** is 12 months after the quarter date following the actual filing date.

11   A   (650 × 12) – 7,500 = £300
                 Deducts the rent-a-room relief limit from the rental income received as this produces a lower result than the normal property income calculation of £4,500 (7,800 – (275 × 12)).

12   C   Chelfry Ltd is a large company for the first time in its current accounting period, so does not have to pay its corporation tax by quarterly instalments.

13 A

		£
Property income		20,000
Interest		2,400
Dividends		2,400
		24,800
Personal allowance		(11,500)
		13,300
(20,000 – 11,500) × 20%		1,700
Interest	(1,000 × 0%) + (1,400 × 20%)	280
Dividends	(2,400 × 0%)	0
		1,980

14 B

	£
House	390,000
Chattels and cash	70,000
Shares in an ISA	60,000
Income tax owed	(25,000)
Total estate	495,000
Less: Spouse exemption	(100,000)
Chargeable amount	**395,000**

15 C

	£
Proceeds (MV)	98,000
Less: Cost	(41,500)
Gain before relief	**56,500**
Gift relief (balancing figure)	(45,000)
Chargeable gain (53,000 – 41,500)	**11,500**

Section B

16 Minor Ltd: Holding period – not owned for one year.
Major plc: Size of shareholding – is less than 5%.

17 A $(117,000 + (22,500 \times 7.40)) \times \dfrac{20,000}{22,500 + 22,500} = £126,000$

18 D £154,880 (½ × (£9.62 + £9.64) × 16,000 shares) (being higher than £152,000 actual proceeds).

19 **12 months**

Tutorial note: The disposal would have fallen into the tax year 2018–19 rather than the tax year 2017–18 and the due date of payment of the resultant CGT would accordingly have been 31 January 2020 rather than 31 January 2019.

20 C $(11,300 \times 20\%) + (10,600 \times (20\% - 10\%)) = £3,320$

21 A $((190,000 - 3,000) - (325,000 - (210,000 - 3,000 - 3,000))) \times 40\% = £26,400$

22 D

23 C $(100,000 \times £8) - (25,000 \times £5) = £675,000$

24 A $80 + 195 + 460 = £735$

25 B Roman: $(560,000 - 300,000) \times 40\% = £104,000$
Paris: $840,000 \times 40\% = £336,000$

26 $(24,800 + 30,100 + 42,600 + 28,700) = £126,200$

27 A $(120 \times 6) + 200 = £920$

28 D $(125,700 \times 20\%) - (56,400 \times {}^{20}/_{120}) = £15,740$

29 B

30

Period after 31 March 2018	VAT scheme
12 months	Annual accounting scheme

*Tutorial note: A company must submit their VAT returns on time and pay the related VAT on time for **12 months** in order to break out of the surcharge period. As the **annual accounting scheme** reduces the administrative compliance burden of filing quarterly returns, this may help Ardent Ltd to avoid further defaults.*

TAXATION (TX-UK) (F6) – REVISION QUESTION BANK

Section C

Answer 31 JACK

(a) **Immediate lifetime cash gift**

- The gift will be a chargeable lifetime transfer of £294,000 (£300,000 less annual exemptions of £3,000 for 2017–18 and 2016–17).   1

- No lifetime IHT will be payable because this is less than the nil rate band and, if Jack survives for seven years, there will be no additional IHT liability either.   1

- The value of Jack's estate will therefore be reduced by £300,000, which will mean an eventual inheritance tax saving of £120,000 (300,000 × 40%).   1

                                                                                                   3

Tutorial note: Although it might itself be fully exempt, the chargeable lifetime transfer will have to be taken into account when calculating any inheritance tax liability arising on any further lifetime transfers which may be made within the following seven years. After seven years, a further gift can be made to a trust.

(b) **Pension contributions**

    (i)   *Additional amount for tax relief*

- For 2017–18, £49,000 (100,000 – 11,500 – (33,500 + (500 × 12))) of Jack's income is currently taxable at the higher rate of income tax.   1

- This is less than the available annual allowances of £136,000 ((40,000 – (500 × 12)) × 4) for 2017–18.   2

- Restricting the amount of personal pension contributions to the amount qualifying for tax relief at the higher rate will minimise the cost of pension saving because each £100 saved will effectively only cost £60 (£100 less 40% tax relief).   1

                                                                                                   4

Tutorial notes:

(1)   *Unused annual allowances can be carried forward for up to three years.*

(2)   *Although Jack's approach to pension saving will maximise the available tax relief, it will mean that some carried forward annual allowances are wasted.*

    (ii)   *Unused pension allowance*

Jack will have unused allowances of £68,000 being £34,000 (40,000 – 6,000) from 2015–16 and £34,000 (40,000 – 6,000) from 2016–17 to carry forward to 2018–19.   1

Tutorial note: The pension contribution will clearly use all of Jack's remaining annual allowance for 2017–18, with the balance utilising part of the remaining allowance for 2014–15.

(c) **Maximum investment in stocks and shares ISAs**

- Jack can invest in an ISA for 2017–18 by 5 April 2018, and another ISA for 2018–19 between 6 April 2018 and 5 April 2019.   1

- The maximum possible amount which he can invest into stocks and shares ISAs during the next 30 days is therefore £40,000 (20,000 × 2).   1

                                                                                                   2

                                                                                                   10

Answer 32 ARRAY LTD

(a) Taxable benefits reporting and submission deadline

- Details of employees' taxable benefits are reported to HM Revenue and Customs using a form P11D for each employee. — 1

- The P11D submission deadline for 2017–18 is 6 July 2018. — 1

                                                                                                                 — 2

(b) Taxable benefits

Alice

- The relevant percentage for the car benefit is 22% (18% + ($\frac{115-95}{5}$)%). — 1

- The motor car was available throughout 2017–18, so the taxable benefit is £4,312 ((24,600 − 5,000) × 22%). — 2

- The fuel benefit is £4,972 (22,600 × 22%). — 1

Tutorial notes:

(1) The amount of capital contribution which can be used to reduce the list price when calculating a car benefit is restricted to £5,000.

(2) The proportion of business mileage is not relevant to the calculation of car benefit.

Buma

	£	
½ (30,000 + (30,000 − (1,000 × 12)) × 2.5%	600	2
Interest paid	(240)	½
Taxable benefit	360	

Claude

- The provision of one mobile telephone does not give rise to a taxable benefit even if the telephone is a smartphone. — 1

- The taxable benefit for the use of the home entertainment system is £160 (3,200 × 20% × ³/₁₂). — 1½

Tutorial note: *The home entertainment system has not been given to Claude, so the market value on 5 April 2018 is irrelevant.*

Denise

- Only £8,000 of the relocation costs is exempt, so the taxable benefit is £2,400 (10,400 − 8,000). — 1

- The payment of medical costs of up to £500 does not result in a taxable benefit provided the medical treatment is to assist an employee to return to work following a period of absence due to ill-health or injury. — 1

                                                                                                                 — 11

TAXATION (TX-UK) (F6) – REVISION QUESTION BANK

(c) **Class 1A NIC**

- The employer's class 1A NIC payable by Array Ltd for 2017–18 is £1,684 ((4,312 + 4,972 + 360 + 160 + 2,400) × 13.8%).

- If paid electronically, this would have been payable by 22 July 2018.

Answer 33 WRETCHED LTD

(a) **Residence**

Companies which are incorporated in the UK are resident in the UK regardless of where their central management and control is exercised.

(b) **Profits and losses for the period ended 31 March 2018**

Trading loss

	£
Trading loss	(141,200)
Advertising expenditure	(7,990)
Deduction for lease premium (34,440 ÷ 10 × $^8/_{12}$)	(2,296)
Capital allowances (W1)	(4,424)
Revised trading loss	(155,910)

Tutorial note: *The advertising expenditure incurred during April 2017 is pre-trading and is treated as incurred on 1 August 2017. It is therefore deductible, and an adjustment is required.*

WORKING

(1) **Capital allowances**

	£	Main pool £	Special rate pool £	Allowances £
Additions qualifying for AIA				
Laptops (£400 × 3)	1,200			
AIA – 100%	(1,200)			1,200
Additions – Motor car [1]		8,300		
– Motor car [2]		12,300		
– Motor car [3]			14,100	
		20,600		
WDA – 18% × $^8/_{12}$		(2,472)		2,472
WDA – 8% × $^8/_{12}$			(752)	752
WDV carried forward		18,128	13,348	
Total allowances				4,424

Tutorial notes:

(1) *The original cost of the laptops is irrelevant.*

(2) *Although motor car [1] has CO_2 emissions up to 75 grams per kilometre, it is second hand and therefore does not qualify for the 100% first year allowance. It instead qualifies for writing down allowances at 18%.*

(3) *Motor car [2] has CO_2 emissions between 76 and 130 grams per kilometre and therefore qualifies for writing down allowances at 18%.*

(4) *Motor car [3] has CO_2 emissions over 130 grams per kilometre and therefore qualifies for writing down allowances at 8%.*

Property business loss

	£	
Rent receivable (1,400 × 3)	4,200	½
Advertising	(2,100)	½
Repairs	(5,900)	½
Property business loss	(3,800)	

Capital loss

	£	
Disposal proceeds	21,400	½
Cost	(26,200)	½
Indexation allowance	0	½
Capital loss	(4,800)	

11

Tutorial note: *Where a company makes a capital loss, then no indexation allowance is available because it cannot be used to increase a loss.*

(c) **Loss reliefs**

- The trading loss of £155,910 will be carried forward and relieved against the first available trading profits of the same trade. — 1

- The property business loss of £3,800 will be carried forward and relieved against the first available total profits. — 1

- The capital loss of £4,800 will be carried forward and relieved against the first available chargeable gains. — 1

3

15

TAXATION (TX-UK) (F6) – REVISION QUESTION BANK

MARCH/JUNE 2017 EXAMINATION – Section C

Answer 31 ZHI

(a) Claim to reduce payment

- The balancing payment for 2016–17 due on 31 January 2018 cannot be reduced. ½

- A claim can be made to reduce the payment on account for 2017–18 due on 31 January 2018 by £5,040:

	£	
Current POA (27,600 + 4,204) × 50%	15,902	
Revised POA (18,000 + 3,724) × 50%	(10,862)	
Reduction	5,040	1½

2

(b) Reduction in CGT for rollover relief claim

	£	£	
Current CGT liability		12,940	½
Revised CGT liability			
Proceeds not reinvested (210,000 – 164,000)	46,000		1
Annual exempt amount	(11,300)		1
	34,700		
CGT liability (34,700 × 20%)		(6,940)	½
Reduction		6,000	

3

Tutorial note: *Equivalent marks will be awarded if the reduction is alternatively calculated as: (76,000 – (210,000 – 164,000)) × 20% = £6,000.*

(c) VAT payable

- The basic tax point for goods is the date when they are made available to the customer, which in the case of Zhi's sale is 12 December 2017. ½

- An invoice date of 1 February 2018 will not affect this because the invoice will not have been issued within 14 days of the basic tax point. 1

- Zhi therefore cannot reduce the amount of VAT payable on 7 February 2018. ½

2

(d) **Delaying payment of employee bonuses**

	£	
First employee		
PAYE (1,500 × 20%)	300	½
NIC – Employee (1,500 × 12%)	180	
– Employer (1,500 × 13·8%)	207	½
Second employee		
PAYE (5,000 × 40%)	2,000	½
NIC – Employee (5,000 × 2%)	100	½
– Employer (5,000 × 13·8%)	690	½
Reduction	3,477	

The postponed PAYE and NICs of £3,477 will be payable one month later on 22 February 2018. ½

―
3
―
10

Answer 32 PETULA

(a) **Taxable income 2017–18**

	£	
Employment income		
Salary	230,000	½
Bonuses (18,600 + 22,400)	41,000	1
Mileage allowance (W1)	8,350	W1
Pension contributions	0	½
	279,350	
Professional subscription	(630)	½
Golf club membership	0	½
	278,720	
Property income (W2)	11,340	W2
Savings income (250,000 × 3% × 4/12)	2,500	2
Interest paid	(140)	1
	292,420	
Personal allowance	0	½
Taxable income	292,420	

Tutorial notes:

(1) The bonus of £21,200 will have been treated as being received during 2016–17 because Petula became entitled to it during that tax year.

(2) Under the accrued income scheme, Petula must include the accrued interest from the gilts as savings income for 2017–18, even though she has not received any actual interest.

(3) No personal allowance is available because Petula's adjusted net income of £292,420 exceeds £123,000.

WORKINGS

(1) Mileage allowance

	£
Reimbursement (26,000 × £0.60)	15,600
Tax free amount	
10,000 miles × £0.45	(4,500)
11,000 miles × £0.25	(2,750)
Taxable benefit	8,350

(2) Property income

	£
Rent receivable	12,000
Replacement furniture relief	
Washing machine	(420)
Dishwasher	0
Other expenses	(1,640)
	9,940
Furnished room (8,900 – 7,500)	1,400
Property income	11,340

Tutorial notes:

(1) No relief is given for that part of the cost of the washer-dryer which represents an improvement over the original washing machine. Relief is therefore restricted to the cost of a similar washing machine.

(2) No relief is available for the cost of the dishwasher because this is an initial cost rather than the cost of a replacement.

(3) Claiming rent-a-room relief in respect of the furnished room is more beneficial than the normal basis of assessment (8,900 – 2,890 = £6,010).

(b) Unused pension annual allowances available to carry forward

Petula has unused pension annual allowances of £20,000 available to carry forward to the tax year 2018–19:

Tax year	Annual allowance £	Contribution £	Carried forward £
2017–18	10,000	20,000	0
2016–17	10,000	20,000	0
2015–16	40,000	20,000	20,000
			20,000

Tutorial notes:

(1) Petula's adjusted income for the tax years 2016–17 and 2017–18 exceeds £210,000, so she is only entitled to the minimum tapered annual allowance of £10,000 for these years.

(2) *The pension contributions of £20,000 for 2017–18 and 2016–17 have utilised all of Petula's annual allowance of £10,000 for those years and also some of the unused annual allowance from years before 2015–16. The £20,000 unused allowance for 2015–16 is available for carry forward to 2018–19.*

Answer 33 ONLINE

(a) **Corporation tax computation for the year ended 31 March 2018**

	£	
Operating profit	896,700	
Depreciation	21,660	½
Amortisation	9,000	½
Deduction for lease premium (W1)	(7,380)	W1
Capital allowances (W2)	(9,824)	W2
Trading profit	910,156	
Chargeable gain (W3)	59,494	W3
	969,650	
Property business loss brought forward	(12,500)	1
Qualifying charitable donations	(6,800)	½
Taxable total profits	950,350	

WORKINGS

(1) Deduction for lease premium

	£	
Premium paid	90,000	
Less: 90,000 × 2% × (10 – 1)	(16,200)	
Amount assessed on the landlord	73,800	1
Deduction (73,800 ÷ 10)	7,380	1

(2) Capital allowances

	Main pool £	Special rate pool £	Allowances £	
WDV brought forward	56,700	12,400		½
Addition – Motor car	13,700			1
Disposals – Motor car	(17,200)			1
– Pool		(9,300)		½
	53,200	3,100		
WDA – 18%	(9,576)		9,576	½
WDA – 8%		(248)	248	1
WDV carried forward	43,624	2,852		
Total allowances			9,824	

Tutorial notes:

(1) The motor car purchased has CO_2 emissions between 76 and 130 grams per kilometre, and therefore qualifies for writing down allowances at 18%.

(2) The proceeds for the motor car which was sold are restricted to the original cost figure of £17,200.

(3) Although all of the items included in the special rate pool have been sold, there is no balancing allowance because the business has not ceased.

(3) Chargeable gain

	£	
Disposal proceeds	90,600	½
Indexed cost (W4)	(26,406)	W4
	64,194	
Capital loss brought forward	(4,700)	½
Chargeable gain	59,494	

(4) Share pool

	Number	Indexed cost £	
Purchase June 2011	40,000	49,300	½
Indexation to October 2014 (49,300 × 0·096)		4,733	½
		54,033	
Disposal October 2015 (54,033 × 22,000 ÷ 40,000)	(22,000)	(29,718)	1
	18,000	24,315	
Indexation to March 2018 (24,315 × 0·086)		2,091	½
		26,406	
Disposal March 2018	(18,000)	(26,406)	½

13

(b) Effect of acquisition of Offline Ltd

- The profit threshold for establishing whether Online Ltd is a large company will be reduced to £750,000 (½ × 1,500,000), so it is likely that the company's corporation tax will have to be paid by quarterly instalments.   1½

- The dividends received from Offline Ltd, being group dividends, will not form part of Online Ltd's profits.   ½

2

15

ABOUT BECKER PROFESSIONAL EDUCATION

Becker Professional Education provides a single solution for students and professionals looking to advance their careers and achieve success in:

- Accounting
- International Financial Reporting
- Project Management
- Continuing Professional Education
- Healthcare

For more information on how Becker Professional Education can support you in your career, visit www.beckeracca.com.

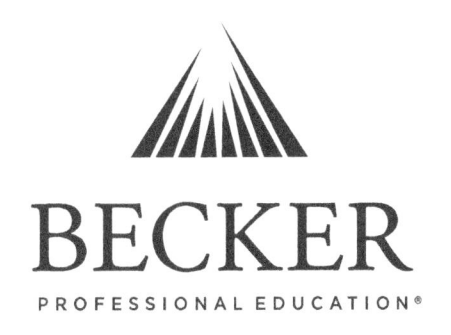

Becker Professional Education is an ACCA approved content provider

BECKER
PROFESSIONAL EDUCATION®